W9-AYP-543

CLAYTON KLEIN

COLD SUMMER WIND

COLD *"The force of the rushing water spun us around...the drop of the rapids only thirty feet downstream. There was no room for error."*

This true-life adventure story, set in the wilds of Canada's Northwest Territories, is the narrative of a father and son team who have canoed more than 3,000 miles above the sixtieth parallel.

Cold Summer Wind takes the reader down three of the major rivers of Canada's vast barren lands –

- The entire 920 miles of the Kazan River system from Snowbird Lake to Baker Lake, then out through Chesterfield Inlet into Hudson Bay.

- The Elk River and the Thelon River, through the heart of the Thelon Game Sanctuary.

- The wild and seldom-travelled Back River, from Muskox Rapids to within ninety miles of Chantrey Inlet on the Arctic Ocean, in the land of the midnight sun.

This is an action book! And action the Kleins had, shooting through boiling rapids and swirling white water, or while bucking high seas on some of the larger lakes.

MEET THE AUTHOR AND HIS SON...

Clayton Klein lives on a farm near Fowlerville, Michigan, in the house where he was born in 1919. He is a part of the Fowlerville business community, having founded the Klein Fertilizer Company in 1951. He served as its general manager and president for thirty years.

He is a member of the American Canoe Association, the Airplane Owners and Pilots Association, the Audubon Society, as well as several other groups and organizations.

An avid hiker, he has walked more than a thousand miles per year for the past fifteen years, and more than twelve hundred miles each year since 1976. He is an active outdoorsman who enjoys canoeing, exploration and writing.

Darrell Klein, the author's son, is also an active outdoorsman who canoes, golfs, hunts with bow and arrow, and spends a lot of time with his family. He is now the president and general manager of the family fertilizer business with its four locations in Michigan's lower peninsula.

COLD SUMMER WIND

CLAYTON KLEIN

WILDERNESS ADVENTURE BOOKS

Library of Congress Catalog Card Number 83-050047

ISBN: 0-9611596-0-X
Third Edition
September, 1985

Cover photo by Darrell Klein

Typesetting by
Word Processing Services
P.O. Box 10042, Lansing MI 48901

Published by
Wilderness Adventure Books
320 Garden Lane
Box 968
Fowlerville, Michigan 48836

Manufactured in the United States of America

TO OUR FAMILIES

who patiently waited at home

while we explored Canada's vast barren lands

CONTENTS

ILLUSTRATIONS

Note

*All photos not otherwise credited
are by Darrell Klein or the author*

MAPS

ACKNOWLEDGEMENTS

My dream for the book **Cold Summer Wind** became a reality because of the cooperation and hard work of the following people:

Special thanks to my sister, Bernice M. Chappel, who suggested numerous improvements in my writing, and for her most valued counsel.

Special thanks to my wife, Marjorie Nash Klein, for doing most of the typing of my material and for suggesting improvements. Thanks also to Laurene Hayes Nagaj and Debbie Klein, who also helped with the typing.

Thanks to Lorraine E. Brandson, Assistant Curator of the Eskimo Museum of Churchill, Manitoba, for her valuable assistance on numerous facts including her help on information about Fathers Joseph Buliard and Joseph Choque.

Thanks to Bishop Omer Robidoux, O.M.I., of Churchill, Manitoba, and the following Oblate priests of the Churchill-Hudson Bay Diocese for their help in the preparation of the chapters on the missionary life of Fr. Joseph Buliard:

Charles Choque, O.M.I., Archivist, Fort Smith, N.W.T.

Théophile Didier, O.M.I., Official Inuit Translator, Churchill, Manitoba.

Guy Mary-Rousselière, O.M.I., Editor of **Eskimo**, Pond Inlet, N.W.T.

Thanks to Eric DeJaeger, O.M.I., of St. Paul's Roman Catholic Mission in Baker Lake, N.W.T., for his help in securing the details on the final years of the life of Fr. Joseph Choque.

Thanks to Allan Simpson, Manager of Program Development and Policy Analysis, Department of Communications, Government of Canada, for his valued assistance in providing historical insights on the early history of Baker Lake.

Thanks to Verlen Kruger of Lansing, Michigan, for the kind words he has to say on the dust jacket of **Cold Summer Wind.**

Thanks to Robert G. Ferguson, President of Parsons Airways Northern, Ltd., of Flin Flon, Manitoba, for his valuable help on recent happenings in the life of Ragnar Jonsson.

Thanks to both Tom and Pat Boufford of Word Processing Services in Lansing, Michigan, for their excellent assistance in helping produce this book.

Thanks to Tom Weber of Cushing-Malloy in Ann Arbor, Michigan, for his helpful suggestions.

Thanks to Gage Publishing, Ltd., for permission to quote from **The Legend of John Hornby.**

Thanks to the Dupont Company for granting the rights to use the photo of Verlen Kruger and Steven Landick on this book's dust jacket.

INTRODUCTION

While growing up on the farm during the Depression years in Livingston County, Michigan, I could only dream of ever being able to see some of the north country. It then seemed nearly impossible, and so far away. In those days, my very best day of the year would be if Ken Chappel or Lyle Glover were to take me fishing at Cook Lake or Chase Lake, only a few miles from our home north of Fowlerville.

Our earliest canoeing was done in the late 1940's with rented canoes on the Au Sable, Manistee, Rifle, Pere Marquette, Pine, Tahquamenon and Presque Isle Rivers in Michigan. Most of these were weekend trips because we could only take a day or two at a time away from work.

Then during the fifties and early sixties, we made a few brief canoeing trips in the Algoma District of Ontario. Canoeing partners during the early years were Ld W. Marshall, Kendall Hoisington, Robert Parsons, James Parsons, Earl Flegel, Virgil Zeeb, Elwood Copeland and his sons, David and Kenneth Copeland.

Then in 1960 my son, Darrell, and I began to camp and canoe together. He was fifteen years old at that time and already a good camping partner. Since then, the two of us have frequently taken time to canoe and camp together. He is a great canoeist and a man who really knows how to read a river.

Basically, **Cold Summer Wind** is the story of our wilderness canoeing adventures in Canada's north country. We begin with a run across Wollaston Lake in Saskatchewan, down the entire length of the Cochrane River and across Reindeer Lake in Manitoba. Then comes an overland canoe journey from Snowbird Lake in the District of Mackenzie down to Jackpine Narrows in Reindeer Lake.

Then we enter the deep wilderness as the setting moves to above the sixtieth parallel for the balance of the narrative. There are travels down the entire length of the Kazan River and out through Chesterfield Inlet. The Thelon River trip follows, and then it's down the mighty Back River from Muskox Rapids to the Meadowbank River less than ninety miles from Chantrey Inlet on the Arctic Ocean.

Other rivers canoed and included in this story are the Elk, the Kunwak, the Little Partridge, the Thlewiaza and the Meadowbank. All are wild, free rivers which still remain unspoiled by the encroachment of civilization.

Darrell began to work in the family fertilizer business while still in school. The two of us have used our canoeing as a retreat, discussing and thinking about things which needed to be done to improve our business. Consequently, we were able to make what has often turned out to be wise and intelligent decisions during those biannual sojourns into the north.

We have developed a real interest in the Inuit peoples of the barren lands. We have found that especially while living out on the land, they were indeed excellent and amazingly intelligent people. They certainly were "the men *par excellence.*" Our primary regret is that we didn't get down their rivers while the Inuit were still living along those waterways.

You are invited to join us in our travels. Come along now. Bring only your lightweight camping equipment, some warm clothing and a paddle. We'll supply the canoe. Our first journey begins as we cross Wollaston Lake where the shorelines disappear into the surface of the lake on the far horizon. Then it's a bouncy ride down the Cochrane River into Reindeer Lake.

1

THE IMPOSSIBLE
DREAM

> *Destiny is not a matter of chance,*
> *But of choice;*
> *It is not a thing to be waited for,*
> *But a thing to be achieved.*
>
> — *William Jennings Bryan*

Halfway across Reindeer Lake, we began flying into heavy smoke. Our pilot, Eddie Dick, soon began to circle the Norseman. Within a few minutes, it became evident that we were lost. We dug maps out of the pack to help locate ourselves, but Eddie kept circling and asked where we would like to be put down. He was obviously nervous. He knew that we planned to start our journey in Compulsion Bay of Wollaston Lake. By the time we had found our location, we were over Swan Lake, which is about ten miles west of Reindeer and nearly on our course to Compulsion Bay.

Eddie turned back east again saying, "I won't fly any farther in this smoke." We again circled over Reindeer Lake, when he saw some familiar islands below. "I'm going to hammer her down right here," he announced and back came the throttle. We landed and he taxied us up to the dock of Reindeer Lake Lodge.

Forest fires had been running wild for the past three weeks, burning over a huge area in eastern Saskatchewan to the south and west of Reindeer Lake. With daily winds from the south and southwest for the past week, the entire area was full of smoke.

This was our first big canoeing adventure. The year was 1964. The month was July. My son Darrell and I would be in one canoe. Elwood Copeland and Frederick Reyhl would be in the other. Our plans were to fly from Lynn Lake, Manitoba to Compulsion Bay, then to canoe north across Wollaston Lake to its Cochrane River outlet, and down that river into Reindeer Lake to Kinoosao, Manitoba.

Reindeer Lake Lodge was owned and operated by John Ivanchuk. John has spent most of his life in the sub-arctic. He told us that he had, for over 20 years, run a trap line in the Nueltin Lake area of Northwest Territories. Then he moved south to build his fishing camp on one of the four thousand islands in Reindeer Lake. John was also a commercial fisherman, and a most interesting man. He told us the meaning of several Chipewyan words. For instance, "Mississippi" means "big river," "Chicago" means "skunk," and "Kinoosao" means "big fish."

After arriving at the lodge, Eddie declared through a cloud of cigarette smoke, "We'll have to wait for a wind change to the east or north." Later that afternoon the smoke thickened, so we stayed overnight. There was no change in the wind direction during the night. By mid-afternoon of the next day, Eddie announced that he wanted to try to get back to his base at Lynn Lake.

Inasmuch as we had paid for our flight in advance, we decided that we were going to stay with the plane until the Chiupka Airways people delivered us to Compulsion Bay, even though Eddie strongly suggested that we stay where we were. That evening, after the third take off of the day in about five-mile visibility, we located Kinoosao on the east shore of Reindeer Lake, and followed the dirt road east, to the Chiupka air base.

Fred Reyhl and Elwood Copeland

Another Chiupka pilot met us at the dock. His first words were "Hey! Where have you fellows been? We were over at Compulsion Bay yesterday afternoon, looking for you!"

Eddie only said, "The smoke was too thick. I had to hammer her down." Eddie didn't appear embarrassed.

A heavy thunderstorm blew through before the next morning. The wind swung to the northwest and cleared the air, but it was another hot day. On the third day, we were finally flown into Compulsion Bay. Thus the big adventure began.

When we arrived at Wollaston Lake settlement a couple of days later, we were met by Alphonse Mercier, manager of the post. Mrs. Mercier came out and invited us into their house for dinner. While she was preparing it, Al showed us through the fish filleting plant and "the point" where several families of Chipewyan Indians live. These people fish in the summertime for the filleting plant, and the men run trap lines during the winter. Each family had several scrawny sled dogs tied along the lake shore.

Al said, "The dogs are fed only about once a week in

The Alphonse Merciers of Wollaston Lake

the summertime." They looked it, too. He went on to say, "They feed them every day in the fall to get them in working condition by trapping season." We talked with several of the Chipewyans and photographed them as they were baking bannocks, mending nets and drying moose hides, while Al acted as our interpreter. These people called us *Ogemaw*, which means white man. There was a sign in front of the Catholic Mission in Chipewyan symbols which, according to Al, said "Keep your sled dogs out of the church yard." The priest was visiting some of his people across the lake, so we didn't get to meet him.

Mrs. Mercier served us a scrumptious dinner complete with homemade bread, tossed salad, pork chops, corn, potatoes, Jell-O and cake. The Merciers had been at Wollaston Lake post for over two years. Al remarked, "As far as we know, you chaps are the first canoeists to ever pass through here heading for the Cochrane. You're also the only group to visit us by canoe."

Mrs. Mercier told us that her nearest neighbor, other than Indians, lived at Co-op Point on Reindeer Lake, about eighty miles to the southeast. She said, "I've never met this neighbor, but we talk to each other occasionally by

Chipewyan Women of Wollaston Lake

radiophone." Their nearest doctor was 225 air miles to the south, at Lac LaRonge. Shortly after dinner and our visit with these friendly people, we headed north again across the lake. It was a fine day for canoeing.

Wollaston Lake is a large lake, with a most unusual feature. It is located exactly on the height of land. For this reason, it has two outlets. The one on the west side of the lake is the famous Fond du Lac River, which flows into Lake Athabaska and down the Mackenzie River into the Arctic Ocean. The other outlet, on the northeast side of Wollaston, is the little known Cochrane River, which we chose. The Cochrane water flows into Reindeer Lake and on down the Churchill River, draining into Hudson Bay.

When planning this journey, we had written to the travel bureaus of Saskatchewan and Manitoba requesting information on the Cochrane River, as part of this river flows through both of these provinces. The travel bureaus responded similarly. Mr. W. E. Organ, Director of the Tourist Development Branch for the province of Manitoba wrote, "To our knowledge, nobody has ever made the canoe trip outlined in your letter and we would suggest you peruse large scale maps of the area in order to ascertain the feasibility of such a trip." Consequently, we received little help. This made us wonder whether or not such a canoe run was really feasible. There was only one way to find out. That was to go and do it!

Paddling across Wollaston Lake, each stroke of the paddle took the four of us farther north than any of us had been before. One night, when we camped on an island in the central part of the lake, a terrific storm came up. Elwood was the first to get out of the tent to check our equipment. He made it to the shoreline just in time to catch one of the canoes before it was blown into the lake. The same gust of wind also swept our entire cook kit into the lake. What a blow!

And what a blow it would have been if we had lost one of our canoes! Our chances of finding the canoe in Wollaston would have been very slim, as the lake is about forty miles wide, seventy miles long, and filled with hundreds of islands. The wind continued to blow and shifted to the north, dropping the temperature to the low forties.

We were out shortly after daylight, and soon saw parts of our cook kit and silverware scattered across the rocks at the bottom off shore in four to eight feet of water. Elwood and Darrell volunteered to retrieve as much of our equipment as they could find. Soon they started coming up with different items of equipment which they tossed up on the rocks to Fred, where he stacked them and took inventory. The outfit was scattered over an area twenty-five feet across.

Finally after a half hour of diving and searching, Fred reported that everything was accounted for. By this time we had a roaring campfire going, as the boys were cold and hungry.

Darrell shivered as he crawled from the water, his teeth chattering. As he dried himself by the fire he mumbled, "I'm freezing! This is the last time I'm going swimming on this trip!" That was true for he didn't get into the water again all summer.

We learned a valuable lesson from that experience

which all campers should never forget. Regardless of the perfect weather you may be having as you turn in for the night, be sure to secure your canoe to a tree or rock with a rope, and put all equipment well back from the shore, where a sudden gust of wind cannot blow it into the lake or river.

During the next few days, we moved on out of Wollaston Lake and began our descent of the Cochrane river. Whenever the wind was from a favorable direction in the lakes, we raised the sail to gain some time and conserve energy. This is one of the advantages of canoeing with even numbers of canoes. We lashed the two canoes side-by-side catamaran style, with the gunwales about a foot apart, and the bows slightly closer together than the sterns. Then, a sail was raised on two poles and held by the bow men, Fred and Darrell, while Elwood or I used a paddle as a rudder from the stern. When a strong gust of wind hit the sail, or we were going too fast for safety, our bow men could let the top of the sail forward, thus spilling some of the pull from the sail.

Above Bigstone Rapids, we had been moving through a swampy area for several miles. Approaching the end of an expansion in the river, we came upon a solitary sandpiper circling overhead, uttering his sharp weet-weet-weet call. Then he perched on the terminal leader of a black spruce while keeping up his ear-piercing chatter.

We had been in need of a shore break, so we pulled ashore on a sandy rise just beyond the sandpiper's tree. The bird kept up its constant noise. Occasionally he left his tree to circle over us for a closer look. Then he returned each time to the same treetop. We were ashore for nearly fifteen minutes and that solitary sandpiper continued its incessant shrill weet-weet-weet the entire time. The bird did not quiet down until we re-embarked and again headed down river.

The fishing was superb along our route of travel for fish could be caught at any time. Northerns were the most common. Grayling were also plentiful, as well as lake trout and walleyes. Here's an entry from our journal:

Friday, July 17 — Arrived at Bigstone Rapids at 7 P.M. The Cochrane's a big river and the portage around Bigstone was about two miles long and a difficult trail to follow. We portaged until about 11:30 and still have the canoes and a couple of packs to move the final one-third of a mile in the morning. Camp is set up near the foot of the rapids. We are a tired group tonight. The northern lights are brilliant and an echo type satellite moved across the sky above us as we were eating our supper, a little after midnight.

Saturday, July 18 — Up before 8:00 and brought the canoes out of the bush before breakfast. We wanted fish to eat, so Darrell and Fred volunteered to catch them. We told them to take only five minutes, and if they didn't connect by then to forget it, as we couldn't spare any more time. They cast from the rocks along the shore, just below camp, and were back within five minutes, each carrying a northern pike. These fish DeLiared out at six and six and one-half pounds respectively. Both were taken on their first casts.

When we finished breakfast, we decided to take an extra thirty minutes to do some serious fishing for pictures, so the folks at home would know that we were not just telling another fish story. All of us fished from the large rocks below Bigstone Rapids. In thirty minutes we had landed seven more northerns. One sixteen pounds, one eleven pounder, two eight pounders and the smallest weighed in at five pounds.

Those fish were released as soon as our pictures were taken. Nearly every day we would take one or two for food. Fred said, "I've heard stories of good fishing before, but I never dreamed it could be as good as this, with a big fish on just about every cast. This certainly is the trip of a lifetime!" Enough said about fishing. Now back to working our way out of the bush.

For the next two or three days, we had intermittent showers with a few brief sunny intervals, and one thirty-hour downpour. The only good thing about all the rain was that it extinguished the forest fires. When these remote areas of taiga catch fire, they're allowed to burn themselves out, because there is little commercial value to the timber. The Canadian government believes that the cost of fire fighting in these northern areas would be more than the loss incurred by the burning of the trees and other vegetation.

We wondered if they were right, as it seemed a great loss to us. It would probably take at least a century for this forest to again mature to its former state for trees grow very slowly here just below the barren lands.

THE LOWER COCHRANE

In the wilderness,
our scientific progress
fades into trivia.

— Col. Charles A. Lindbergh

On July 20 we were able to move out of Saskatchewan and into Manitoba. We also rounded the northernmost bend in the Cochrane and made camp above the 59th parallel.

Weather can be the disappointment of a canoeist. Bad weather is something one doesn't plan on, but foul weather is something one usually gets, on an extended canoe trip. Disagreeable weather comes in many different ways. There is the occasional thunderstorm when one doesn't want to be caught out on a lake or under a tree, but an even greater problem is wind, especially a wind when you're crossing the larger lakes and it's on the nose or from either side.

During the next five days we struggled along down the Cochrane into continuous foul weather. We rounded the northernmost bend in the river, which is sixty-two miles south of the 60th parallel, and headed mostly south, crossing Misty Lake in a downpour of rain. The wind blew out of the east and south each day, with temperatures ranging from the mid forties to the low sixties, with many periods of rain.

Later we were to learn that these winds which stopped us on the Cochrane and impeded our progress, were really minimal when compared to the cold summer winds which blow across the barrens above the tree line.

Between showers one night at a campsite on an island in upper Lac Brochet, while we feasted on fresh-caught walleyes, hash browns and hot biscuits, we wondered whom the Republicans had nominated for President at their convention in Miami the week before. This was the first time ever that any of us had been out of touch with civilization, for we had received no news from the outside world in nearly three weeks.

Moose were plentiful along this part of the river and they were a joy to see. Frequently, we would watch as they waded in the river to escape the insects and browse on underwater plants. We had no telephoto lenses on our cameras. So, at times we would move in very close for pictures. We used a stalking technique which works, and it can be improved with practice. Here is the way it's done.

When you see a moose in the river or along a lakeshore feeding on bottom grass or lilypads, you hold perfectly still until the animal's head goes underwater for a mouthful of food. Then, you paddle forward until the head comes up, at which time you freeze your position, with the person in the stern of the canoe using his paddle underwater as a rudder to keep your craft headed directly at the moose. This procedure is repeated as many times as necessary to close to a satisfactory distance. Remember, each time the head goes down, paddle forward. Each time the head comes up, freeze your position. Moose usually will notice only a moving object while their heads are above the water surface.

On an earlier trip down the University River in

Ontario with Elwood, the two of us moved in so close to a bull moose that Elwood was able to reach out of the bow and slap the animal across the back with his paddle, before the river erupted as the animal splashed toward the shore.

The French Canadian voyageurs and fur traders of the early days had a name for the moose that seemed appropriate. They called him *L'orignal,* which conjures up in its meaning words like "awkward, freak, fantastic and grotesque." Their name was fitting for the appearance of the moose, which under adverse conditions, is anything but beautiful. But in good weather and at his best, the moose is a magnificent animal.

A moose would make an easy target for a person with a rifle. Fred said, "I don't understand how there's sport in killing such a beautiful animal." After considerable discussion, we unanimously agreed that the only justification for moose hunting should be for people who really need the food and were unable to get meat in any other way.

Elwood said, "I've heard of trigger-happy canoeists who shoot moose just for the fun of it, or to get a few steaks and then leave most of the carcasses to spoil."

"What a repulsive thought!" Darrell exclaimed. Our group did not carry firearms, as we didn't plan to kill anything, except a few fish for food.

We crossed Lac Brochet and continued on down the river in a steady drizzle of rain. The southeast breeze gradually increased in intensity until the wind became so strong that we could make no progress. We put up the tent and crawled in, thinking that the rain would surely let up in a little while so that we could cook supper and dry out some of our soaked clothing. But there was no let up, so no supper. That night a terrifying thunderstorm with heavy winds continued for hours, and the tent offered little shelter from the rain.

Here's an entry from our journal of the following day, which was July 24:

Rain! It's now 11 A.M. and we hope it lets up

soon so that we can get something to eat. It's been over twenty-eight hours since we've had anything in the way of food. To make matters even more distressing, due to all these delays, our food supply is getting rather low.

The rain finally let up at noon, so we immediately fixed a double-size pot of stew. The wind has now shifted to the north. We ate and dried things out until 3:30, when we left camp. This campsite had been used for drying fish this spring by a band of Chipewyans, and we used their fish drying racks to dry out our duffel. We paddled down some heavy swells in the lakes and portaged Chipewyan Falls at about 5 P.M. As soon as we entered Sandy Hill Lake, we rigged the sail and the good northwest breeze carried us down the lakes. The sun came out at about 6:15, and everyone's spirits improved after our ordeals of rains and bad winds for the past several days. We made camp on an esker at around 9 P.M. This is a beautiful campsite. We moved twenty miles this afternoon, since about 3:30.

That evening, around our campfire as we relaxed and sipped an extra cup of tea, we discussed eskers in general, as well as some of the eskers upon which we had camped. Eskers like these were formed more than ten thousand years ago. They are remnants of the last ice age. They were formed from the sediment which settled in river bottoms which then flowed over the ice. As the glaciers melted, these long, sandy gravelly ridges remained.

Most eskers in this part of Canada run in a northeast to southwest direction. Many of them are several miles long. They're usually not much over three hundred yards wide, and frequently less. Many eskers meander through spruce forests, where the trees grow relatively far apart in the sandy soil. The spruces are often interspersed with birches, which seem to grow well with so much space and light. The widely spaced trees, with the forest floor covered with caribou moss, British soldiers and other lichens with clumps of bunchberries, wintergreen and dwarf blueberries, reminds one of being in a picnic area of a state or provincial park.

Eskers make excellent campsites along the top of their ridges, especially near the places where they intersect lakes or streams. That is, they make good campsites if you don't mind packing your tent and sleeping gear up their twenty to sixty feet of elevation to the top of the ridge. Such a campsite is usually more free of insects, as it's up in the breeze above the surrounding tree tops.

These eskers are beautiful places, not only to camp, but also to walk on. Being high, you can overlook much of the surrounding wilderness. Nearly always, one will find well used game trails to follow, and walking an esker ridge is most enjoyable.

July 25 was certainly a day to remember. We were on the river by 8:15. The Cochrane moves rapidly through the area below Sandy Hill Lake. Lunch time found us in the north end of Easton Lake. There were arctic grayling surfacing all around, but we were unable to land a single one. Elwood hooked a nice one, but lost it as he attempted to lift it into the canoe. Darrell played a large northern for about ten minutes, before he lost it. This fish actually towed the canoe around. We took movies of the lunker, whenever Darrell was able to bring it to the surface. Too bad to lose that one. It probably would have weighed in at more than thirty pounds.

That same evening, we crossed the 58th parallel going south, and made camp below an unnamed rapids twelve miles northeast of Brochet. So far this was our best day of canoeing. We moved down river for forty-eight miles. Late in the afternoon, Darrell relieved me in the stern, as I took over the bow position. This worked so well that we kept those same positions in all of our canoeing from then on.

The following morning, about halfway into Brochet, we stopped and visited a group of Chipewyans who were camped along the shore. These were the first people we had seen since leaving Wollaston Lake post about two

Chipewyan Family of Cochrane River

weeks earlier. In this group there was only one boy, named Dona, who could speak English, and he acted as interpreter. These people were very friendly. They prepared tea for us as Dona showed us around their camp. His elders' faces showed amazement as he told them that we had canoed all the way down from Wollaston. They asked if we had seen any moose or caribou. We told them that we had seen moose, but that they were a long way up the river. At one point, there was considerable laughter in the group. We asked Dona what they were laughing at, and he said, "They make jokes about your tin canoes." Elwood asked Dona if his group lived there along the Cochrane all year long. "No!" came the reply. "We move around to wherever the hunting and fishing are good."

Later, when we arrived in Brochet, we learned that most of the Chipewyan people were now settled in a permanent-type log cabin or tent, and almost all lived in or near one of the trading posts. Very few groups, such as the one we had visited along the Cochrane, still remained on the land. These people, who speak a dialect of the Athabasca language, originally inhabited all of the country north of the Churchill River inland from Hudson Bay.

Their neighbors to the north were the hated Eskimos and to the south, the Crees. Hostilities were frequent between the Chipewyan and the Eskimo. As these people invaded the barrens each summer, in search of caribou, frequent skirmishes with the Eskimo took place. The Chipewyans also had a tendency to look down on the Cree, because their southern neighbors lived basically on hares, not caribou.

In the early days, caribou occurred in tremendous numbers, and upon these animals the Chipewyan depended almost entirely for existence. The caribou supplied not only food, but also materials for making most of their equipment. Each spring, the caribou migrate northward into the barren lands to spend the summer. Since the Chipewyan are primarily hunters of caribou, they adapted their way of life to the yearly cycle of these animals. Their winters were spent in the forested areas, and their summers on the barren lands.

On Sunday, July 26, we finally arrived in Brochet. We looked up the manager of the Hudson's Bay Post. He opened the store for us, and we were able to buy a few needed supplies.

We decided to look up Father Adrien Darveau to see if he could find a Chipewyan or a Cree who would tow us down the east shore of Reindeer Lake to Kinoosao where we planned to terminate our canoeing. This we wanted to do, as we were already several days behind our schedule.

As it turned out, we missed Fr. Darveau by a few minutes. He had just left for Kinoosao. "That's our usual kind of luck," said Darrell.

Next, we went to the Department of Transport station, and sent a wire home. From there, we contacted Bud Elford, a missionary working with the Chipewyans and Crees for the northern Canada Evangelical group, and told him of our problem. In a little while, he had talked a young man, Raymond Marasty, into towing us down the lake the following morning with his nineteen-foot freighter canoe powered with a ten-horse outboard motor.

We set up our final camp on a site beside the Trading Post, and then cleaned up as best we could inside a tent in town.

We visited with several of the Indian boys in the settlement who came along to look at our "tin canoes," as they called them.

One boy asked, "Where are you from?"

"We live down in Michigan," Elwood replied.

"Where's that?" asked another.

"Down near Detroit where all of the automobiles are made," Fred added. "You know — automobiles are the things we ride up and down the roads in."

Those boys had blank looks on their faces and had no idea what we were talking about until Elwood added, "We're from down in the United States."

"Oh!" came the reply. "The United States. That's way down south."

Further discussion with those boys revealed that not only had they never seen a road or an automobile, neither had they ever seen a pig or a chicken or a cow, and all they knew about milk was that it came to Brochet in tin cans.

That evening we went back to Elford's house. Mrs. Elford (Marge) had invited us over for a snack, and to take part in a hymn sing with about fifteen young people. Bud played a mandolin and the organ, and we sang songs in both Chipewyan and English. They were hymns which Bud had translated into their language, such as "How Great Thou Art" and "The Old Rugged Cross." In all, it was a most interesting evening and the home-cooked meal was a real treat.

Next day was cloudy, cold and windy. We rode up and down over the more than five-foot waves, towing our canoes behind us. We made good time on the eighty-mile ride to Kinoosao. The whole distance, with a short stop at Jackpine Narrows, took about seven hours.

Though this was a cold, rough ride, none of us complained as we were happy that we would be home before the following weekend.

THE FRINGE OF
THE BARRENS

Something hidden. Go and find it.
Go and look behind the ranges —
Something lost behind the ranges,
Lost and waiting for you. Go!

— *Rudyard Kipling*

It had been four years since our descent of the Cochrane River from Wollaston to Reindeer Lakes. Now it was mid-July in the summer of 1968. During the previous winter, Darrell and I had found two new camping mates for our first expedition into the Northwest Territories of Canada. Neither Fred Reyhl nor Elwood Copeland was able to get away from their work to travel with us into the Northwest Territories. Bryan Beasley of Utica, Michigan, and Lauren Jonckheere of Howell, Michigan, were now our partners. Bryan grew up on Guilford Avenue in Detroit and had an Eagle rating in the Boy Scouts of America. He was nineteen years old. Lauren also had considerable camping and canoeing experience in the northern part of our state. He was the youngest member of our group at age eighteen. Both of these young men were cousins of Darrell.

On any wilderness camping trip, it is important to have the right kind of people as your canoeing partners. One person in the group who is a loafer or who lacks discipline and courage can take all the pleasure out of an undertaking. Fortunately, Darrell and I have selected only top-quality canoeing partners for our adventures. When we have been unable to locate this properly qualified type of mate, we prefer to travel alone. True, it is safer to travel with two or more canoes in a group in case of mishap. We strongly recommend that journeys of this kind only be attempted by well-qualified, experienced persons who don't "fold" or "blow their stacks" at the first sign of adversity.

The four of us met at our house a couple of times during the early part of the summer to discuss the proposed journey and to complete our plans in detail. One of the topics discussed at those meetings were costs, including our flight from Lynn Lake, Manitoba to our starting point at Snowbird Lake. We also prepared lists of personal items, equipment and food menus for each meal for twenty-one days. We estimated that we should be able to paddle out and down to Brochet Post at the north end of Reindeer Lake in about three weeks. We also spent considerable time discussing the importance of our maps and in making certain that our new partners understood how to read them. We had obtained two sets of topographical maps of the area between Snowbird Lake and Kinoosao, covering our entire route. One set was to be carried in each canoe and used to make sure that we stayed on our route.

Northwest Territories of Canada is a unique part of the North American Continent. It lies north of the 60th parallel and is an area of land larger than all of the United States which lies east of the Mississippi River. The total population of this huge area, including Eskimos, Indians and all other Canadians, consists of only about 46,000 people. That's about one person for each twenty-eight square miles, and nearly one-third of the population lives in the capital city of Yellowknife.

Northwest Territories is divided into three districts. The District of Mackenzie, where our canoeing would begin, runs west to Yukon Territory and north to the Arctic Ocean. The District of Keewatin includes everything else west of Hudson Bay and east of the 102nd meridian on the Canadian mainland as well as all of the islands within Hudson, James and Ungava Bays. The other is the District of Franklin. It includes the islands to the north of the mainland, Hudson Bay and Hudson Strait.

The four of us had driven to Cranberry Portage in Manitoba on July 6th and 7th. After staying overnight at "Cap" Anderson's Caribou Lodge, we drove to the Canadian National Railway Station, where we loaded canoes, camping gear and ourselves onto the train and headed for Lynn Lake. The 184 miles on the CNR was completed as we pulled into Lynn Lake Station twelve hours later.

The following morning, we were met by the people from Parsons Airways Northern whom we had previously engaged to fly us to Snowbird Lake. They told us that our plane would arrive from Flin Flon at about 11:00 A.M. We reported in at the Royal Canadian Mounted Police station to obtain our travel permits. Then we purchased our fishing licenses for both Manitoba and Northwest Territories. When the plane arrived, we learned that it was a 1946 model, single-engine Fairchild Husky. It was the first one we had ever seen. Both of our canoes went inside of the aircraft through a door under the rear of the fuselage.

We took off promptly and flew north over Brochet and set down on Charcoal Lake in Saskatchewan where the Parsons people had a cache of gasoline on an island. After refueling, we were so overloaded that our pilot was unable to get the Husky back into the air. After three attempts he stopped and pumped the water out of the pontoons. On the next try, the old girl finally took off and we headed north barely clearing the hills. We couldn't get any extra altitude for the next fifty or sixty miles — just enough to clear each ridge by only a few feet.

At top speed, the old girl cruised at eighty-five miles per hour. As we approached and crossed the 60th parallel

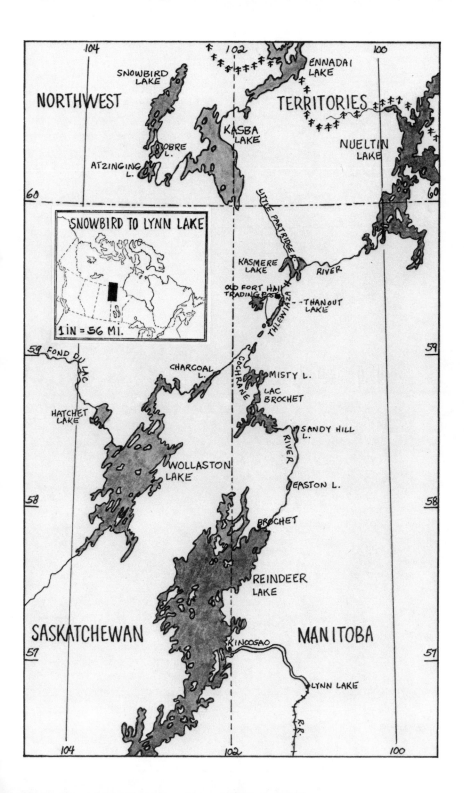

into the District of Mackenzie, we flew through several snow showers. Finally after 265 bouncy air miles, five hours out of Lynn Lake, we settled down on the surface of Snowbird Lake. Our pilot put us ashore on an island in the southwestern part of the lake. We paddled a couple of miles to the west shore where we set up our camp.

That evening, in the clear cold weather, we had our first opportunity to enjoy wilderness camping in the Northwest Territories. We established regular duties for each of us. Bryan and Lauren would do the preparation of our meals. Darrell and I gathered firewood and did the dishes. At times we had a problem with our fuel supply as our first few days were spent on the fringe of the barrens. True, there were some areas of small trees, but also many barren areas where no trees grew. We talked about the fact that the tree line runs across this lake. Most of the islands in Snowbird are without trees of any kind.

The tree line west of Hudson Bay begins near Churchill, Manitoba and runs in a northwestern direction to the mouth of the Mackenzie River. There are few places along this great distance that it is a clearly defined line. Temperature determines the tree line location. In general, trees grow north to the point where the average temperature during the warmest month of the year exceeds 50 degrees. The trees and tundra merge into one another in an erratic interlinking fashion, as local conditions of soil, moisture, elevation, humidity and permafrost either favor or foil the growth of trees. Islands of trees cluster in valleys on the tundra far to the north of the tree line and areas of tundra occur deep within the forest. In the past, Eskimos from the treeless north traveled to the clusters of trees along the Thelon River to get their much-needed wood for kayaks, sleds, tent poles and other necessities. Some came from as far away as Victoria Island, north of the Canadian mainland. Wood was one of the Inuit people's most valued possessions.

By next morning the temperature was down to 38 degrees. While eating breakfast of bacon, eggs, toast, jam and coffee, Bryan recalled how our pilot had told him that he had flown over Snowbird Lake on July 5th and the lake was still covered with slush ice. "That was only six days ago," he said. "No wonder it's so cold here!" We broke camp and headed north along the shore line. It was a good feeling to be back in the canoe again.

For more than ten years, back trouble had given me many problems. Twice I'd been hospitalized and put in traction to ease the pain. I have found that whenever I'm able to canoe, the backache goes away. In my case, there's something about canoeing that must have a therapeutic value. I'm reminded of the wilderness experiences of Sir George Simpson who was Governor of the Hudson's Bay Company back in the days of the voyageurs. He wrote in a letter to his friend J. G. McTavish, "It is strange that all my ailments vanish as soon as I seat myself in a canoe."

"That's exactly the way I feel now," I told the boys just before we stopped for lunch near the mouth of a stream flowing in from the west.

By mid-day the weather had warmed to the upper 50's with bright sunshine. Darrell and I pulled our headnets out of our packs as soon as we went ashore for lunch. Mosquitoes and black flies swarmed around us. Then we learned that neither Lauren nor Bryan had brought headnets!

We knew we were in trouble. It is impossible for anyone to survive in this part of the north in July and have any comfort or enjoyment without headnets for protection from the insects. Fortunately, we did have an aerosol can of "Off" for each canoe. We would now have to ration it. Consequently we didn't stay ashore for lunch. We paddled back into the lake where there was enough breeze to blow most of the little critters away.

While lunching, we decided to explore up the little stream to try the fishing just below the rapids which we could hear in the distance. There was too much current to enable us to paddle up this stream, so we took our fishing rods and walked to the rapids after securing the canoes on shore. But the black flies were so treacherous that we were unable to do any serious fishing. All we could think about was to hurry back to the canoes and get out on the lake again, away from the horde of insects.

At this point we were about eighteen miles east of Wholdaia Lake, which is on the Dubawnt River system. Our location was 60 degrees, 36 minutes north latitude and 103 degrees, 8 minutes west longitude. This was as far north as we were able to get in the summer of '68.

With no headnets for our partners, we decided it would be best to cross the lake and head for the outlet as soon as possible. Until that time, our plans had been to travel to the northern end of Snowbird Lake taking a couple more days to explore.

We paddled east to an island which still had a lot of snow on it from winter. The boys had a snowball fight and all faces were washed with snow before the battle ended. We didn't linger long after the battle, as the insect horde promptly closed in. We moved across Snowbird to a long island in the south central part of the lake. We decided we would like fish for supper, so Lauren caught us a six-pound lake trout before we arrived at the island.

We set up camp behind a sandy beach. After supper, Darrell and I took a quick dip in the lake. Wow, that water was cold! We crawled into our tents with the sun shining brightly. The wind died down at 9:30. Inside the tents was the only place we could go to get away from the swarm of insects. We were in a one-on-one situation with those insects. One million of them to each one of us.

The following morning we broke camp by 8:30 while the surface of the lake was still calm. Just east of the island we had camped on, we came across hundreds of lake trout feeding on insects on the surface. In some places the water was almost covered with insects which had fallen onto the water during the past few hours. All that the fish needed to do was swim along the surface with their mouths open to scoop in all of the food they could handle.

We decided to try to catch some of these lakers as it was just too much of a temptation to resist. We cast our red- and white-striped spoons into the group and three of us landed our trout after the first cast. They were good sized and most required a five- to ten-minute fight to

Lauren Jonckheere and Bryan Beasley

bring them to the canoes. Darrell had a big one hooked which he battled for fifty minutes before he could bring it in.

We decided to put our catch on stringers for picture taking purposes and then to release them. It was about two miles to the nearest point of land on our route where we could take pictures. Unfortunately, the largest fish on each stringer broke loose before we had proceeded very far towards shore. We had only the smaller ones left for our pictures. These little ones weighed in between six and ten pounds each. We estimated that Darrell's "lunker laker" would have weighed in at more than twenty pounds.

So, our experience was typical of all fishermen, the biggest ones got away!

THE UPPER KAZAN

> *And so it fell on me a spell*
> *Of wanderlust was cast.*
> *The land was still and strange and chill*
> *And cavernous and vast.*
>
> — *Robert Service,*
> ***The Ballad of Gum-Boot Ben***

We paddled to the south end of Snowbird where we again lunched in the canoes. The carrying place around the rapids at the outlet of the lake was on the left, the trail was good. That night we camped on an esker along the northwest side of Obre Lake. We used our headnets all evening due to the hordes of insects. Except to rub more insect repellent on their faces, necks and hands, Bryan and Lauren had but one option — to get used to the mosquitoes. Without headnets they went inside their tent as soon as we finished supper.

Darrell and I went for a walk on an esker and along the shore. We came upon an old Chipewyan camp where we found two abandoned log cabins which were still standing. We found the date of 1954 in one and the name of William Youya followed by some symbols under his name. There were several old porcelain dishes laying around partially covered with moss. We also found lots of bones, antlers and floats for fish nets.

The following morning the wind was blowing strong out of the east and we could see many signs of rain. Due to this cold wind we decided to change our route and make a portage out of the southeast corner of Obre Lake instead of following the Kazan River down into Atzinging Lake, as the lake would have been difficult to cross in the strong wind. We arrived at the far corner of Obre Lake just as a downpour of rain began. We put up a little shelter between two trees and lit a small fire to smoke away the insects. It was a five-hour wait before the rain began to let up.

While waiting we discussed some interesting things about the weather and how to forecast it. Darrell started the discussion by saying "Sundogs like the ones we saw yesterday are a forewarning of a storm within a day or two. Also, the smoke from our fire drifts off near the surface and that tells me that we're in for some bad weather soon. And rising smoke is a sure sign of fair weather."

"Then I hope this smoke starts rising soon," Bryan said.

"You've all heard the old saying," I said. "Rainbow in morning, sailors take warning. Rainbow at night, sailors delight. Another weather indicator is that when distant sounds are louder than usual, you can look for rain. At home, whenever we can hear a train, and that's six miles from the nearest railroad, it nearly always storms within the next day or two. Of course, I don't expect to hear a train today as we're at least 240 miles from the nearest railroad."

Bryan said, "High clouds won't rain on you, no matter how threatening they look. It's the lower clouds that drop the rain. And leaves on trees show their backs before a rain, and birds perch more before a storm because the low air pressure is less dense, making it more difficult for them to fly."

Lauren added, "Ducks and geese tend to fly higher in

good weather than in bad."

"I've heard that low barometric pressure affects their ears," Darrell added.

"Dew on the grass in the late evening or morning is always a sign of fair weather," Lauren concluded.

I told them, "My father used to say, 'When you see a ring around the moon, there's rain on the way. Then if you can count the stars which appear inside the ring, you'll know how many days away the rain is as each star represents a day.' When I'm at home I've noticed that my back aches more just before a storm than any other time. Since I've been here on this camping trip, I haven't had an ache of any kind. Canoeing surely agrees with me, but it's even nicer when the sun shines. An old guide in Ontario once told me that when the loons are vocal in midday, they are saying, 'Tomorrow's going to be a windy day'."

The rain finally let up enough for us to make the portage into a small lake east of Atzinging. This was difficult as we found an error in our maps. Two small lakes which are not shown confused us for an hour or two. By 7 P.M. we had completed the portage back into the Kazan and canoed a couple of miles south when more rain forced us to make camp on an island.

The boys had trouble getting a fire started as everything was wet. When Bryan was unable to do it on his second attempt, Darrell said, "Let me try. I think I can do it. At least so far I've always been able to start a campfire in any kind of weather." It took him about five minutes to find and prepare the tinder which he carefully placed. He set up more small dry splinters in tepee form around the tinder. Then with one lighted match, he touched it off between cupped hands and we soon had our fire burning.

This was proof of the old adage, "Experience is the best teacher." Darrell had more experience at camping than Bryan, our Eagle scout, for Darrell had camped out in the woodlots around home from the time he was a young boy, in all kinds of weather, and at all times of the year.

After another delicious supper prepared by Bryan, we dried out our wet pants, boots and socks by the campfire.

Then the rains started again. It rained all that night and all the following day until late afternoon. Finally we cooked up a combination breakfast and supper in the light drizzle. While eating, we saw an encouraging sign. The smoke from our campfire was going nearly straight up through the trees!

We broke camp and moved down into the Kazan again. Darrell and I took a little water over the bow while shooting a small rapids. This was definitely a no-no! "From now on, we're going to look every rapids over ahead of time from the shore," Darrell said. "We can't afford to take unnecessary chances when we're this far from civilization." We all agreed that we would be more cautious.

During the next couple of days we moved down the Kazan in good weather. We portaged around three sets of rapids and were able to shoot several others without further mishap. One evening, Lauren baked us a delicious cake and a supply of hot biscuits in the reflector oven. We also took time to go for a swim which was refreshing and enjoyable, even though the insects let us have it as we were drying off and getting our clothes on again.

Then we found another error on our maps. We canoed on past the falls, which are shown on the Snowbird Lake map, without even slowing down for a portage for these falls are nonexistent.

On July 16th we entered Kasba Lake. Inasmuch as the wind was blowing strong out of the northwest, we set up an early camp on an esker which runs along the west side of the lake. The spot we chose for our campsite had been used as a burying ground in the past. There were three or four marked graves as well as several human bones laying around nearby.

Someone had built a wooden fence around nearly every grave and erected a small wooden cross at one end of each grave.

That evening a boat with four Indians stopped for a visit. Their leader was Louis Baker from Cranberry Portage down in Manitoba. They had arrived in Kasba six days before us and were working for Canadian Federal

Fisheries. Their assignment was to check out the fish in the lake for possible future commercial fishing. They told us that they were catching lots of lake trout but the size of these fish was smaller than that of lakers taken in the south. One of the young men in the group was Raymond Marasty of Brochet, the same fellow who towed our group from Brochet to Kinoosao back in 1964. Raymond told us that he now had a wife, but would not get to see her again for about two months as their group would not leave Kasba Lake until just before freeze up.

Louis Baker informed us that the Chipewyan people called Kasba Lake *Cossed Whoie*, which means Partridge Lake. He also said, "We call the Kazan River Cathow-hachoga, which translates to, 'where fish are plentiful in the river'." Again it started to rain and our guests headed for their camp and we into our tents after saying some speedy good-byes.

The rain stopped in less than an hour. We again went out around the campfire as the wind was strong enough to blow the insects away and it was too early to turn in for the night. We sat around the fire sipping tea and smoking our pipes. We talked over plans for getting across the lake the next day and allowed as how we really needed a good day with gentle breezes from the northwest.

We discussed some of the early explorers of this area and I read a little to the boys from Samuel Hearne's journal of his crossing of this lake. Samuel Hearne was the man who made it on his own from Prince of Wales Fort at the mouth of the Churchill River overland all the way to Coppermine on the Arctic Ocean. He was sent by his employer, the Hudson's Bay Company, to find the copper mines which were the source of pieces of copper which were brought into the fort by Chipewyan and Cree traders. These mines were thought to be only a few hundred miles to the west. Hearne made three attempts between 1769 and 1772. In the search, he walked nearly five thousand miles, usually in the company of Indians. He was the first European to see the land between Churchill and Coppermine. His journeys were so difficult that some of his areas of discovery were not revisited by white men again for over 140 years. Hearne has been called by Farley Mowat and others "The Marco Polo of the Barren Lands." In fact, it was Hearne who named these vast treeless plains, the Barren Lands. Here is a direct quote from his journal.

> *Having got across the Cathawhachaga River we came to Cossed Whoie, or Partridge Lake, and began to cross it on the 7th of February. It is impossible to describe the intenseness of the cold we experienced that day, but the dispatch we made in crossing fourteen miles was almost incredible, for the greatest part of the men performed it in two hours; though the women, being heavier laden, took much longer.*
>
> *Several of the Indians were frozen, but none of them more disagreeably than one of Matonabbee's wives, whose thighs and buttocks were encrusted with ice so that, when they thawed, several blisters arose which were as large as sheep's bladders. The pain the poor woman suffered was greatly aggravated by the laughter and jeering of her companions, who said that she was rightly served for belting her clothes so high. I must admit that I was not of the number who pitied her, as I thought she took too much pain to show a clean heel and a good leg; her garters always being in sight which, though not considered indecent here, is by far too airy for the rigorous cold of the severe winter in a high northern latitude.*

Matonabbee, the Indian woman's husband, was Hearne's guide on his final attempt to locate the mine.

"Wow!" Lauren exclaimed. "That was 197 years ago. I'm glad that it isn't that cold here tonight!"

At that time it began to rain again so we called it a day. The downpour didn't let up until the following forenoon. Finally we were able to break camp about midday with a brisk, cold, summer wind out of the north which continued throughout the day.

Kasba Lake is a good-sized lake which lies on the 102nd meridian north of the 60th parallel where the provinces of Manitoba and Saskatchewan join. The lake is about twenty-four miles wide and forty-eight miles long. We needed to cross Kasba a little south of center from the place where the Kazan flows into the lake, to a small unnamed stream which flows into the east side of Kasba. On our maps this small stream seemed to be the most likely place for us to ascend to cross the height of land between Kasba and the Little Partridge River.

We had moved south, keeping behind the islands near the west shore until late afternoon. We were several days behind our planned schedule due to the high winds and downpours of rain, so we needed to keep going whenever we could. While eating our supper of fresh-caught lake trout on White Partridge Island, the wind dropped off. We decided to cross to the east shore that evening while the wind was not blowing.

There were no islands in the lake along this route, so the crossing was risky business as thunderstorms were rumbling to the north of us. When we were about midway across, a thunderstorm swept past us with a downpour of rain and wind.

We should have taken more compass readings and studied the maps better but in our haste we headed for a high hill on the horizon with a compass heading of 95 degrees; the small stream we wanted to find was just slightly south of being straight east of our landfall on the north shore of White Partridge Island. We held our heading at 90 degrees as we wanted to be sure to stay to the left of the small stream. At 11:30 that evening, we arrived at the east shore. It was a few minutes past sundown, but we soon found a level spot above the rocky shoreline to set up camp.

The next morning after more rain, we headed south hugging the shoreline, expecting momentarily to find the mouth of our small stream. We checked out the deepest part of every bay we came to. By 11:00 that morning, another huge thunderstorm closed in on us. We went ashore on a small island and set up our tents in time to get inside as the deluge hit. Four hours later we resumed our search for the inlet which was to be our exit point from Kasba Lake.

We worked our way south along the shore. Nothing looked the way it should have according to the map. We were certain that the first stream we came to would be the one we should ascend, so we kept going, even though we were having second thoughts as to why we were unable to find our exact location. Finally at about 6:00 P.M. we arrived at the first little river. We worked our way past a couple of rapids and came into a large lake. This confused us even more, as the map showed no lake at all in the little stream we had searched for all day.

Paddling south we saw a cleared strip of the small trees which grow on the fringe of the barrens. It looked like the clearing ran straight east and west.

"Dad, look at that! Remember the day we flew into Snowbird Lake, our pilot showed us the strip of trees which had been cleared off along the 60th parallel? I think we're on the 60th right now."

"You're probably right," I replied. "Let's go ashore and size up the situation."

So we went ashore, climbed a high hill in the clearing and that narrow strip ran to the horizon, both to the east and across the lake to the west.

What a blow! Downright disgusting! Now we knew where we were anyway. Right smack on the 60th parallel! As the two of us returned to the lake, we told Bryan and Lauren where we were.

"Can you imagine?" Darrell said shaking his head. "Four experienced canoeists! We've been lost all day and didn't realize it until now."

We did plenty of head shaking that evening as we paddled back north again. Nothing foolish would have surprised us after that. We had been in the most northwestern lake in the province of Manitoba which was about fifteen miles south of where we now knew we would find our small stream. By 11:00 that evening we were setting up camp a short distance north of where we had spent the previous night.

Instead of taking the blame for being lost, we each had an excuse. We tried to blame it on the weather, the swarms of insects at White Partridge Island and not allowing for the difference between true north and magnetic north when setting up our compass heading the previous evening. Actually, instead of crossing Kasba Lake going nearly east, in reality we went nearly southeast, thus arriving on the east shore to the south of the small stream instead of north of it as we had supposed we would.

That evening while waiting for supper, I bragged to the boys that this was the first time I'd been lost in over forty-six years. The last time was when I was four years old. My thirteen-year-old sister, Bernice, told me that we were going to walk from our house across the section to visit our relatives, the Killingers. Their farm joined ours along the back. To get there, we had to walk through our corn field, climb a rail fence, go through the woods and finally through their corn field to get to their house. Actually, she and I walked through our corn field into their woods, made a circle, and walked back through our corn field. Just before getting to our house, Bernice said, "We're almost to Killinger's. You walk straight up this corn row and you'll come out right in their yard. I'll be along in a few minutes."

I walked on into what I expected would be our cousin's yard. To my amazement, when I came into a yard, it was not Killinger's, it was our own yard. My sister thought that was very funny! When she finally recovered from laughing, she said, "Now let that be a lesson to you. Always pay attention to where you're going. Remember things like big trees, fences, other landmarks and where the sun is so that you can find your way back from wherever you go." Well, she certainly did teach me a valuable lesson, a lesson which served me well until that day forty-six years later when we four became lost on Kasba Lake.

The next two days were long and busy ones as we worked our way up the little unnamed stream and over the height of land which separates the Kazan River waters from those which flow down the Little Partridge River, on into the Thlewiaza River through Nueltin Lake and into Hudson Bay south of Eskimo Point. We knew that a trail had, at one time in the past, existed between those two watersheds and from studying our maps, were quite certain that we would find this old trail along our little stream. We lined the canoes for a distance along the shore as the stream flowed much too fast for us to be able to paddle. Then with so much brush along the shore, we waded, then portaged, then paddled and finally portaged again.

By lunchtime, we had found no sign of the old trail, and as the stream swung back to the south and was becoming more and more difficult, we decided to strike off east in as straight a line as possible. This was the shortest way for us to intercept the upper reaches of the Little Partridge. What's more, the little stream was becoming impassable even along its shores.

Our maps showed several small lakes to the east. All we needed was to find them to be able to paddle nearly half of the distance. So we left the little unnamed stream and found a small lake after a portage of nearly one half mile. Darrell and I then scouted ahead to find the next lake which was nearly another mile east of us. When that portage was completed, we all agreed that we'd had about all we could take for one day so we camped on huge fragmented rocks along the east side of the second lake.

The black flies had followed us by the millions all day. Bryan and Lauren suffered pathetically from the insects without headnets. That evening whole armies of mosquitoes waited to ambush us. Following a rushed supper we all disappeared inside the tents almost immediately to escape the hungry horde until the following morning.

Then more of the same the next day. Darrell and I would leave our partners in the canoe on a lake where they could escape the full fury of the insects. We would strike out to the east with our backpacks, maps, compass and axe to find the next lake, blazing a trail through the thick forest. Thus we could easily find our way back and then pack the canoes and other camping gear across to the next lake.

The second day we made seven portages from lake to lake and by evening had arrived in Lake 1313 which is the uppermost big lake on the Little Partridge River. The total distance overland was only eight miles. In those two days we each walked more than twenty miles to make the crossing.

One of the few enjoyments of this crossing were those drinks of delicious "wild water" from each lake. Between lakes the going was tough around the huge jagged rocks and through the boggy wet muskeg. The one thing we looked forward to as we struggled on was to get into our canoes again, get out on a lake away from those swarms of insects and indulge in a big drink of that ice cold, clear and delicious "wild water." "That stuff's always good, but it tastes even better in these little lakes," said Darrell.

We camped that night on an island in Lake 1313. We called it Lake 1313 because that is an elevation in feet above sea level which showed on our maps. Elevation figures are used on maps on some of the larger unnamed lakes. A terrific thunderstorm woke us up early the next morning with a downpour of rain which didn't let up until early afternoon. We finally broke camp and began our descent of the Little Partridge shooting some fast water and making five short portages during three more rain showers.

We found a good place to camp on an island which was only a couple of miles to the north of the 60th parallel. Lauren baked another fine cake and a double batch of biscuits to go with the fish and other delicacies which Bryan had prepared for supper.

Each time that Lauren baked a cake for us, he would push down the top of it with his hand when it was nearly finished baking. Finally, we asked him what he was doing.

He answered, "I'm checking to make sure it's done."

Darrell said, "Why don't you check it with a toothpick or matchstick so you don't flatten it down so much?"

Lauren said, "My mother always checks her cakes by pressing them down with her fingers. They're done if they bounce right back up again."

The three of us had a good laugh over that one. Soon the skies had cleared and there was enough breeze to keep the insects at bay. As we enjoyed the food, we talked about how that should be our final campsite in the District of Keewatin and the fact that we were more than three days behind our planned schedule.

To make our food supply last we were going to have to eat more meals of fish. Those young fellows seemed to have an almost endless appetite. Our food packs were beginning to look empty and at best we expected it would be another ten days or more before we could reach Brochet Post.

Darrell commented that we should travel longer each day and keep going even though it rained. He said, "Starting tomorrow morning, let's break camp earlier and stop only for thunderstorms or high winds on the lakes. We need to pick up some time if we're going to get out of here before the snow flies."

5

THE OLD NORTH TRAIL

The strong life that never knows harness
The wilds where the caribou call
The freshness, the freedom, the farness
Oh God! How I'm stuck on it all.

— *Robert Service,*
The Spell of the Yukon

The next morning, July 22nd, in sunny weather we again entered Manitoba. This time, however, we were not lost for we were on our planned course. We made a couple of portages, picked our way over some huge underwater rock piles and were able to shoot or line our way down several other sets of rapids. We made two more portages before entering Kasmere Lake by midafternoon of the following day. We crossed the lake and by late that evening were setting up camp on an esker along the west side of an arm of the lake leading to the upper Thlewiaza River and Kasmere Falls.

At about ten the following day, as we worked our way up the river, it began to rain again. We made a portage a few miles below Kasmere Falls and when we arrived at the falls we had difficulty finding the portage in the constant rain. Eventually it was found on our right and had once been a well-used trail. We soon entered Thanout Lake and passed the old and abandoned Fort Hall Trading Post. We should have stopped to look it over but didn't due to the continuing rain and our haste to keep going.

By the time the rains let up it was late and we were ready to camp. We picked another esker about one-third of the way down Fort Hall Lake. Bryan and Lauren prepared another feast for us that evening. While we dried out our wet outfit we decided that the insects were not quite as vicious as they had been when we were farther north.

There was another Indian burying ground across the narrow lake.

A nearby spot on a little peninsula was also a caribou crossing as someone had built a corral of poles across it. This corral was probably built by the Canadian game management people and used in their study of the barren land caribou which winter in the forests of this area.

Following much discussion and map study that evening, we made a decision as to which might be the best route from Fort Hall Lake to the Cochrane River. There were three possible choices and we were unsure which was the correct one. Lauren finally said, "I think if there is a trail, it would be the most direct route between those lakes right down through there." He pointed to the map. We agreed that his idea made good sense and that we would go that way, right or wrong.

With more heavy rain the next morning we were late getting away from camp. Winds were strong out of the southwest as we paddled to the south end of Fort Hall Lake. After moving through Blue Lake we picked up a good trail between the lakes to the southwest. We were overjoyed to learn that we had made the correct decision about our route to the Cochrane. By hustling down the connecting lakes and up and down over the hills along the trail, we reached the Cochrane by nine that evening. This was indeed the old highway which had been used for centuries by the Indians, trappers, traders and the occasional brave Eskimo.

Along the west side of the final lake before crossing the hill into the Cochrane, we passed a bald eagle nest in a treetop which had a large young bird in it while the pair of adult birds circled above us. At about eleven that evening, while washing up just before crawling into our sacks, we saw a large white wolf along the shore of the Cochrane just below our camp. This was the first wolf we had seen, even though we had listened to their howls on several different occasions.

On July 26th, we again headed down the Cochrane. We had intercepted it just below its northernmost bend. The cold summer wind was strong out of the northwest. Rain showers mixed with sleet hit us every little while with brief sunny intervals between showers. The temperature at noon was up to 46 degrees, which was the high for the day.

In early afternoon we saw a wolverine, and what a treat it was! This was the first wolverine any of us had ever seen. They no longer exist in the continental United States. They are scarce everywhere but are still occasionally found in the far north. Wolverines are the largest member of the weasel family, but they look more like a small bear with a bushy tail. The one we saw was dark brown in color with a light brown head and a sandy colored stripe down each side. They usually weigh between twenty and fifty pounds. This was a large one which came bounding out of the bushes and galloped along the riverbank just a little way ahead of us. We were moving along down a fast part of the river and we just about kept pace with this rare and beautiful animal as it ran along the shoreline less than one hundred feet away.

Wolverines are constant and restless travelers, always looking for food. They eat birds, eggs and any animals they can overpower including amphibians. They also feed on berries, fish and anything they can steal from man. They are best known for the havoc they play on the human residents of the far north where they follow trappers, stealing bait and destroying trapped animals. Thus they are the enemy of most trappers. Only a few wolverines are trapped or shot each year. Their fur is a valuable trimming for winter clothing as it doesn't freeze up with moisture in very cold weather.

Early that afternoon we arrived at the large unnamed lake just above Misty Lake. We were forced to put ashore as the high winds out of the northwest had increased to gale force. We built a fire and had tea with our lunch while warming up and trying to dry ourselves. During the afternoon we shivered and huddled around the fire to keep warm as the cold wind and frequent sleet showers continued. We were literally held prisoner by the wind.

We had an early supper so that if the wind velocity dropped that evening we could soon be on our way. We inventoried our food supply and were shocked at the small amount of stock remaining. Those young guys had terrific appetites. They were almost always hungry. We would surely have to eat more fish as we only had enough food remaining for about three days. It was most unlikely that we would be able to paddle down to Brochet Post in such a short time, even if the wind was to quit blowing immediately.

There were a couple of whiskey jacks, sometimes called Canadian jays or gray jays which hung around close to us that afternoon. Those birds were tame and would almost take scraps of food out of our hands. This reminded me of the time years before, when in Ontario north of Lake Superior, Ld W. Marshall and I had a whiskey jack actually sit on our hand and eat out of it. Then I recalled another year, even before that, when Kendall Hoisington and I were on a brief fishing trip west of Hawk Junction, Ontario. Kendall and I had hired a guide to show us how to catch speckled trout in a lake. This old gentleman also told us that whiskey jacks are edible in case you really run out of food. He then proceeded to tell us how to prepare one of these birds for a meal. He said, "You clean it as you would any other bird. Then to cook it, you put the bird in a pot of boiling water along with a rock, and salt to taste. You then boil the bird along with the rock. You can tell when the bird is ready to eat. It's ready when you've boiled it until the rock is soft enough so that you can prick into the rock with your fork." The boys didn't seem to appreciate my story. They must have been too hungry to think it was funny.

There was no letup in the wind. The sleet changed to rain. We decided to set up our tents and get some sleep. Then whenever the wind dropped in velocity, we would break camp and be underway. Lauren woke us at six the next morning. The wind had slackened. We embarked within a few minutes. By the time we were well out on the lake it again started blowing strongly. Finally after battling some high seas we did make it to the trail around the rapids at the entrance to Misty Lake.

After completing the portage, Darrell and I caught fish for breakfast while Bryan and Lauren built a fire. Darrell caught a two-pound grayling while I took a northern. This was the first arctic grayling we had ever caught and it tasted delicious. Following breakfast we went back to the base of the rapids and caught more fish to take along for future meals. By mid-afternoon, following our lunch of fish and cornbread, the wind slackened enough so that we could get going again. We crossed Misty Lake, riding south on and between some very high swells in the open areas of the lake. We were able to shoot Whitespruce Rapids before we rounded a bend in the river and were caught in a whirlpool along the right side of the rapids. This whirlpool spun us around and around. It was shaped like a huge dish with its circumference being two or three feet higher than its vortex. It was about a hundred feet in diameter. Fortunately by doing some hard paddling we were able to break out of the whirlpool as it spun us 'round and 'round.

We moved right along down the river for fifty-six miles during the next two days in much improved weather. We crossed Lac Brochet, portaged around three sets of rapids and slid the canoes past Chipewyan Falls, where we caught several more fish. We had some favorable wind and were able to set the canoes side by side in catamaran style and sail about ten miles before the wind gave out. We camped just before entering Easton Lake on an eskerlike mound.

Following supper of more fish we heard an outboard motor and saw a canoe approaching from down stream. Two Chipewyan men from Brochet came ashore. They did not speak English; however, they did know a few English words such as caribou, moose and go. We tried to communicate with them while they ate their supper of pilot biscuits and jam around our campfire. They were moose hunting and wanted to know if we had seen any moose. We had seen several during the past three or four days. These men were Pierre Ansanie and Alphonse Saphier. Alphonse had badly sprained his ankle earlier in the day and could hardly step on his foot. We gave him aspirin to ease the pain. I helped Pierre set up their tent and learned the Indian style of doing it while the boys and Alphonse drank tea and smoked their pipes. These fellows also taught us the word for mosquito. It's *julisaw*.

Tuesday, July 30th, turned out to be our last day on the Cochrane. Bryan rolled us out at six o'clock. Our Chipewyan friends were up shortly thereafter and following their breakfast of pilot biscuits and jam, they left us and headed up the river by seven.

"I guess we should learn a good lesson from them," Darrell said as the two men in their freighter canoe disappeared around the bend above camp. "They took less than three-quarters of an hour from the time they came out of their tent until they were on their way up the river. It takes us more than twice that long every morning." We all agreed. We would try to do better in the future.

Our first portage of the day was just below Easton Lake. There was plenty of fast water along the way including a couple sets of rapids just below the 58th parallel. By five that afternoon we were paddling on the surface of Reindeer Lake, having progressed over thirty-six miles during the day.

A strong wind was blowing out of the north that afternoon and we were unable to cross the large bay east of Brochet so we set up camp on the Indian reservation. Inasmuch as we were only a little over four miles from the post, Lauren baked up the last of our biscuit mix while Bryan cooked all of our remaining food for supper.

After a discussion that evening we decided that we would again try to hire someone to tow our outfit down to Kinoosao as three of us were due back at work by the following Monday morning. It would require perfect weather if we were to paddle that eighty miles of lake in three days. Our chances of catching the train south from Lynn Lake before the following weekend would have been slim indeed, so we decided to attempt to secure assistance.

By nine the following morning we had arrived in Brochet. We sent a wire home and purchased a few snacks from the Hudson's Bay store. There we found a man who said he would take us south on his thirty-foot inboard. What he didn't say was how far he would take us or at what time he would leave the post. After hours of waiting, finally, at three in the afternoon, he informed us that he was ready to leave.

Three hours later we arrived at Jackpine Narrows where after an hour of stalling around, the man informed us that he couldn't take us any farther south as that was as far as he was going. Finally, however, he did find a friend who agreed to tow us the remaining fifty-five miles for $75 plus the cost of gasoline. This man said we would be able to leave right away so we agreed to accept his offer.

By nine that evening we were heading south with three of us in the little fourteen-foot motor boat, Darrell in one canoe and Lauren in the other on tow ropes behind. As we rounded the south end of the island at Jackpine Narrows and headed toward the open lake, a terrific thunderstorm was moving in on us. Our boat operator didn't like the looks of it and neither did we so we told him that we would like to be put ashore so that we could set up our tents before the storm hit. He put us ashore on the south end of the island and headed back to his settlement after saying that he would pick us up again at five o'clock the next morning. Our tents were raised just in time to crawl in as the downpour of rain and strong wind hit us. Lucky for us we were not out on the open lake.

We were up at 4:30 the next morning as we wanted to be ready when our motorboat man showed up. When he didn't come by 6:30 we decided to paddle back to Jackpine Narrows and attempt to get a radio message out to Lynn Lake, requesting a plane to fly in and pick us up. We arrived at Jackpine by 7:30. There was no sign of life. Everyone was still sleeping.

An hour later a chunky gentleman walked from the house beside the icehouse to the outhouse. He didn't see us. On his return to the house, we walked up to him and told him about our situation. He invited us to follow him inside.

He got his wife out of bed by telling her that they had company. As soon as he had his pants on we introduced ourselves. His name was Ingevar Stolberg and he had first settled in the Reindeer Lake area in 1929 after arriving from Denmark. While Mrs. Stolberg was making fresh coffee and serving us cookies and hot biscuits, Mr. Stolberg was on his two-way radio calling Chiupka Airways in Lynn Lake. They agreed to pick us up about eleven.

While we waited for the Chiupka aircraft, the Stolbergs told us interesting stories of their life in the sub-arctic. Mr. Stolberg asked where we had been in the north and we told him that we had come down from Snowbird Lake. He was familiar with all the places we had been. He asked, "Did you happen to see anything of my old friend, Ragnar Jonsson while you were up there?" Of course we had not. We asked if he knew where Mr. Jonsson lived up there. He replied, "I think he's somewhere up around Nueltin Lake."

Ragnar Jonsson is the man we heard about while in Brochet in 1964. He only comes south to Brochet once each five years to pick up his mail and trade at the Hudson's Bay post. While we were there that summer, the post manager told us that they were expecting Mr. Jonsson to arrive soon as it had been five years since he last came down to pick up his mail. There were several boxes of mail waiting for him at the post.

The Bay manager had told us that the old fellow

roams around somewhere up in the Northwest Territories with his dogs and does some trapping. He said that when Mr. Jonsson came to pick up his mail in 1946, people were still talking about the war and finally Mr. Jonsson asked why they were discussing the war as it had been twenty-eight years since the war had ended. They told him that there had been another World War. That was the first time he had heard anything about World War II, as he had been out of contact with civilization since he had picked up his mail in the summer of 1941.

We asked Mr. Stolberg if that story was true. "Yes!" was his reply. "That's a true story. Old Ragnar just doesn't like it outside where there are lots of people."

Mr. Stolberg went on to tell us that back in the thirties he and Ragnar made a trip together down to Flin Flon for supplies. "That was before there was a Lynn Lake or a railroad. Back in those days the only way to travel in the summertime was by canoe. It was about 250 miles each way."

Mr. Stolberg continued, "We got a room in the hotel in Flin Flon to stay overnight before heading back north again. We turned in early as we wanted to get a good night's sleep before starting back. At about two in the morning, Ragnar woke me up to tell me that the town was just too noisy for him. He couldn't take it any longer, he couldn't get to sleep and so he was leaving. He went on to say that he would wait for me on the east side of the third island up the lake where we had left our dogs. That's where I found him the next afternoon. Old Ragnar just wasn't comfortable in town."

"It sounds to me like your friend is a living legend," said Bryan.

"Well," said Mr. Stolberg, "I wouldn't say that, but he is a successful trapper who really enjoys his life up there."

We asked more questions about Mr. Jonsson and learned that he was born in 1900 and came from Sweden. "Both of us came to Canada when we were young," said Mr. Stolberg. "We were here around the Reindeer Lake area for a while. Then this area became too civilized for Ragnar, so he went on up around Nueltin Lake. I don't really expect he'll ever leave the north, except when he comes down to Brochet for his mail every fifth year. He's a wilderness man if there ever was one."*

Following another cup of coffee and more cookies served by Mrs. Stolberg, Ingevar told us that the old trading post we had passed on Thanout Lake and known as Fort Hall was already closed when he first saw it back in 1929. About then our visit was interrupted by the sound of an airplane. It was a little before eleven. Within a few minutes we were saying our goodbyes to the Stolbergs and thanking them for their generous hospitality. We quickly loaded our gear and ourselves into the Norseman and with one canoe fastened to each side of the aircraft we winged our way over the lakes and hills to Lynn Lake.

What we didn't know as we left the Stolbergs and flew away from Jackpine Narrows was that Ingevar Stolberg had been one of the pioneer bushpilots of Canada. Later he had built up the business known as Chiupka Airways, Ltd., which is now called Calm Air International, Ltd. This company operates scheduled as well as charter flights into settlements all across north central Canada. We had been guests that morning of another of the living legends of the north and didn't realize it until several years later.

Even though we were happy to be heading for home, it was easy to understand why men like Ragnar Jonsson and Ingevar Stolberg wanted to live out their lives in their beautiful north country. Compared with the rest of the world, the sub-arctic seems like a vast realm of peace.

See Epilogue for an update on Ragnar Jonsson and Ingevar Stolberg.

THE RIVER OF MEN

> *The mighty river snatched us up*
> *And bore us swift along.*
> *The days were bright and the morning light*
> *Was sweet with jewelled song.*
>
> — *Robert Service,*
> ***The Ballad of the Northern Lights***

In the fall of 1971, Verlen Kruger of Lansing, Michigan, appeared at a meeting of the Commercial Club in my home town of Fowlerville. He showed pictures and talked of his experiences during a most unique canoe journey. He and Clint Waddell of Minneapolis had recently completed a Cross Continent Canoe Safari. They had paddled from Montreal across Canada and Alaska to the Bering Sea, a distance of seven thousand miles, during one summer. Never before in history had anyone completed a canoe journey of that magnitude in one season. These two men averaged nearly forty miles a day for 176 consecutive days. This was an outstanding accomplishment.

That story told by Verlen Kruger inspired Darrell and me to do more serious canoeing. We would never attempt to establish any canoeing records, but we decided to try to get to some of the more out-of-the-way places on the North American continent.   We both liked to get off the beaten paths and away from the rat-race of civilization. Verlen Kruger and Clint Waddell were not men who just followed the crowd.   They had the courage to do something different.   They were not afraid to get off the beaten path.*

So by the spring of 1972, Darrell and I were making plans to see more of the north.   This time we would travel alone in our seventeen-foot Grumman canoe.   We had decided to explore the remaining 590 miles of the Kazan River from Kasba Lake down to Baker Lake, which we had not seen on a previous journey.   This river would take us through the barrens where the inland Eskimos had lived for many centuries until the early 1950's.

Early that summer we repainted the canoe.   We named it the *North Star*.   This was the same canoe we had used on our earlier travels.   The *North Star* was originally owned by Ld Marshall.   It had been wrecked in a rapids on the University River north of Lake Superior in 1962 by Darrell and Keith Lillywhite when as canoe mates they got their signals crossed.   Darrell, who was in the stern, called out, "Right!   Right!" as they approached a large rock in the middle of the rapids.   Keith pulled to the left. Consequently, they broadsided the rock, and the canoe filled with water with the topside facing upstream.   The force of the rushing water wrapped both ends of the canoe around that rock, spilling them and most of their equipment into the river.

The force of the water swept them downriver but they managed to make it safely to shore at the foot of the rapids.   Their packs floated downstream and we soon pulled them ashore.   The fishing rods and camp axe, however, could not be found.   Fortunately, Elwood and I carried the food packs in our canoe.

"What are we going to do now?" Keith asked as he stood there dripping wet.

See Epilogue for an update on Verlen Kruger.

"We have no choice but to attempt to pry the canoe off that rock. Then we'll see if we can get it to float again," Elwood replied.

"That's right!" Darrell chipped in. "We have no choice. We're forty miles from the nearest road and the four of us could never make it out of here in one canoe."

So we went to work. Darrell volunteered to try to swim out and attempt to get the canoe loose from the big rock. He tied one end of a forty-foot line around his shoulders and gave Elwood the other end. The two of them made their way upstream to the head of the rapids, where Darrell waded into the river until he was swept off his feet by the swift current. He swam down to the wrecked canoe and tied his end of the line around the stern seat. We tied another forty-foot line to the end Elwood was holding and the three of us moved upstream, along the rocky shore, to gain more leverage against the current. Then we pulled as Darrell lifted but the wreck wouldn't budge.

Above the roar of the rapids, Elwood shouted, "Let's all pull together! Let's pull on three!" Then he counted, "One! Two! Three!" That time it moved a little. Then he shouted, "Let's do it again. One! Two! Three!" The canoe moved a few inches more. That pull on three count was repeated several more times. Finally the wreck did come loose and we pulled it up on the rocky river bank.

We sat the hunk of aluminum right side up in as level a place as we could find. Together we bent the center down. Elwood stepped into it first but he needed more weight. Soon all four of us were inside. By bouncing together it began to regain the shape of a canoe. Most of the large dents were then popped out, but there was still a problem. There was an eight-inch hole in the left side near the bottom. We cut down a tree and wedged a block of wood into the hole, sealing the leaks with chewing gum and tape. In that condition, Darrell and Keith were able to complete the run down to Lake Superior and along the north shore to Michipicoten.

We decided that when we returned home, the fair thing to do was buy Ld Marshall a new canoe because we had borrowed it from him for the University River run. Weeks later we had a patch of aluminum welded over the hole in its side and the *North Star* has been good for thousands of miles down many rivers and lakes since that time. This trip had been in the planning stage for many years. In fact, the Snowbird to Reindeer Lake journey in 1968 was somewhat of an exploratory trip so that we could become acquainted with conditions on the fringe of the barrens. Apparently in '68 we had extremely good weather, because we certainly were not prepared for the cold temperatures and high winds encountered on the lower Kazan.

The river which we were to follow for so many miles appears on white man's maps as the little known Kazan, but we will always favor the Eskimo name, "Inuit Ku," which means "The River of Men." The main purpose of this journey was to see the land and experience some of the conditions under which the inland Eskimos had lived for so many centuries.

Up to this point in time only a few parties had descended the River of Men. Recorded travel on the river began in 1894 when explorer J. B. Tyrrell surveyed the river from Kasba Lake to just below Yathkyed Lake where he turned east and out to Hudson Bay. Only five other groups made the Kazan River run between then and 1968, and all except one of these groups used either experienced Chipewyan or Eskimo guides. Darrell and I do not use guides on our travels. We like the challenge of being on our own in the wilderness.

On July 4 we were dropped into a nameless lake in the extreme northwest corner of the province of Manitoba by a pilot from Parsons Airways Northern. We soon named the lake Boundary Lake as the north end of it crossed the 60th parallel into the District of Keewatin. We had been in the north end of this lake four years earlier. This was the place where we had found a cleared line of trees along the boundary between Manitoba and Northwest Territories.

From an esker along the southeast shore of Boundary Lake we waved goodbye to our pilot. Little did we know

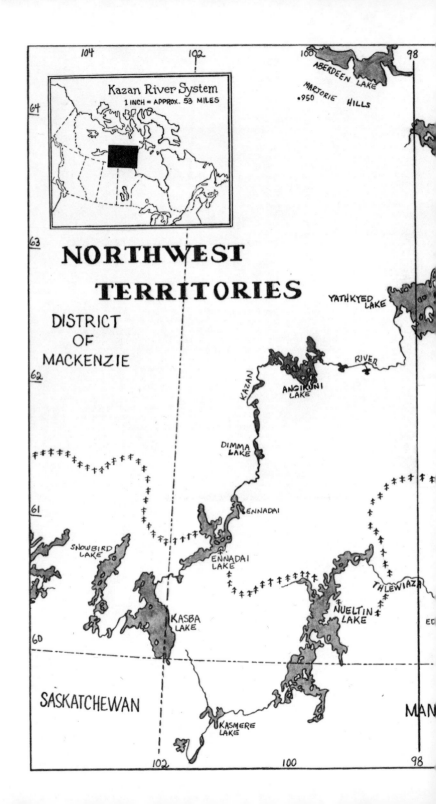

104 · 102 · 100 · 98

64

Kazan River System
1 INCH = APPROX. 53 MILES

ABERDEEN LAKE

MARJORIE HILLS
·950

63

NORTHWEST
TERRITORIES

YATHKYED LAKE

DISTRICT
OF
MACKENZIE

62

RIVER

KAZAN

ANGIKUNI LAKE

DIMMA LAKE

61

ENNADAI

SNOWBIRD LAKE

ENNADAI LAKE

THLEWIAZA

NUELTIN LAKE

ED

KASBA LAKE

60

SASKATCHEWAN

MAN

KASMERE LAKE

102 · 100 · 98

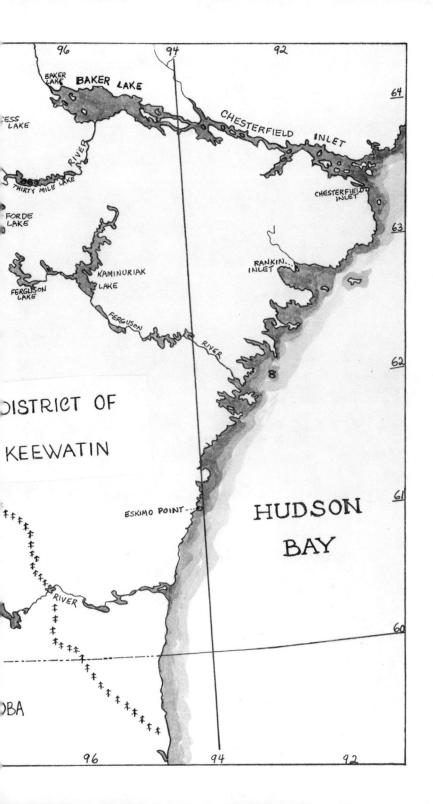

that this was the last plane we would see until our arrival at Kazan Falls nearly five weeks later.

We set up our first camp on the esker. There were some Indian graves nearby with the usual little old wooden fences around them. It was a delightful campsite but with more than an ample supply of insects. That first night in camp we experienced a feeling of exhilaration at being finally liberated from traffic, telephones, timetables and all the other trappings of civilization.

We went for a paddle along the lake shore while the sun's rays cast a spell in the bright light with reflections of clouds, blue sky and trees onto the surface of the water. "This is called the Ross light," said Darrell. "As you know, it happens frequently in the north just before sunset." The glassy light made every object stand out in stark relief. Like ghost trees, the birches along the shoreline emerged in shimmery whiteness against the dark spruces, while the deep blue sky with an array of cumulus clouds reflected onto the surface of the lake. It was a beautiful evening. Certainly it was a fitting way to begin our descent of the Inuit Ku.

That first evening we had checked the temperature of the water in Boundary Lake and found it to be 62 degrees. We then discussed the fact that with the water temperature so warm, we surely wouldn't be bothered with ice anywhere along our route. The following morning we crossed the 60th parallel and moved down the little stream into Kasba Lake. Due to a stiff breeze out of the north we paddled close to the east shore all day. By mid-afternoon we were surprised to see some large ice floes drifting down the lake. Late that same day we came upon a huge area along the shore that was covered with ice to a depth of several feet, and which was still solidly anchored to the bottom of the lake.

We made thirty-two miles during the first day on Kasba Lake before we set up camp. By then the water temperature was down to 42 degrees. We were astounded at the change in conditions in so short a distance.

By mid-afternoon of our second day we arrived at the outlet to Kasba Lake and began our descent of the Inuit

Ku. Our first portage was a short one over the rocks along the right bank. The second portage was on the left bank over a hill through a thick growth of small trees. This second portage was nearly one-half mile long and required over an hour to complete as we each had to make three round trips. From there on down into Ennadai Lake the canoeing was very good. The river, except for its expansions, moves fast and is already a good-sized river between Kasba and Ennadai lakes. Darrell strung up his fishing rod below the second rapids and immediately caught an eight-pound lake trout for our supper. That evening we camped on an esker at an expansion in the river beside an old spruce tree which held a bald eagle's nest in its top. The nest was vacant but we saw an adult eagle leave the tree as we approached the esker.

On July 7 we moved down through Tabane Lake where we saw a moose swimming between two islands. We soon entered Ennadai Lake. Just west of the entrance to Ennadai we found the ruins of an old log cabin settlement. We went ashore. There were five buildings in all, and each was pretty well caved in and rotted down. We did not find anything of value other than some fishnet floats. We estimated that the buildings probably had not been used for the past fifty years or more. Darrell remarked, "I wonder what this place was used for?"

"It might have been a base camp for a trapper or a prospector, or it may have been a trading post."

"It would be nice to know who it was that lived way up here and something about the place including its reason for being here."

Later we learned the truth. The place had been the original trading post operated by Husky Harris from 1909 until 1916. Then in 1917 he moved his business sixty or more miles east to the mouth of the Windy River where it flows into Nueltin Lake. At that time the buildings at Ennadai were abandoned.

These were the years when furs from the north were much in demand. Prices were high. The traders did everything possible to encourage the Eskimos to trap more and more of the fur-bearing animals. By the '20's, for example, the fur of an arctic fox would bring forty to fifty dollars, which in those days was a considerable amount of money. The Eskimos were taught to trap the white foxes and to bring them to the trading posts where the traders paid with goods. Payment was usually made with items such as traps, repeating rifles, ammunition, flour, tobacco, tea or various other supplies. Nearly all of these items were new to the Inuit people. Naturally they were anxious to obtain them. The rifles made it easier to hunt caribou, for the animal supplied them with their main food items, skin for their clothing and tents, and many other essentials.

So the Inuit trapped the white fox and brought it to the trader. Husky Harris was the first trader to come to the area to trade with the Inuit people from the north. He also traded with the Chipewyans from the south. According to Charles Schweder, Jr., whose father once operated the Windy River post, "Husky Harris remained in this region at one time for fifteen years without going outside. He then took his Eskimo wife for a visit, down to Winnipeg."

With a strong wind blowing from the west, we detoured to the northwest shore as soon as we passed the tip of the esker at the entrance to Ennadai. We hugged the shoreline for the next seven miles before finding a good campsite along the esker to the north.

That evening we walked a mile or more on the esker and found it to be criss-crossed with caribou trails most of which ran parallel with the lake shore. We were camped just above a fine long crescent-shaped beach curving around our little bay. The water temperature was a cool 56 degrees but much warmer than the 42-degree temperature registered in Kasba Lake. We decided to go for a swim.

The mosquitoes descended on our bare skins by the thousands. The only way to escape them was to dive completely underwater and then stay under. When we came up for air, there they were, ready to swoop in immediately. But the big struggle came when we wanted to get back on the beach to dry off and put our clothes on.

The Author with Natural Star of David

That was sheer agony! Darrell and I with our towels were trying to get dried off fast while running away from the swarm and struggling to get back into our pants. At the same time we were swinging towels and trying to get our socks and boots on so we could get some protection from that hungry horde.

The following day was another beauty, with a gentle breeze out of the southwest. We paddled along the north shore for a while, then crossed over to be near a series of islands close to the south shore. Our lunch break found us on a rocky island where a number of gulls were nesting. Apparently they thought we intended to rob the eggs from their nests as the Eskimos and Indians did, because they put up a terrific fuss, squawking and diving at us in great agitation. Finally we found ourselves fighting adult gulls off with our canoe paddles as they dove at us time after time. Their diving bomb runs continued until we were once more underway.

When we first entered Ennadai Lake, trees were still very much in evidence, but during our second day of paddling, our surroundings changed within a few miles. First only the distant hilltops were barren, but then all of a sudden we noticed that the trees had disappeared. We seemed to have crossed the literal "tree line," although we would still see stragglers for another hundred or more miles. "There's no doubt about it," Darrell said. "We have entered the barren lands." This was our first real view of the barrens and it would prove to be a challenge.

The tree line defines the general northern limit of the Chipewyans' hunting grounds from the southern limit of the territory claimed by the inland Eskimos. The Eskimo people formerly lived all along the Kazan and its tributaries from Ennadai Lake on down to Baker Lake and beyond. These Inuit, as the Eskimos called themselves, were still plentiful as late as the 1920's and early 30's, but now they are gone. They have virtually passed out of existence.

That evening we set up camp on the west shore about eight miles north of the 61st parallel. We could see for miles in any direction with not a tree of any size in sight, just bare tundra dotted with a few brush and many rocky knolls. About one half mile to the northeast was a ravine white with snow, and some large rocks in the lake southeast of us also had ice lodged on their tops, probably blown there by the wind as the lake ice broke up.

To the east we could plainly see the buildings and radio tower of the Canadian Department of Transports, Ennadai Lake station. "Those buildings are about six miles from here," Darrell said as he checked our maps. "It sure doesn't look that far. Distances are going to be hard to judge until we get used to it here in the barrens."

I agreed with him and said, "Another thing hard for me to get used to is the fact that here the word 'down' means 'north'." All of our lives the word 'down' had been connected with phrases like 'down south' or down any place south of us. Now we were traveling downstream on a river system flowing north to the sea, so we were going 'down north.' We would have to refer to places already passed as 'up south.'

Earlier that day we had stopped to stretch our legs on a most unusual island. Instead of being composed of rocks and gravel, this island was made up almost entirely of peat moss. From a distance it appeared much as any of the other islands in this lake, with a flat, nearly level top. Two things caught our attention — the island's dark reddish rust color and the fact that the east side was eroding away and had fallen in large chunks into the lake.

We went in for a closer look. It was indeed made up of a great pile of peat moss. Along the face of the eroded area, the solid humus extended from the surface of the lake for fifteen to eighteen feet to the highest elevation of the island. Huge chunks of the dark organic material had fallen into the lake as it had been gradually undercut by the action of the water and ice. I commented to Darrell, "That material had to have been formed thousands of years ago, at a time when temperatures remained nearly tropical for a long period of time. It's almost inconceivable that so much humus could form at this high northern latitude where it now stays frozen the year around except for the top few inches."

Darrell said, "It would be interesting to learn the scientific explanation of how an island such as this one could be way up here." Then he quipped, "You could say that this is one humungas island."

The next day was Sunday, the ninth of July. The weather remained fine as we crossed over to the east shore. By mid-forenoon we arrived at Ennadai Lake station from where we planned to send a telegram home. We wanted to let Marjorie, Millie, Debbie and the girls

The Crew of the 'Ennadai Hilton'

know that we were on schedule and in good condition.

We saw no one outside, so we walked up the hill to the main building. A sign over the door read ENNADAI HILTON. We knocked. For nearly a minute all was quiet from within. Then we could hear sounds of moving feet and shuffling inside. After nearly another minute the door was opened. There stood three of the most surprised gentlemen we'd ever seen. One of them held a rifle. It took another minute or so for them to recover enough to answer our "good morning" greeting. We had to tell them twice how we happened to be at their door because they kept saying, "We didn't hear an airplane." Finally they began to relax and we introduced ourselves. The man with the rifle set it behind the door. They invited us in and told us they couldn't imagine who could be knocking at their door as they had no neighbors within several hundred miles. The whiskered man who had been holding the rifle said he thought we might have been some renegade Eskimo knocking at their door.

The three men were Ernie Philstrom, station operator from Winnipeg; John Risco, assistant operator from Vancouver; and Bill Campbell, the cook, from The Pas. They soon had the coffee pot going and Bill made up some delicious individual hot raisin pies. One man told us that we were the first people that any of them knew of who had ever arrived at their station by canoe. These men were part of a four-man crew who were operating the station at that time. The night operator was sleeping while we were there. They usually staffed a five-man crew, but ten days before our visit, their fifth man drowned only a little distance from the station when their motor boat was swamped in a bad storm. They found his body tangled in the anchor rope, floating near the boat.

These men were overjoyed that we were there, and wanted us to stay on all day. They must have led a lonely life because they stayed at the weather station for a year at a time without getting a visit "outside" to civilization.

They told us that we were 290 air miles from Baker Lake. We also learned that none of them had even been to the north end of Ennadai Lake. They couldn't seem to comprehend how it was possible that we could make it all the way down to Baker Lake in our little *North Star*.

Finally, just before noon after taking pictures of the crew and they in turn taking pictures of us, we said our goodbyes. They each called out to us as we paddled away, "Now you fellows be careful!"

THE WINDSWEPT
BARRENS

The more we received a modern education, the more spiritually illiterate we were becoming . . . We might know some physics, or astronomy, but we did not notice if the moon waxed or waned, and we were losing wonder at the visage of the stars.

—*Gerald Wallop, Earl of Portsmouth,*
A Knot of Roots

That afternoon the north wind began to whip up, so we hugged the east shore all the way to the outlet. It was difficult paddling. It also began to rain, and turned cooler from the high of 53 degrees in the early afternoon.

At the outlet we found a little cabin. We stopped, and removed a shovel from the door latch. The building belonged to the Water Survey of Canada. By checking the log book we found that we were at their Kazan River outlet of Ennadai Lake. They had recording instruments set up to keep track of the amount of water flowing down the river. The log book also recorded that the place was checked on July 6.

Darrell Klein with Arctic Grayling

Darrell remarked, "That's only three days ago."

Their previous visit was dated 12 May, 1972, and both entries were signed by E. R. Engstrom of Churchill.

We replaced the shovel in the door latch, and moved on down the river for about eleven miles before we decided to call it a day. Just before setting up camp, we stopped below a little riffle in the river to catch a fish for supper. We each made only one cast. Darrell caught a two-and-one-half-pound grayling and I brought in a ten-

and-a-half-pound lake trout. I guess you know what we had to eat that night, and they were delicious! As we enjoyed the fresh-caught fish, Darrell remarked, "I think I prefer the lake trout. It seems to taste better than the grayling."

"Ya, me too."

"This is sure one big, fast flowing river, isn't it?" Darrell remarked.

"It certainly is! This is the biggest river we've ever been on. I hope the weather fairs up tomorrow so we can see the eclipse of the sun. It should be almost total here at this latitude above the 61st parallel, and it will be the last total eclipse to be seen in North America until the year 2017. I won't be around to enjoy that one, but you should be around to see it. Let's see. By then you'll be only seventy-two."

"Yup! I might make it if I live to be an old man."

The strong northeast wind continued all night, and by the following noon it was raining. We went ashore on a little beach and quickly put up our tent as we were making very little headway paddling into that strong, cold wind. We crawled into the tent to keep warm as the rain continued and the temperature climbed to its high for the day of 44 degrees.

When the downpour finally stopped that evening, we immediately rolled out to fix some food. "Sure enough, we have missed the total eclipse of the sun," Darrell remarked as he gathered little wet sticks to light a fire.

I was so disappointed that I found myself unable to reply. Finally, to get it out of my mind, I said, "Do you think you're going to be able to get a fire going for us?"

"Absolutely," he replied. "I've never seen it fail yet, but this one is going to take a little doing. Everything's so wet." Sure enough, he soon had a nice fire burning and while supper cooked, I began to recover from the disappointment of missing my last possible total eclipse.

On the beach about forty feet from our tent was a bird who cried out at our movements as we brought sticks in for our fire. She resembled a killdeer but was only about half the size. The bird, with a band of black feathers around her neck, was trying to lure us away from her nest by pretending to have a broken wing. She dragged it pathetically over the sandy beach just as a killdeer does in our fields at home. Her nest was soon located. Three eggs lay in a little saucer shaped depression in the sand. Each time we approached the nest she flew a few feet and again tried to distract us with her broken wing trick. Neither of us knew what kind of bird this was, except we were sure she was a member of the plover family. Later we learned that we had been watching the antics of a semipalmated plover.

The wind continued from the north all the next day, but we kept digging our paddles into the water, making it all the way down to a peninsula in the center of Dimma Lake. The Inuit Ku really moves along down hill toward the sea. We made only one portage over the rocks on the left as the river swings to the east just a couple of miles above Dimma Lake.

That same evening as we were finishing our meal, a large caribou came trotting along the shoreline towards us. By the time the animal had approached to within thirty feet, we had shot it several times. The shooting was done, of course, with our cameras. We have made it a practice never to carry firearms of any kind on our travels in the north.

We were forced to remain on the peninsula in Dimma Lake until late the following afternoon by a gale out of the northwest. This gave us ample time to do our laundry, and to sew up some holes in our pants.

"The only good thing about all of this wind is that there's no insect problem today," said Darrell. "I would rather have it calm, and battle the bugs. At least then we would be making progress down the river."

We needed to progress at least a reasonable distance each day to maintain our schedule, because we were due to be back at our work in Michigan by the first Monday in August. We were only packing enough food to last until that time, and now we were beginning to fall behind in our travel plan.

While walking across the peninsula, we found where

someone had lived for a time, long ago. There were seven old tent poles, a fuel can, and two pots with patches in them. Two kerosene lanterns nearly covered by moss lay nearby.

On July 13th, we broke camp at about 4:30 in the morning. We wanted to move while the wind wasn't blowing. Two hours later the lake was rolling so high that we were forced ashore to bail water out of the canoe. While waiting for a wind change in the 36-degree temperature, we again walked to try to keep warm. One hundred yards from shore we came upon a large area of stone rings where Inuit had once anchored their caribou skin tents. In years past, it had been a sizeable settlement as there were actually hundreds of stone rings. They were either circular or oval in shape, and some measured up to thirty feet in length. In some places three or four tents joined each other, with little connecting tunnels so the people could go from tent to tent without going outside.

"It's hard to imagine how this area must have looked when the people used to live here," Darrell remarked.

"Wish we could have seen it back in those days. Think of the thousands of caribou hides it took to make all of those tents!"

"Yes! Plus all the additional hides these people used each year for their clothing, blankets, boots and other things."

Caribou, which the Inuit called *tuktu,* had literally provided the life blood of the human residents of Canada's northern plains since time immemorial. Caribou were also the main source of food, and life itself, for the Inuit. The people had relied on caribou for nearly everything they owned. It is estimated that when the Europeans first arrived along the fringes of the barrens, about two centuries ago, the caribou herds consisted of over five million animals. By 1950 the herd had dwindled to about 650,000, by 1955 to 280,000, and by 1960 to less than 200,000 animals.

With the decline in caribou, there was also an accompanying decline in the Inuit population. There always was uncertainty in these people's daily lives, because a hunter might be unfortunate enough to miss these animals in their migratory maneuvers. This uncertainty, along with the utterly inhospitable winter climate, placed a limit on supportable population. With this natural balance, the introduction by the white traders of firearms was certain to affect both man and animal. This swap of spears and bows and arrows for repeating rifles brought a few years of plenty. Then the great herds of caribou dwindled, and the people starved and died.

In the early 1920's, there were well over five hundred people living along the shores of Inuit Ku. By that time, some of them were making annual visits to the trading posts to the south, swapping caribou skins for supplies. For several years the traders, such as the Hudson's Bay Company and Husky Harris, paid the Inuit people good prices for the pelts of the arctic fox.

Then in the 1930's, the price of the white fox pelt declined to a point where there was no sale for them at any price. By that time, however, the Inuit people had learned to live the easier life and had given up hunting for the trapping of these fox. With the decline in fur prices, the trading posts were soon locked up, and the people had nothing to do but return empty handed and without ammunition for their rifles.

These people tried desperately to spear the caribou. They no longer had bows and arrows, nor were they able to make bows, because the muskoxen had been shot off along the Kazan many years before. The people had made their bows from the horns of muskoxen.

A desperate and terrible struggle to survive went on, but it was a losing battle. Without caribou, no food was available and no tents could be built. Caribou hides had always been used to make shelter when snow conditions were not right for building igloos.

A very small number of these people were all that managed to survive in their homeland on the barrens until 1957. At that time, the Canadian government moved the few survivors to one of the trading posts on Hudson Bay, where a few of them and their descendants still remain.

Until mid-forenoon we occupied ourselves by talking as we covered the old settlement, and looked for artifacts without finding anything worth taking with us. Then the wind velocity slackened somewhat so we were soon back on the lake. Frequently we took on water even though we hugged the shoreline as closely as possible. Progress was very slow paddling into that northwest wind.

"It's amazing how these winds in the barrens blow so hard," Darrell said. "I never realized how much a stand of trees could slow down the velocity of the wind."

That evening we crossed the 62nd parallel and camped on an island in the river about two miles beyond. On a small hill near our tent we found a kayak paddle and some wooden parts for the frame of a kayak. An inukshuk also stood on the same hill.

We first started seeing inukshuks, which in the Inuit language means "Stone Men," along the shores of Ennadai Lake, and we found them all along the way from there on. They are built of rocks and made to resemble a man. From a distance they look like people, varying in height from two feet to more than six feet. The Inuit built them on nearly every hill where caribou might pass in their migrations. Caribou are nearsighted animals, and the reason for the inukshuks was that a hunter with a bow and arrow or spear, and standing still in his fur clothing alongside an inukshuk, would also resemble an inukshuk. He could then often spear the animals as they passed by. Later we found that inukshuks were also built in prominent places to mark a trail or crossing place between lakes, or around impassable sections in rivers.

By evening of the next day, after a continuous battle against the cold summer winds from the northwest, we finally arrived at the final bend in the river above Angikuni Lake. We set up camp beside the Eskimo's Mount Kinetua. This mountain is a very large dome-shaped rock standing about seventy-five feet above the surrounding area.

There had been many geese and ducks along our route. Now, a large white tundra wolf watched as we rounded the final bend in the river above our camp. Then he followed along on the opposite shore, keeping us in sight until after our tent was set up. Two inukshuks stood on the hill across the river, seemingly watching our every move as we prepared our meal of delicious lake trout.

On July 15th, the strong wind picked up to gale force shortly after we broke camp at six in the morning. We decided to try hugging the north shore of the bay in the southwest part of Angikuni. That day turned out to be difficult, hazardous and disappointing as the gale continued to blow along with intermittent showers. Several times we were forced to put ashore and bail out the canoe.

At mid-day we discovered that, in our haste to break camp that morning, we had left behind the metal cooking grid used to set up on rocks over the fire while cooking the meals. What a blow! There was no way we could paddle back into that wind! From now on our cooking would have to be done by setting rocks closely together so that the edges of the pots and pans could rest on the rocks. It would be more difficult but we immediately agreed that we could manage without a cooking grid. We both accepted the blame. We had learned another costly lesson. Never again would we leave a campsite without a final look around to make certain everything had been picked up.

By 5:30 we made it to the east end of the bay and crossed the peninsula into the large part of the lake. That was it for the day because the gale howled on. In the wet 42-degree temperature that evening, we again discussed the wind. Believe me we had no good words for it, because our tent flapped, whipped and rattled throughout the night.

The wind and showers continued until about 8:30 the following morning. Then as the sky cleared the wind tapered off. We crossed the main part of Angikuni before camping that evening just to the left of the lake's outlet.

There were several large patches of snow around the eastern part of the lake. "This certainly has been a gorgeous day," said Darrell. "I hope we can have a week or more of this same kind of weather."

"That would be what we need, but two weeks would even be better. Two weeks could easily see us into Baker Lake. We've now covered about half of our total distance."

Inukshuks stood on several islands along the way as we crossed Angikuni. Just above our tent on a little hill three more of them stood, and it seemed as though they were constantly watching our every move. That was a perfectly enjoyable evening, the first we had had in many days. There was no wind, bright sunshine, and with the 36-degree temperature the mosquitoes didn't bother. We stayed close to our little campfire, and there was ample fuel nearby to keep it burning.

We talked about J. B. Tyrrell who was the first to explore this part of the Kazan River back in 1894. At that time the Inuit were plentiful all up and down the river. I read to Darrell a copy I had brought along from Tyrrell's journal of his travels along this part of the river. His entry for August 21, 1894 said:

August 21 — Paddled out into Angikuni Lake. Shortly five kayaks came to meet us, then seven and then three, all the men wanting presents of tobacco. As we crossed the lake we were surrounded by a swarm of 20 – 30 kayaks, all the men anxious to see the first white men to descend their river. On the western shore was said to be the village of Outoowiack with 5 tents. We reached the village Enetah with three tents and as a high east wind was blowing, with a big lake ahead we were obliged to camp among a swarm of inquisitive Eskimos. We bought some boots and a coat chiefly with needles, though our supply was not nearly as large as it should have been. One man, Anuleah, came in in the afternoon from a short distance up the river. He says that he goes every winter to Du Brochet Post (Lac du Brochet) to trade, and that all the Eskimos bring their furs to him. He is going as soon as the snow comes, and will take a letter from me . . .

August 22 — On account of the high wind we were only able to travel six knots today, and we were alone with our two Eskimos for the first time. As we were eating lunch a fine big caribou appeared in the distance. Taking my Lee-Metford rifle I fired two shots at him, the first falling short, and the second hitting him. After lunch I went to him, and he was lying dead just where he had fallen when I shot him. I paced the distance to our lunch place at seven hundred yards. From that time onwards both the Eskimos as well as the canoemen thought that there was no limit to the range of that rifle. Ferguson shot the nearer game with the Winchester, while I took the longer shots with the Metford.

I spent a couple of hours with our Eskimos getting the name of things around us. They said that there were no Eskimos on the streams south of here. In winter there are no deer in this vicinity, and the Eskimos live on the deer that they kill and cache in the summer.

Ahyout (Tyrrell's guide) said that he had seen white men four times, at Churchill, Du Brochet, and at two other places further west. He has travelled over all the country from Dubawnt Lake to Churchill. His son, Kakkuk, saw white men when he was a little boy. He then came in the spring overland from Churchill to here . . .

August 23–24 — Windbound on this island. Kakkuk went hunting but could find no deer. Took some photographs around camp, among them the two Eskimos standing on each side of the head of the buck that I had shot at seven hundred yards . . .

August 25 — Paddled seven miles to the end of the lake . . . Then three miles of rapids down to Ungalluk with three large tents containing 20 people. Here Ahyout wanted to talk and to

*arrange for crossing the long portage ahead so he
kept us about three hours. One of the Eskimos
riveted the handle on our frying pan very nicely.*

*From there taking four more men to help us,
we ran down the river about 2 miles to the head
of a portage a mile and a half long past three
rapids. We got the canoes over, and camped at
10 p.m. at the first of the portages 60 feet above
the river. Some of our things were left scattered
along the portage covered by tarpaulins, and
Ferguson was very much distressed about them.*

*August 26 — This morning the rest of our
things were brought over the portage. Four
miles lower down the river we came to Pasamut's
camp with seven tents, and 42 people in all. The
weather was cold but the children were playing
about quite naked. A woman had a baby, and a
man had shattered his arm by accident with his
gun. It was mortified up to the elbow and was in
a dreadful condition. They asked me to help him
but of course I could do nothing.*

Darrell explained, "Boy! Things have really changed
since then. It's hard to imagine — all those people who
used to live around here and now they are all gone."

"Sure is! How would you have liked to have been
canoeing down through here about seventy-eight years
ago?"

"I would have liked to have seen it then. What a thrill
it would have been to see twenty kayaks of Inuit people,
paddling in here to visit us! If we were fortunate, they
would probably have supplied us with a feast of boiled
caribou."

"Yes! That would have been great! We might have
been able to trade them something for a couple of nice
warm coats. We sure could use them! And maybe they
would have held a drum dance for us."

"That would have been nice, but we are really
dreaming. Those days are gone forever, and it could never

happen again because the Inuit are now gone," Darrell concluded as he pulled out our Tulemalu Lake map.

Every evening, part of our daily ritual was to study our maps to learn as much as possible about what we could expect to encounter during the following day. From Angikuni, the river flows mostly east for about eighty miles before it swings north again towards Yathkyed Lake. In that distance the Inuit Ku drops over three hundred feet nearer to sea level.

There was solid ice on our kettle of drinking water when we prepared breakfast the next morning. The wind soon picked up and true to form, it was not about to co-operate with us. It came up the river out of the east all day. Here is a quote from our journal of July 17 —

This is a beautiful, large, fast-flowing river. The average width here is about a quarter mile. It would certainly be a great canoe ride down if it were not for the gale which we faced all day. We had more rain showers today but they were only a small problem compared to the wind. In all today we proceeded only about twenty-five miles. With the speed of the river we could have doubled twenty-five without the headwind. Tonight we are camped on one of the poorest possible campsites. We are only here because we were 'blown off' again this evening about 8:30.

Tonight while stepping out of the canoe onto a large rock, it rolled over and I fell flat on my back into the shallow water. It gave Darrell a real scare. He hollered, "Are you hurt? Are you hurt?" as I picked myself up. Fortunately for both of us I was OK except for a wet back side. He said later that he was afraid I'd broken my back.

We made no portage today and the river probably dropped about one hundred feet nearer to sea level. We are sure hoping for a wind change by morning. We need it. We're falling too far behind our schedule.

That wind did, however, continue to blow from the east at a high velocity all night, and all day for the following three days. A steady rain began during our first night and continued until mid-afternoon of our second day there. It took Darrell over a half hour to get a little fire started because everything was wet. We huddled beside the fire, downwind from some short willow bushes which grew near the river, while we cooked some food. It had been more than twenty hours since we had last eaten.

Shortly thereafter, another downpour hit us, and it continued without letup until forenoon of the second day following. Believe me, we were two miserable guys. The water rose around our tent in those three days until we were actually lying in our sleeping bags in the water by the third morning. We had been unable to find a better place for our tent.

Our thermometer readings for that period varied from lows of 34 degrees to a high on the third day of 44 degrees. With that cold wind and our thin jackets, we had a real problem keeping warm enough to carry on. That was the first time in all of our canoeing experience that we had been forced to spend three days in the same place.

The rain seemed to be letting up by the third morning so we decided to try and move while we could. We loaded everything into *North Star* and were underway by 5:30. The wind was still strong out of the east. We managed to make about three miles and then went ashore to have a quick breakfast. We both felt weak from the lack of food for our last hot meal had been forty hours before. Fuel was nearly impossible to find, but we did locate enough for a small fire. We cooked up a double batch of cream of wheat. That, along with coffee, biscuits and jam, and our strength began to return. While eating, the rain started again, so we set up the wet tent and crawled back inside to escape the cold summer wind.

ICEBOUND IN
LATE JULY

We watched the groaning ice wrench free,
Crash on with a hollow din,
Men of the wilderness were we, freed
From the taint of sin.

— *Robert Service,*
The Ballad of the Northern Lights

Good weather finally arrived! The morning of July 21 began with a portage of about one and a quarter miles past a couple of drops in the Inuit Ku. As we made the traverse a pair of rare peregrine falcons who were nesting on a rocky ledge high above the river flew in circles overhead screaming at us. Terns and gulls also darted in and chattered. The River of Men continued untamed, as the remainder of the day was spent running an almost continuous twenty mile rapids, making six portages and rounding the bend where the river swings north again. It seemed great after being weather bound for such a long time. Along the way hundreds of geese strained their paddles and wings ahead of us, honking continually. Flocks of them pattered up the shore to hide behind rocks or in the dwarf vegetation.

Inukshuk Overlooking Yathkyed Lake

By mid-afternoon of the following day we saw a large inukshuk standing on a rise on the left side of the river. We went ashore and walked up the hill to investigate. From the inukshuk's vantage point looking northeast, we could see out over Yathkyed Lake. It appeared that most of the lake was still covered by ice. The only open water we could see was a mile or so where the Inuit Ku emptied into the lake. A little way from the inukshuk we found a large area of stone tent rings. This was another place where the people had lived. More than likely this was the old settlement the Inuit called Palenah. J. B. Tyrrell described Palenah as "near a place where the river was deep and narrow (which it is) and the caribou in their migrations regularly swam across the stream."

It is also probable that this was the same place where Samuel Hearne crossed the river back in 1770. The river was called Cathawhachaga in Hearne's time. Cathawhachaga is a Chipewyan word meaning "where fish are plentiful in the river." The Yathkyed Lake area was, at that time, the summer hunting grounds of the Chipewyans. This happened because the Indians came in contact with the trading posts many years before the Inuit people. The Chipewyans had used their guns to successfully drive the Eskimos away from their former homeland in the barren grounds. By 1894, on Tyrrell's trip, this area was again inhabited by the Inuit.

In his journal Hearne had written —

On the 26th of June we again proceeded northward and on the 30th arrived at a river called Cathawhachaga, which empties itself into a very large lake called Yathkyed Whoie, or White Snow Lake. Here we found several tents of Indians who were employed spearing deer from their canoes as the animals crossed the river on their journey north. On preparing to leave, my guide informed me that a canoe would be absolutely necessary to cross some of the unfordable rivers ahead of us, and this induced me to purchase one from the strange Indians at the easy rate of a knife, the full value of which did not exceed a penny. The canoes made by these people were extremely small and scarce able to carry two men, one of whom had to lie full length on the bottom. Nevertheless, this additional piece of luggage obliged me to engage another Indian; and we were lucky to get a poor, forlorn fellow who was used to the office, never having been in a much better state than that of a beast of burthen. Thus provided, we left Cathawhachaga and continued our course over open rocky plains toward the north and west.

We paddled out in the direction we had planned to go to cross Yathkyed Lake, hoping that what we had seen was only slush ice with a few large floes in it. But no such luck! When we arrived at the floe, it was far too solid to ever get a canoe through. Most of the ice was about a foot thick along its edge where the warm Kazan River water had been flowing under it. The remainder of the lake appeared to be completely frozen over, from shore to shore. We paddled back to a little peninsula on the east side of the river mouth. This was at the place where the Kazan entered Yathkyed Lake. Our spirits were low as we set up camp on the rocky point, and talk that night was of the ice, and of our chances of completing the journey before having to be rescued.

It was already July 22. We still had about two hundred thirty miles to go. We estimated that if we could get across the lake without too much delay and the present near-perfect weather continued, we might still be able to reach Baker Lake by August first. When we registered with the RCMP in Lynn Lake we had given them the date of July 28 as the latest date we would check in with their detachment at either Baker Lake or Churchill. That night we speculated that they probably wouldn't launch a search for us before the first of August.

Darrell said hopefully, "If we can find a way around or through that ice tomorrow, we still may make it out on time. The river below the lake is certainly open and we are sure due for some more good weather." We inventoried our food and found that we still had enough to last another six or seven days.

"By eating lots of fish, we should be able to stretch our food supply by several extra days, if we have to," I added.

"There are also plenty of geese around here that are in molt and we should be able to catch one or two, if we need them," Darrell remarked, as geese honked it up on an island about one-half mile away.

After breakfast the next morning, we shoved off in *North Star* to check on the ice conditions and to see if there was a possible way to cross the lake. First we tried the shoreline east of camp. We managed to work our way through some ice floes past a small bay which was filled with solid ice. Within one-half mile we came to a place where the ice was still solid against the shore. We walked along the rocky shore for some distance but could see no more open water, either along the shore area or across the lake. Back in the canoe again, we followed the edge of the ice to the west where there were lots of trout swimming, their dorsal fins frequently showing above the surface of the water.

We saw three islands about one-half mile north of our campsite and paddled to the one with the highest elevation. At its highest point, we looked for an opening or lead in the ice, but found none in any direction other than the open water back to our camp and on up the Kazan. Two of those three islands were still frozen into the edge of the solid ice leaving only the smallest island in the center in open water.

"Dad, this doesn't look encouraging. Let's paddle along to the west shore and have a look from there," Darrell said. On the way to the west we also decided to try to get the canoe up onto the surface of the ice to see if we could pull it across the ice with a rope as we would have pulled a toboggan. That attempt was futile! We could not find an area where we could put our weight onto the ice without breaking through. It was full of little holes like honeycomb, and just wouldn't support any weight even though it was about twelve inches thick.

When we reached the west shore where we had hoped to find some open water close to shore, we again found solid ice.

"What a disappointment! There's no way we can carry everything around this big lake," Darrell sputtered.

"We're really trapped. We'll just have to wait. Maybe this stuff will break up in another day or two and we can go on," I replied. "Especially if this warm sun keeps shining as it has today."

Back in camp, we settled in around the huge inukshuk that dominated the point. We designated the northeast tip as our laundry and fish-cleaning area, the northwest part of the point as our canoe-parking area, the level area south of the inukshuk as the tent area, and the kitchen area was just to the northeast of the inukshuk. This entire area covered not much more than one hundred feet in any direction.

The temperature of the water flowing past our point checked out at 51 degrees. In the bright sunshine the air temperature rose to 58 degrees. There were a few dead dwarf willow bushes on the peninsula, so we had an ample supply of cooking fuel. We gathered up some of these little sticks, and then could no longer resist the urge to try the fishing. We cast our lures from the rocky ledge along our campsite. On the first casts we each hooked and landed nearly identical seven-pound lakers. We caught and then released several more trout, varying in size from five to a little over ten pounds. Darrell also caught a grayling. We selected a small five-pound laker to keep for our lunch.

That afternoon, following a siesta, we walked south on the tundra. There were several kinds of birds in the area. We watched a pair of sandhill cranes and listened to the strange sounds those long-legged birds made as they hurried away from us. We were both surprised to see a robin hopping along near some dwarf willows. We certainly didn't expect to find robins north of the tree line.

"That's a turdus migratorus, the technical name for robin," I said.

"Dad, did you say turdus?"

"Yes, I did! Turdus migratorus!"

Darrell chuckled and replied, "That's a good name for them! You remember the old saying 'you're full of —— like a young robin'." To that we both laughed. Other birds we saw were ptarmigans in their brown and white feathers, while jaegers occasionally swooped overhead. We also discovered another group of stone rings indicating

Lake Trout Were Easy to Catch

where the Inuit used to live.

We were warmed up when we returned to our "point," the first time we had really been warm in nearly two weeks, and it sure was a pleasant feeling. Then some fool suggested that inasmuch as it seemed warm and the day was so nice, we should go for a swim. There was no question whether or not we needed to clean up because we had been unable to wash off since our swim in southern Ennadai Lake back on July 7, so we really needed that bath. The shock nearly took our breath away! That swim turned out to be two of the fastest baths in history. Believe me, it was refreshing, and it was good to get into some clean clothes.

We had lost considerable weight on the journey and were now wearing our belts in the last holes. "That's from eating so many fish along with all of the exercise," I said as I used my pocket knife to punch yet another hole into my belt.

"Those lake trout, called *islug* by the Inuit, sure do taste good. There's no comparison in flavor to the lake trout shipped to restaurants in the south," Darrell remarked.

"You are making me hungry again, son. What shall we fix for supper?"

"Let's have another trout. I'll catch it if you'll clean it."

"You've made a deal. I'd like trout for supper too. Do you think you can catch one?"

"Watch this," he said as he picked up his rod, walked over to the end of the rocky ledge and made a cast. The lure no more than hit the water when he jerked the rod to set the hooks. Sure enough he had one on. In about five minutes he lifted out another eight pounder. The fish was soon cleaned and within the hour we were feasting on fried trout, hash browns, and warm biscuits. The meal was topped off with vanilla pudding and coffee. The strange thing was that we devoured the entire islug with that meal.

Here is a quote from my journal of July 24 —

Today we paddled out to the ice north of camp and visited a couple of the islands. We did some fishing which was simply great along the edge of the ice. Today we were more hunting fish than fishing. The four to ten pounders can be caught on practically every cast, consequently we would only cast when we sighted a large one in the water. We are hoping for a trophy fish but didn't see one today. To land one of these lakers

*requires at least five minutes of tiring them
enough so we can lift them out of the water and
release them.*

*The geese on the center island north of camp
are beginning to honk it up again as they have
been doing every evening we've been here.*

*Not only do we have our own private river,
the several hundred miles of the Kazan, we now
have our own private lake, Yathkyed. This lake
is larger than Lake St. Clair near Detroit, and we
are the only people to fish it this year — and the
fishing's sure great!*

It did in fact seem like our own private river and lake
for we had seen no other people since leaving the three
men at Ennadai Lake. Neither had we even seen or heard
any airplanes other than a high-flying jet which flew over
the area three times each week, probably on the polar
route from the United States to Europe. We were alone
for hundreds of miles, cruising down what seemed like our
own private river.

Time was slipping away from us with each day more
or less the same. And still we waited. Perfect weather,
and nearly twenty hours of sunshine each day. The solid
ice just couldn't last much longer. We settled into a
routine of sleeping when we were tired and eating when
we were hungry. The eating, however, consisted mainly of
trout as we stayed on short rations of our supplies. Once
each day we paddled out to check on the condition of the
ice, which was slowly receding, but no leads developed
either into the lake or along the shores.

One afternoon as we looked north across the lake, we
saw what looked like lake ice continuing up and over the
hills on the north shore. This was a mirage. Mirage
effects are a common phenomenon in the far north, and
frequently occur over cold water and ice, and usually on
clear, sunny days. We had seen mirages before, over large
bodies of water, but this one was the most spectacular.
We watched this beautiful mirage for nearly an hour. At
times the ice seemed to move slightly up and over the far

northern horizon. We decided to photograph it to see if our camera could also see the phenomenon we had been watching; and sure enough, it did! The camera saw the same mirage we had been watching, so we have this proof on film that we had indeed been enjoying a most spectacular mirage.

On Wednesday, July 26, during our daily trip out to inspect the ice conditions, we stopped for lunch on a small rocky island that had been freed from the solid ice pack within the last twenty-four hours. The little island was still completely covered with ten to twelve feet of pulverized ice which must have been pushed there by a storm.

We also stopped on the center island north of camp to look at the geese. We planned to try to catch one to add to our diminishing food supply. We searched that entire island where we had been seeing and hearing geese since our arrival at Yathkyed, without success. The geese were gone! We didn't see or hear them again during our remaining days in the lake.

Darrell remarked, "Those geese left just in time. They must have known our plans for them and anticipated 'fowl' play."

We continued our watchful waiting for some change in the ice conditions. Each day some time was spent fishing and hunting for dry sticks for fuel. The fishing never failed and we caught trout as we wanted them. They were delicious fish, firm and fat as they are in all northern lakes where the water temperature remains near the freezing point all summer. They are so tasty that we always looked forward to our next meal which usually consisted of more fish. We enjoyed them fried in bacon grease, we liked them broiled over the open fire, we relished them in stew with dehydrated carrots or corn and flavored with onion, and we also liked to eat them cold after having boiled them in a bucket of water.

One afternoon we found ourselves discussing the former residents of the area. Darrell said, "I remember reading somewhere that the Inuit people used to call this lake 'Hikoliguak.' That was a good name for it, because in their language, *hikoliguak* means 'great water with ice that never melts'."

"I hope enough of it melts this summer so that we can soon be on our way," I replied.

"Me too!" Then, after a thoughtful pause, Darrell continued, "The Inuits used to call people like us 'Krabloonak,' which in their language means 'the big eyebrows.' They also had a name for the Indians from the forests to the south, calling them 'Irkrelret,' which is the Inuit word, meaning 'the lice.' To these people who used to live around here, they, and they alone, were the men, the only real men. They thought of themselves as the men par excellence and they looked down on all other peoples."

"It's easy to understand why they thought of themselves as the greatest," I replied. "Any group of people who had the intelligence required to survive in the harsh environment of the barrens for countless centuries certainly deserves a lot of credit. I'm afraid that you and I wouldn't last long out here in the winter."

"That's for sure! We'd better not be around here when winter comes. The Inuit are probably the only people on earth who could survive up here."

"Back in 1922, the Arctic explorer Knud Rasmussen spent more than a month visiting the settlements of the Padlermuit people who were living here along the shores of Yathkyed Lake. He called them 'the most remarkable people in the world'."

"Rasmussen was from Greenland, if I remember correctly," said Darrell.

"That's right! He grew up in Greenland and spoke the Inuit language. Subsequently, he had no trouble conversing with these people. In those days, the chief of the Padlermuit was a man named Igjugarjuk. He and Rasmussen took a liking to each other from the outset. The chief declared that Rasmussen was the first Krabloonak he had ever seen who was also an Inuit."

"Those two men spent hours together discussing many topics. While discussing education, Igjugarjuk said something that gives a little insight into the intelligence of those primitive peoples. According to Knud Rasmussen, the chief said to him,

*All true wisdom is only to be learned far from
the dwellings of men, out in the great solitudes,
and is only to be attained through suffering.
Privation and suffering are the only things that
can open the mind of man to those things which
are hidden from others.*

"That's amazing," declared Darrell. "The Inuit people
must have been a highly intelligent people."

"Yes, they were. Much more so than we white men
have generally given them credit for being. Our educators
in southern Canada and in the United States could well
have learned from the Inuit people, but they didn't. The
problem is that they wouldn't humble themselves enough
to listen. They could never admit that these people might
have an idea worthy of their consideration."

Darrell grinned and said with a moan, "You know the
old cliche, 'misery loves company.' Civilization is what its
leaders have made it, and the leaders are what modern
education has made them. Our civilization is in a 'higher
education' rut, all right, and it isn't likely that it will
change in our lifetime."

We spent a lot of time in the tent, because it was
usually warmer inside the sleeping bags, especially when
the weather was overcast or windy. We became well
rested, and this caused us to daydream a lot. Most of the
dreams were of the people who used to live along the Inuit
Ku; or of the people back home whom we had known in the
past. We had many interesting conversations as a result
of those daydreams.

There were strange things happening to our health
that we didn't understand. Not only had we lost a lot of
weight, but Darrell developed a badly ulcerated tooth.
His jaw and the left side of his face were swollen until one
eye became nearly closed. We both developed large areas
of blisters on our noses, cheeks, lips and hands. When the
skin came off these blisters, the sores remained opened
and raw, even though we tried everything we had in the
first aid kits. Nothing was effective! We thought our
sores were caused by the constant exposure to the cold

and wet conditions experienced since leaving Kasba Lake. When these open sores didn't improve during the good weather of the past several days we grew more and more concerned. Of concern also was numbness in our hands and feet.

We learned later that those problems were caused by the steady diet of fish and freeze-dried foods, plus a lack of fresh fruits and vegetables. Even though we did not really go hungry, we had developed a serious vitamin deficiency and were suffering serious malnutrition.

The fine weather continued for nearly a week, and we were constantly hoping for a change in the weather to break up the lake ice.

Here is a quote from our journal of July 28 —

Thunderstorms caught us last night, with lots of lightning all around. Here we are with aluminum tent poles and less than a rod away stands the large inukshuk. We are fortunate indeed that we didn't catch a bolt of lightning because the poles and inukshuk are the highest points in our area. The storm cracked, rumbled, and snapped around us in a downpour of rain, and gusts of rain hit us time after time nearly blowing us and our tent into the lake.

The storm continued throughout the night. By mid-morning the rain let up for awhile, but a strong north wind blew all day with intermittent showers and clouds right down to the ground.

In fact, it was nearly five this afternoon before we could see to the nearest island a half mile away.

For supper tonight we had another trout, plus Rice-a-Roni, hot biscuits with jam, and the last of Marjorie's good pickles. I caught another ten-and-a-half pounder from the rocks along our camp, and had a much larger one hooked but it got away when it broke my new fifteen-pound test line.

*Today is the date the RCMP in Churchill are
expecting us to report in to them. We expect
that they may launch a search for us if they don't
hear from us within the next few days. The
weather is looking somewhat better tonight, and
it appears as though the lake may now be open
along the west shore. The cold summer wind is
still strong out of the north and the temperature
stands at 39 degrees. We will break camp early
in the morning and attempt to work our way
around to the outlet, wind and ice permitting.*

For Saturday, July 29, our journal says —

*The wind and ice didn't permit us to leave
today. In fact, the good Lord made certain that
we stayed here. The wind continued all night and
became a howling gale out of the northeast. It
has continued all day today also. At about five
this morning, it began to pour and continued
raining all day.*

*We ventured out of the tent for the first time
at 3:30 p.m. The temperature was 37 degrees,
and in this cold wind it seems like zero. We did
manage to heat a pot of water and have a bowl
of soup along with some crackers. Then it was
back into the sleeping bags to keep as warm as
possible. The wind began to taper off a little
around 9:30, so we were out again for a few
minutes to grab cookies and candy for snacks.
That was it for the day, and what a horrible time
it has been!*

*All day long the gale force winds kept moving
the ice in on us and past our camp and up into
the river mouth. A steady flow of ice moved
along at a speed which we estimated at between
three and four miles per hour. Some great
chunks of ice floes were several hundred feet
across, and they made a tremendous, grinding
roar as they slid over the giant rocks around our*

camp.

We sure hope this rain lets up so we can get dried out tomorrow. We are also wondering how things are going at home, because we had intended being there by now. We know our family must be worried. We're also wondering about unimportant little things such as, whom did the Democrats nominate for the presidency in Miami three weeks ago, and how have the Detroit Tigers been doing?

The long–wished–for gale had come at last. There was no question about it. The Yathkyed Lake ice was finally breaking up. We would be off and underway just as soon as the storm subsided and the broken–up ice field moved away from the shore along our camp.

Our journal entry for Sunday, July 30th says —

The rain let up for awhile during the night, but started again this morning as the northeast wind continued. It rained steadily until mid-afternoon. We braved it outside the tent at 1:30 to pick up something to eat. We were both weak from lack of food since Friday, and also from so much time spent on our backs in the sleeping bags trying to keep warm. We soon had some food prepared. The wind shifted around to the northwest. It warmed up to 42 degrees. There were acres and acres of ice at our doorstep, but during the afternoon it all moved back east into the lake from where yesterday's gale had blown it. The wind is losing some of its velocity tonight, so we may be able to break camp early in the morning.

That evening we had a pleasant surprise. We could hardly believe our eyes when we saw a canoe headed our way from the west side of the river mouth. We welcomed our two visitors ashore. They turned out to be Jim Arnold and Gary Heiling from Minneapolis. We told them that we had been ice bound on this point for the past eight days, and Jim said, "This is the first ice we've seen since we left Snowbird Lake over a month ago." He went on to say, "There are six of us in our group. We were paddling north over there along the west shore when we sighted your camp here. The other two canoes are continuing on and will set up camp for the night, but Gary and I wanted to come over to say 'hello'." Gary Heiling then added, "You two are the first people, other than our own group, that we've seen since we were dropped off at Snowbird back on June 28th. It's good to have someone else to talk with."

Darrell and I both agreed. We asked them where they sat out the terrific storm. "In the sand flats about eight miles upstream," was Jim's reply. "That gale blew our tent down twice." They were soon into their canoe again and heading back to join their group after visiting with us for about half an hour, taking their leave just as darkness began to settle in.

The following morning dawned clear, calm and cold. We broke camp before six and decided to gamble on crossing Yathkyed in a direct line from our campsite to the outlet. There were a few islands along this route and no ice in sight as we started. This direct crossing cut the distance in half when compared to following the shoreline as we normally would have done. This reduced the distance to only twenty and a half miles in the open area of the lake to the tip of the peninsula which forms the west shore of the outlet.

The weather remained perfect most of the day as we made the traverse. We could see plenty of ice in the southeast part of the lake, however. When we stopped for lunch on the larger island along our route, a snowy owl sat atop a pile of large rocks blinking big round eyes at us, and probably wondering if we were creatures from another planet. This was the first snowy we had seen, and it reminded Darrell of this little rhyme by Farley Mowat —

> *The Snowy Owl, I've heard it said*
> *Lives on the entrails of the dead.*

It loves to gorge on rotting bowel
Which spoils it — as a table fowl.

By mid-afternoon we rounded the tip of the peninsula in the northeast corner of the lake just as the first breezes came sliding by out of the east. Low clouds soon moved in, and a cold wind then began to whip up. We were both tired and hungry as we finally approached the rapids at the outlet of Yathkyed at about seven that evening. Nearing the rapids, we made what easily could have been a fatal mistake. We didn't take time to go ashore and look the area over. Instead, we looked the rapids over from the canoe and thought there was only a small drop. We decided to shoot it! We were in mid-river and the powerful current soon carried us close enough to the drop so that we realized we had made a faulty decision.

"This doesn't look good," I hollered above the roar of the rushing water, as we both slid to our kneeling positions on the canoe bottom. By that time there was no turning back because we were being sucked into the rapids at an ever-increasing speed. We shot over one drop of about three feet and through a standing wave below, taking on half a canoeful of water over the bow and gunwales. About thirty feet ahead was another, larger drop.

"We'll never make it," Darrell yelled. "Try to pull her to that big rock!" Fortunately for us we were able to slide the bow onto the rock which lay at the next drop and which was covered by only an inch or two of water. As the bow slid solidly up on the rock, the water inside *North Star* completely submerged the stern seat where Darrell was kneeling. We managed to keep her right side up while we baled her out. We were both wet, but Darrell was completely soaked with icy water. Our problem was what do we do now? We were stranded on a submerged rock in the middle of rough rapids. It was about eighty yards to either shore, but with all of the Kazan's icy water rushing along on either side of us, we had but one choice. That was for both of us to get out on the rock without losing our footing, bail the water out, and manually lift the loaded *North Star* over the rock and slide her down into the eddy below. Then we would have to shoot on down to the foot of the rapids.

Before embarking into the eddy below the rock, we discussed and agreed on what appeared to be our best possible proper procedure for descending to the bottom of the cascade. We would try to keep along the right, out of the heaviest chutes of water, to avoid two more sets of standing waves about one hundred fifty feet below. Our plan was to work our way down while keeping as close as possible to the line of visible protruding rocks, then to cut back hard to the right just above the final drop. We would have to keep a close lookout for submerged rocks which could be lurking just under the surface. To collide with one of those would have been "curtains." We said a prayer, and finally we were ready.

We shoved off and carefully maneuvered *North Star* around and out into the edge of the chute. We used skulling draw strokes so we would not pick up too much speed. Easing our way along, I kept an eye on the surface watching for hidden rocks. Rapidly we slid along, bumping lightly against a boulder on the right but keeping control. Then came the short turn to the right followed by another drop of more than a foot and we scooted into slower water to avoid the final standing waves.

With the roar of those rapids finally behind us, we made it to shore within the next quarter of a mile. As soon as we set our feet on solid ground we both thanked God for helping us out of that near disaster. We found dry clothing in our pack sacks, changed, dumped water from our boots, and then began to search for fuel for a fire. It was mighty scarce. It took more than a half hour to scrounge up enough twigs and sticks, but we finally did get a small fire going. We then raised the tent so that Darrell, who was suffering the most, could get inside out of the strong 39-degree wind.

While he was trying to warm up, I tried to catch a fish for our supper. Walking down to the river bank, I soon tied into a real lunker of a laker. Following a lengthy battle, I finally landed one that weighed in at eighteen and three-quarters pounds and was the largest lake trout we had caught. Our problem now was that with such a shortage of fuel we needed a smaller fish for our supper. This laker was just too large, so it was released and after a few more casts we settled for a small six pounder. That little trout, along with some hot soup and biscuits, sure tasted good after our long and eventful day, a day that finally saw us out of Yathkyed Lake and, best of all, out of those dangerous rapids below the lake.

BETTER LATE
THAN NEVER

> *Suffering, straining, striving,*
> *Stumbling, struggling on.*
>
> — *Robert Service,*
> ***The Suburbs of the Pole***

When we awoke the next morning a strong wind was whipping the tent, and the rain was falling again. The rain let up by mid-afternoon but the wind howled all that long day, coming up the river at us from the north. This gave plenty of time to analyze the situation as well as to feel sorry for ourselves.

"I'm glad that we brought along the little one-burner Coleman stove," I said as we warmed water for coffee and soup for our late breakfast. It was nearly impossible to find sticks to build a cooking fire. "We should have had a two-burner camp stove. This little one doesn't throw much heat."

"Yeah," said Darrell. "But then we would have had to carry more than this one gallon can of gasoline, which, by the way, is almost empty." We had expected to find plenty of willows and other low bushes for cooking fuel all the way down the river.

Another serious problem was that our food supply was just about gone. We would have to eat mostly fish for the remaining meals. We inventoried our food and found that we still had about a pound of sugar, three packets of instant soup, about one-half pound of candy, a pound of mixed nuts, a pint of instant rice, a small can of Crisco and one package of Rice-a-Roni, plus salt and pepper. We had intended being back in Michigan before the end of July. Now it was August and we still had nearly one hundred forty miles to canoe.

"If we meet up with the group from Minnesota again, we'd better tell them about our food situation," Darrell said. "They might have some surplus we can buy."

"That sounds good to me."

Another problem we discussed almost daily was our inadequate clothing for the weather we were finding in the barrens. Darrell had only one sweat shirt with a parka hood. Most of the time he wore his rain suit over the sweat shirt to break the cold wind. I had one lightweight zippered jacket and a poncho that flapped when the wind blew. Neither of us brought winter underwear, thinking we would find much warmer weather during July.

We also discussed our error in judgement about the rapids the previous evening. There we had definitely committed a "no-no." We had always made it a practice to look over any questionable rapids from the shore before deciding whether to "shoot" or "portage around."

"Maybe our steady diet of fish, plus so much exposure to the cold and the fact that we were low on energy has affected our vision," said Darrell.

"You may be right. The river also looked O.K. to me, until we got too near the rapids to turn back. Let's be sure we take no more chances like that! There are several more drops in the river ahead, and we must be more careful even though we are late, tired and hungry."

"That's for sure," Darrell replied. "It will be better to be late getting out of here than not to get out at all."

When the rain began to let up we were out to prepare

for travel again. Looking back upstream towards the rapids we were pleasantly surprised to see four tents pitched along the shore line just above those rapids. They had to be the men from Minnesota. We would wait until they came along in case they had some extra food we could buy.

We didn't have long to wait. They were soon dropping their tents and heading down our way. Jim Arnold, Gary Heiling and their group came ashore and we talked for awhile as the strong north wind continued to blow. We told them of our short food supply. They opened their food packs, and generously gave us small bags of white and whole wheat flour, prunes, corn meal, Red River cereal, and dried fruit. They also handed us soup mixes and a plastic bag of freeze-dried carrots and sweet corn.

They refused to accept our money saying that some of their group had experienced similar conditions on past trips, and anyway, they were sure they had more food than they could use up. On a previous trip, one of the men had smashed up his canoe in a rapids on the Seal River in Manitoba, and had to wait nearly a month to be rescued. Another of this group had been ice bound on Dubawnt Lake for two weeks and had run out of food.

These were surely kind and understanding men! Soon they headed on down river, and we followed thirty minutes later knowing that our next meals would be vastly more substantial.

Progress was slow and strenuous. After crossing the 63rd parallel, we portaged past the rapids and soon after were blown off the river again. Fuel was nearly non-existent. We searched for close to an hour before finding enough sticks to cook supper.

Our final meeting with the Minnesota group occurred the following day when we overtook them at the entrance to Forde Lake while they were having their lunch break. They insisted that we share their food with them, and they again brought more good things from their food bag. Believe me, we were thankful for their help of the past two days. We departed after lunch to battle the headwind and waves of Forde Lake, leaving our friends behind. We had to move on as fast as possible.

Earlier that day we had paddled past the "bank of boulders" in the little bay on the right where J. B. Tyrrell and R. Monroe Ferguson left the Kazan and headed east toward Hudson Bay on September 1, 1894. Tyrrell could have continued on down the Kazan to Baker Lake, but he had paddled through there a year earlier following his descent of the Dubawnt River and he knew that September was high time for him and his group to head out of the barrens.

In camp that night at the north end of Forde Lake, our talk was of the generosity of the Minnesota group, the Inuit people, and of J. B. Tyrrell. I read aloud to Darrell these entries from Tyrrell's journal of his exploration through the area in 1894 —

> *September 1 — Three and a half miles farther down the river we ran into a little bay of quiet water on the right, and from it, at a bank of boulders, the portage starts eastward. It is 2050 paces long, over wet ground to a little lake drained by a brook northwestward into the Kazan river. At the east end of the portage I took an observation for latitude 63° 7' 48", which was the last that I was able to get for a long time.*
>
> *Six extra Eskimos worked for us on the portages. Ahyout had hired them for a box of caps and a plug of tobacco each, for the whole job, and they were to supply their own food, which they could do without trouble as deer were plentiful.*
>
> *September 2 — Last night it rained heavily, and today a south east wind drove the rain in our faces making travel very disagreeable. The country is a great flat sedgy plain, with patches of dwarf birch here and there. It is wet everywhere. Five of the Eskimos stood a great stone slab on end at our camp tonight, though all eight of them worked hard all day, and were*

*delighted when I gave each of them a little piece
of tobacco about as big as one's thumb nail.*

*September 5 — Portage 900 paces across
very wet flat to the shore of a lake which I
called Ferguson Lake after my volunteer assistant, and I also called the river that flowed from
it to the sea Ferguson River as a tribute to him
for his splendid contribution and assistance to
the success of this expedition.*

"In his entry for September 2 he explained just how
the Inuit erected an inukshuk, didn't he?" Darrell asked.

"Yes, he did. They used a lot of manpower. Another
amazing thing about this man J. B. Tyrrell is how he, after
arriving in Churchill, again walked all the way from there
to Winnipeg, just as he had done the winter before. The
distance between those places is nearly one thousand
miles."

August 3 was one of those excellent days which didn't
happen very often that summer along the Inuit Ku. We
were under way by 4:40 in the morning. Here is a quote
from our journal of that day —

*Today we moved down and all the way to the
east end of Thirty Mile Lake. We didn't take
time for many shore breaks. The only unnecessary stop was on an island where we thought we
saw a small box on a hill. This was in western
Thirty Mile Lake. It turned out to be an exciting
stop because there was a grave under a pile of
nearby rocks. We found a human skull near the
box, a handmade wooden drum hoop called
'Kriloan' by the Inuit people, a toy wooden sled, a
toy sleigh runner carved from a caribou antler,
and a 1947 calendar in a crack in a big rock. The
calendar is still in nearly perfect condition. The
last four items we will attempt to take back to
Michigan. The skull, however, we left snuggled
in the moss just as we found it.*

Our Find in Thirty Mile Lake

Today we actually saw hundreds of inukshuks
along the route. They are standing on almost
every hill and especially on the higher islands in
Thirty Mile Lake.

Tonight we are camped about a mile and a
half south of the rapids that are the exit from
Thirty Mile Lake. Our tent is set up on a large
level tundra area where stone tent rings surround
us. There were thousands of 'the People of the

Inukshuks Were Standing on Most Hills

Deer' living here in the past. Now they are all gone. Instead of calling the Kazan 'the River of Men,' 'the River of Ghosts' now seems more appropriate. It's as though we have been traveling for over a month in a 600-mile-long cemetery.

A nice day tomorrow should see us below Kazan Falls by evening, only about twenty-eight miles down river from here.

August 4 was certainly a day to remember. We portaged past the rapids at the outlet to Thirty Mile Lake. We had narrowed the distance to the falls to eight miles by lunch time. Several inukshuks stood atop the rocky hill near us as we took our break.

Darrell remarked, "With a little luck we could be camping below the falls tonight." Little did we know then just how far below the falls we would camp that night.

The river moved right along. We were soon in some fast water and picking up more and more speed in the final three miles as we approached the falls. We hugged the right shore so closely that we had to make one short portage over some rocks. We continued hugging the shore while gradually easing our way down toward the falls. A misty spiral hung over the falls as we progressed to within a half mile of the rocky cascade where the river plunges more than forty feet into a seething gorge below.

Suddenly above the roar of the surging water, we glanced up and saw a Cessna aircraft on floats, heading upstream directly over the falls. We waved our paddles frantically and latched onto the shore at the first possible place. The plane made a circle and came back over us. We waved the paddles some more. The plane made a turn below the falls and came back upstream again. We thought they had seen us.

They made a landing on calmer river water a couple of miles upstream. We rapidly pulled *North Star* up on the rocky shore and started running back towards the calm water above the rapids, carrying our paddles as we ran. The plane put ashore across on the opposite river bank, nearly half a mile from the nearest point we could get to. We stood on the highest rocks and continued to wave our paddles as two men walked around outside the plane. We thought they had probably seen us but were not absolutely certain. We tried shouting as loudly as possible, and Darrell said, "If they have seen us why did they go ashore across the river?" So we tried shouting together again as loud as we could as we waved our paddles.

After about half an hour we saw one man get into the Cessna and the other stayed on shore. The plane taxied out into the river and we kept waving. Gradually it came towards us. It taxied into a little bay where the current was slower.

The pilot shut down the motor, and leaning out the door he asked, "Can I do something for you fellows?" We told him of our situation in as few words as possible and that our number one problem was that we needed to send word to our families that we were OK. Following some discussion, he decided that he would wait while we packed *North Star* and our camping gear back up stream past all of that very fast water we had just gone down through.

We were overjoyed! We hurried as much as we could and about two hours later the job was completed. In another thirty minutes we were flying out across Baker Lake, which was still mostly covered with ice.

"What a blow it would have been," Darrell said above the roar of the Cessna, "if we had paddled on down to Baker Lake only to find that we were again ice bound."

"That would probably have happened by tomorrow evening, had we not lucked out and caught a ride with this fellow," I answered.

The pilot was Max Shapiro of Rainy Lake Flying Service at Fort Francis, Ontario. For the summer they kept an aircraft based in Baker Lake to serve the customers of Baker Lake Lodge. The lodge also operated Camp Chantrey, a fishing camp near the mouth of the Back river at Chantrey Inlet above the Arctic Circle.

The lake was clear of ice in the northwest part where the waters of the Thelon River pour into Baker Lake just west of the settlement, so we finally arrived at Baker Lake on the afternoon of Friday, the 4th of August.

A few minutes after splashdown and securing the plane to the beach, we made our appearance at Baker Lake Lodge just in time for supper. What a treat that was! And we could have all we wanted to eat! The lodge was operated by R. L. "Pooch" and Helen Liesenfeld, who also were from Fort Francis, Ontario. There was no room for us to stay at the lodge, but they did offer us a bunk in their warehouse. The $10.00 per night price included a

The Warehouse behind Baker Lake Lodge

hot shower which we definitely needed. And what a treat that was after three weeks without even a dip in a lake. We shared bunk space in their warehouse with Max Shapiro and a lad named Pat who also worked at the lodge.

That evening we walked down the graveled main street to the Department of Transport station at the east end of the settlement to send a wire to our homes about our safe arrival at Baker Lake.

There were plenty of motorized vehicles in the

settlement, but very few automobiles. The vehicles consisted mostly of motor scooters, motor bikes, small trucks and snowmobiles. The only road ran from the airport west of the post to the garbage dump east of the settlement.

We had to wait until Monday noon to catch the next Transair flight out to Churchill. So, we passed three days in Baker Lake, just enough time to sample life at the post. The lake itself was first explored by Captain Christopher in 1762 as he sailed west from Hudson Bay through Chesterfield Inlet.

Baker Lake post was originally established in 1915, some sixty miles to the southeast at the outlet of Baker Lake, as a base for the RCMP. By 1920, the Lampson-Hubbard Company were bartering with the Inuit from the same location near the rapids where Baker Lake discharges into Chesterfield Inlet.

During those early years the Hudson's Bay Company operated a post located on an island near the mouth of the Kazan River. Then in 1925 the Company sent W. O. Douglas to the west end of Baker Lake to choose a site for a new post, and to build it. This he did, selecting the present location of Baker Lake Settlement.

When the people were on the land, Baker Lake served as a lonely trading post. Since 1957, however, the influx of the Inuit people and government officials increased the population to over 850, and created the largest settlement in the interior of Canada's vast barren grounds.

On Saturday, we walked around the settlement and visited the "Bay." From there we scheduled *North Star* to be shipped back to Michigan via the annual supply ship expected within the month. The supply ship would take it to Montreal. Then the Canadian National Railroad would take it the remainder of the way to Windsor, Ontario.

On Sunday morning we attended St. Paul's Oblate Mission along with two of the Lodge employees, Nancy Nesbitt and "Pat" from International Falls, Minnesota. Father Joseph Choque was ringing the bell for Mass when we arrived. As we were about twenty minutes early, he invited us into his living quarters which were attached to

The Baker Lake Cemetery

the church. He was a very friendly fellow, and we had quite a chat. He had been in the north since 1938.

"When I first arrived in Baker Lake," he said, "no Eskimos lived here. In those days there were only the Anglican and Oblate missions, the Hudson's Bay Company and the Royal Canadian Mounted Police. The Eskimos came only at certain seasons to trade. They lived on the barren land in little groups, staying put in igloos during the winter, then moving around more with their caribou-

A Woman and Child at Baker Lake

skin tents in summertime. It was only in the mid-1950's that some of them began to stay here permanently."

In the early years Father Choque visited the people living on the land. He went by dog team in the winter. "In the summer," he continued, "they would be on the move with their skin tents and hard to find. Those were the good old days," he said sadly.

"Where did you come from originally, before coming to Baker Lake?" Darrell asked.

"Belgium!" Then he continued, "I served my appren-
ticeship in missionary life and learned the Eskimo lan-
guage under the expert guidance of Father Didier, at
Chesterfield Inlet.   Then in 1939 I went over to Cape
Dorset to work with Father Rio in southern Baffin land.
Then after three years there, I was sent across Hudson
Strait and spent two years at Ivuyivik before coming here
in 1944."

"You've certainly seen a lot of the north," I remarked.

"Yes," he replied.   "Then in 1952 I was sent to Coral
Harbour on Southampton Island and didn't get back here
until 1963. I've only been outside three times but I plan to
go south again next summer."

"You should write a book about your life and
experiences in this area," I remarked.

He replied with a laugh, "No one would be interested
in what I've done here." Of course we disagreed with that!

At eleven o'clock we moved into the sanctuary where
the Mass began. Most of the worshipers were Inuit. In all
there were less than forty of us, but the little church was
full. Father Choque conducted the Mass in Latin and gave
his sermon first in Eskimo, then in English. One of the
native men who could not read music played the little
organ. He had learned the tunes and played by ear, to the
accompaniment of much coughing and crying by the
younger ones.

Following another great meal at Baker Lake Lodge,
we walked up the hill north of the settlement. At the top
of the rocky hill was the cemetery. Most of the graves
were of the Inuit. Because of the rocks and permafrost,
the dead were placed on the surface of the ground, usually
in some sort of box, and then covered with rocks. Most
graves had white wooden crosses on them, and the dead
person's name was often carved into the wood in Inuit
symbolics.

There was a small cut stone monument in the
cemetery also, erected to Father Joseph Buliard, O.M.I.,
who drowned in Garry Lake on the Back River near the
mission he built there to serve the Eskimos of the area.

That evening while Darrell walked back into the

settlement to get some pictures, I attended the St. Aidan's Anglican Mission. The place was packed with about 150 Inuit people. I was the only non-Inuit in the congregation. They really made me feel welcome. I enjoyed the service which was all conducted from beginning to ending in the Inuit language, including the singing of the hymns.

In a small house adjoining the church which was used as a Sunday School room, there was an interesting picture. It was a wall painting showing a fur-clad Joseph and Mary with the baby Jesus bundled in skins, receiving furs and carvings from an Eskimo, an Indian, and a Hudson's Bay Company man, while a husky dog and a caribou watched.

No longer do these men urge their kayaks through the icy waters. No longer do the women serve boiled caribou tongue to mark a successful hunt. The River of Men is now silent.

The People have left their land, their lakes and their rivers for the new life, the life of white man's ways, and the life that has suddenly brought them into the twentieth century.

THOUSANDS OF CARIBOU

Then there were days of drifting,
Breezes soft as a sigh;
Night trailed her robe of jewells
Over the floor of the sky.

— Robert Service,
The Trail of Ninety-Eight

When we returned home from Baker Lake, we were both fed up with the north. "We had suffered enough to last us the rest of our lives. Never again would we go north for more of that kind of punishment." Those were our exact quotes to each other and to our families. By the following summer, however, we were beginning to forget just how miserable we had often been. It was true that the summer of '72 had been the coldest summer on record in the barrens. We had also learned that winter clothing is often necessary for canoe camping north of 60. We found that we had suffered from malnutrition due to our diet of freeze-dried foods and fish. We had both studied Gerry Cuningham's excellent booklet entitled "How to Keep Warm." From it and our experiences on the Kazan we really expected that we would never again have to suffer from the cold summer winds of the barrens.

We found ourselves discussing these matters frequently and before 1974 arrived we had decided that we would like to see more of the north. This time we would be better prepared for the anticipated weather conditions. Early in the year we had selected the Coppermine River. Robert Finley of Howell, Michigan, and a friend of his, Gerry Lynch of Edson, Alberta, would be our partners. A short time later Darrell learned that a commercial outfitter was offering guided tours down the Coppermine. "That spoils it for me," he said. "If commercial outfitters are working the Coppermine, that means people will be in there with lots of canoes and probably even motor boats on the river. Let's try to find a river that's more isolated and not so heavily traveled." So we went back to the maps of northern Canada.

A few weeks later, Robert Finley called to tell us that he would not be able to go along as he had bought a herd of dairy cows and would be tied down with his Holsteins. So, it would again be just the two of us. We decided that we would like to explore the Thelon River. It is another of the major rivers flowing into Baker Lake. The Thelon flows out of the taiga east of Great Slave Lake and into the barrens right through the heart of the Thelon Game Sanctuary.

This time we would ship *North Star* by rail to Lynn Lake and fly our Cessna 210 up there ourselves. This would give us additional camping days and reduce our time on the road. The people at Parsons Airways Northern would then fly us and our outfit into Rennie Lake on the headwaters of the Elk River, the southern tributary of the Thelon in the District of Mackenzie. To make sure that we would come out on time, R. L. (Pooch) Liesenfeld in Baker Lake agreed to meet us at the west end of Aberdeen Lake on August 11 or, if we were not there when he arrived, he would fly on up the river until he intercepted us.

This time we waited until July 15, to give ourselves more assurance that the ice would be out of the lakes. On the flight north from Lynn Lake, our pilot, Bruce Hallock, made a stop at Treeline Lodge on Nueltin Lake to refuel.

From there we decided to be flown to the south end of Damant Lake which is a few miles north of Rennie but still on the Elk. The flight from Nueltin took us right over Kasba and Snowbird Lakes. It was a good day for flying but the air was turbulent and we were indeed happy when we splashed down near a beach in the southeast corner of Damant Lake late that afternoon. We set up camp just above the beach and had a relaxing and enjoyable evening. "It's great to be back up here again," said Darrell.

"And the temperature's just right too," I replied as I checked the thermometer which was showing 65 degrees.

The next morning dawned bright and clear. We broke camp before 6:30 and started our long paddle toward Baker Lake. It was one of those rare and beautiful sunny canoeing days with the lake surface remaining as calm and clear as a mirror. Damant Lake is just a few miles north of the tree line but there are a few pockets of trees along its rocky shores. A couple of eskers also cross the lake. We stopped on one of these for our lunch break but that was cut short by swarms of insects. We had a few kinks to work out of our paddling muscles so we didn't hit it too hard that first day.

By early evening we had left the lake, made one short portage and crossed the 62nd parallel before calling it a day. Just as we began setting up camp, a strong east wind started whipping up. The lake we had just crossed was soon covered with churning white caps. With the wind blowing, our camp was free of insects for the evening.

From this point on the Elk River was wild. For the next several miles it was a continuous series of rapids. We were able to shoot most of them after walking ahead to look them over from the riverbanks but we also made nine portages in that stretch. The portages were short but we were having to make three trips on each portage to move all of our gear, for our load included enough food and supplies to last for a full month. We were taking no chances of running short of food this time.

Our third morning on the Elk saw us across Lake 1164 before breakfast. This is where we intercepted a huge migration of barren ground caribou bulls. We had started

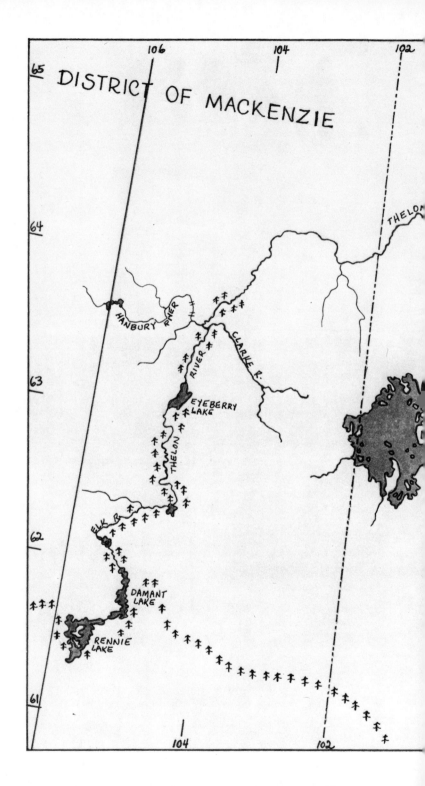

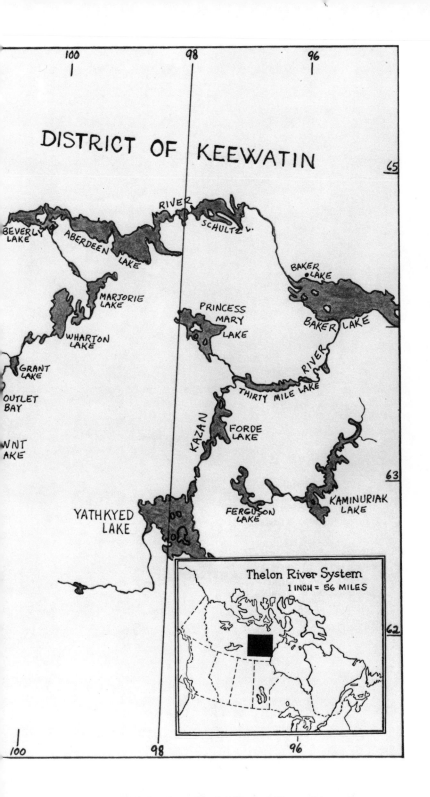

DISTRICT OF KEEWATIN

BEVERLY LAKE

ABERDEEN LAKE

RIVER

SCHULTZ L.

BAKER LAKE

BAKER LAKE

MARJORIE LAKE

PRINCESS MARY LAKE

WHARTON LAKE

RIVER

GRANT LAKE

THIRTY MILE LAKE

OUTLET BAY

KAZAN

FORDE LAKE

WNT AKE

YATHKYED LAKE

FERGUSON LAKE

KAMINURIAK LAKE

Thelon River System
1 INCH = 56 MILES

The Elk River Was Wild

early to get across the lake before the wind came up and were looking for a place to stop for breakfast when we spotted the first group. While we watched in amazement, hundreds of them appeared near the river ahead of us. What a beautiful sight that was! This was the first time we had seen a large group of caribou and these were all males. We estimated that there were around five hundred animals in the herd. Then a few minutes later while preparing breakfast, we watched another herd on the opposite hills. That group stretched out for several miles as it moved away from us. While eating, a third herd moved along the hills on the north side of the river. In all we must have seen more than 2,500 of those beautiful animals that morning and most of them carried large racks of antlers.

The Elk River increases in size as it swings back to the northeast. It also continues to be extremely wild in places. We shot many more sets of rapids that afternoon. Some of the eddies and little quiet places in the river were completely covered with floating caribou hair for the animals had been shedding their winter hair as they swam across the river. "This would be a sight for a trout

fisherman who likes to tie his own flies," said Darrell.
"Maybe we should take a bag of them home with us. We
could sell them, to offset some of our expenses. Better
yet, we could start our own fly tying business. We could
come up here each July to harvest the hair, then
manufacture and sell dry flies the rest of the year."

"That's really dreaming," I joked.

"I'm serious. It could be done. Those hollow little
hairs intrigue me," he said as he scooped up another
handful of them, gave them a squeeze and dropped them
back on the water. "Just look how high they float on the
surface."

Our discussion abruptly ended as we glanced up to see
more caribou antlers moving over the top of a hill north of
us. We watched as another large herd moved down along
the river beside us. They came close enough so that we
were able to get some pictures. In all there must have
been more than a thousand animals in that group.

There were caribou bulls in sight almost all of the
time that afternoon and all the next day as we continued
to move on down the Elk. As we approached a rapids,
suddenly I heard a crash behind me. I glanced back over
my shoulder and I didn't see Darrell. His paddle was
floating in the water behind the canoe. I quickly took a
better look and found him lying in the bottom of the
canoe. The stern seat of *North Star* had broken completely
off its mountings just as he was making his move to stand
up to take a better look at the approaching rapids.
Fortunately for us, I managed to swing the canoe around
and pick up his paddle so that we were able to scramble
ashore just before we would have been sucked over that
drop in the river.

We searched the area and eventually found a small
dead tree stump. We trimmed it and used it to prop up
the canoe seat which then remained in place. Later, as
we moved into one of the small expansions of the river,
we saw something that looked like smoke from a camp
fire rising above some of the low bushes near the shore
about a thousand yards ahead. As we approached the spot
we found that the "smoke" was actually millions of black

flies and other small insects.

That evening we came to a long rapids. We climbed a high hill and the river kept dropping as far as we could see. That called for a portage of two miles which cut off about three and one-half miles of rapids. The black flies and mosquitos were merciless but by sunset we had completed the portage and pitched our tent on the top of a hill above the river. That hill top was the only level spot we could find that was not covered with scrub willows.

The weather had been warm with afternoon temperatures in the 70's every day. During the night a terrific thunderstorm moved in on us and there we were on top of the highest hill in the area with our aluminum tent poles sticking up to attract the lightning. As the storm continued, bolt after bolt of lightning flashed, cracked and snapped near us. We anticipated that any minute could be our last.

The rain poured down and the winds whipped against the tent. Lying inside in our sleeping bags we found ourselves counting the seconds between the time the lightning flashed and we heard the thunder. By making this count of seconds and dividing by five, we knew how many miles away from us the lightning bolts were striking. There seemed to be dozens of them when our count didn't even get one before we would hear the thunderclap. Finally after a couple of hours, the storm began to move off to the east and 'thank the Lord' we had survived.

We were off to a late start the next morning. The high winds had pulled a side tent stake during the storm and the tent sagged so much that water had leaked in. Both of our sleeping bags were wet. We dried them in the strong west wind while we did up our camp chores. The wind remained at gale force as we embarked and moved on downstream to Granite Falls. After looking over the falls we started carrying a load of our supplies along the right shore. There were several sets of chutes and rapids which could not be canoed. We were another mile and a half down stream before we found canoeable water and that was at the junction where the Elk flows into the

Thelon River. We were unable to portage *North Star* until
the following morning as the gale continued all through
the evening.

The wind lost some of its velocity by the next day.
We packed the canoe down into the Thelon and were again
underway by mid-forenoon. We now found ourselves in a
much larger river. We hugged the shores as much as
possible to keep out of the wind but kept digging in with
our paddles until we went ashore for a break in late
afternoon. That's when Darrell strung his fishing rod for
the first time and within an hour we were eating three
nice Arctic grayling for supper.

On July 22nd we again started seeing large groups of
caribou. This time, however, there were no bulls. They
were all cows and calves. The barren ground caribou
spend their winters in the spruce forests to the south.
Each spring they migrate north nearly to the shores of the
Arctic Ocean where the cows drop their calves. The bulls
turn back south at that time. Then within a week or two
the cows and calves follow along behind. This is where we
intercepted them, heading in a southeasterly direction.
They continue to graze across the barrens swinging back
north one more time before fall when the bulls rejoin the
cows and calves, and together they winter in the tree
country, far to the south.

These migrations are an awe-inspiring sight. The
animals spend the summer grazing and moving across the
open tundra. They feed on shrubs, leaves, twigs, flowers,
grass, moss, lichens and other plant matter which they
find.

For the next couple of days caribou seemed to be
everywhere. Sometimes they would appear in small
groups and sometimes in large herds. They seemed to be
tormented by the insects. At times they were so harassed
that apparently they could not take time to rest or eat. In
addition to the black flies, mosquitos, and the huge flies
known as bulldogs which also bothered us, the herds were
pestered by the parasitic warble and nostril flies.

The caribou herds also have other problems which are
more visible than the insects. They are hunted by wolves,

wolverines, bears and man. Wolves and bears prey on the adults but seldom make a kill of a healthy caribou because a healthy animal can outrun a wolf or a bear. It is the old, the sick and the feeble that are picked off by the predators. The wolverines do take an occasional calf.

The selective thinning of these herds by wolves and bears serves to increase the strength of the remaining animals. Killing of the wolf as advocated in the past by so many could not save the caribou herds. The caribou and the wolf are perfectly capable of working out a natural balance good for both if man will leave them alone. They did very well before man showed up with his rifles, his traps and his poisoned bait and attempted to re-organize things as he thought they should be. Nature, the caribou, and the wolf, did not ask for this help. Man, the meddler, can help most by leaving things alone. Caribou taken by the Inuit people for their very important needs do not weaken the herds. The Inuit are learning the need for economy and are no longer killing more of these animals than they can use. Fortunately, the caribou herds once so decimated are now making a substantial comeback in numbers.

The canoeing was easy along the portion of the Thelon above Eyeberry Lake. One day we moved along for thirty-six miles and dropped over one hundred feet nearer to sea level without making a single portage. In most places the clear, fast water really slid along over the colorful rocks on the river bottom. The way we sped along with so little effort was most enjoyable.

The larger rocks have all been pushed or rolled into huge piles at points where the river bends to the left or right. Where the river swings to the right, the rocks are piled on the left shore and conversely where it swings to the left, rocks are on the right. They have been pushed out there by the action of the ice floes in high water during the spring breakup of the ice. Frequently on the bends, these large rocks would be piled twelve to fifteen feet above the level of the river water. This situation is common to most of the rivers in the far north.

All along our way we found Arctic terns. They are

beautiful birds, graceful in flight. They were frequently nesting on islands along the way.

Arctic terns spend their summers along the lakes and rivers in the barrens where the sun shines nearly the clock around. Then in September, they migrate southeast over Newfoundland, across the north Atlantic, south along western Europe and Africa and then down to Antarctica where they spend the winter months. There the sun shines the clock around while we in the northern hemisphere are having our shortest days. Then in March the terns reverse their route back to the Arctic. They travel as much as twenty-two thousand miles in their annual migrations, and see more daylight than any other living creature since they are in both the Arctic and the Antarctic during the periods of the longest days.

Rounding a bend in the river we came across a pair of whistling swans. Then just beyond, as we entered another island of trees along the river, a bald eagle was resting on the top of a broken tree stub. Canada geese were in abundance along this section of the river. Some were still in molt and could not fly. They were very afraid of us for they swam ashore well ahead and scurried up the riverbank and into the dwarf vegetation or behind the large rocks. They had nothing to fear from us as we have made it a policy to carry no firearms on any of our travels.

"They must remember being shot at during their migrations over the United States," said Darrell.

I agreed. "Some of those trigger-happy hunters down there will shoot at anything that moves."

The weather continued warm with highs in the 70's and lows in the low 60's. Winds remained gentle until the afternoon that we entered Eyeberry Lake. There we were met by breaking waves sweeping across the lake from the east. Our only choice was to go ashore, set up camp and wait for the wind to change.

That afternoon we explored the tundra west of the lake, watching small groups of grazing caribou. They were constantly on the move, eating whatever vegetation they came across.

It was there that we started finding a strange-looking yellowish orange colored berry. The berries were more than a half-inch in diameter; they were soft and they had a deliciously sweet flavor. We didn't know what they were, so we ate them sparingly at first. We named them eyeberries because we first found them at Eyeberry Lake. From that day on, we found and devoured eyeberries most every time we were to go ashore.

After completing our Thelon journey, research showed us that our eyeberries were actually bake apple berries, also called cloudberries and muskeg berries (Rubus chamaemorus). We also learned that the Inuit people had a taboo on cloudberries, which says that "women must not eat cloudberries." Little girls and old women, however, were exempt from this rule.

Ten miles below Eyeberry Lake as we passed the end of an esker, we entered the Thelon Game Preserve. For the next 210 miles we would be traveling right through the heart of this huge game sanctuary. The Thelon Preserve was established in 1927. No hunting or trapping of any kind has been allowed in the area since that date. Later, in Baker Lake we were to learn that travel is also banned within the reserve.

On July 25 we did plenty of portaging. That morning we made the first portage since our arrival on the Thelon more than five days before. Then downriver another six miles was where our work really began. About four miles above the Clarke River junction begins a series of rapids where the river flows between towering cliffs. We portaged around two bends in the river over some high hills with steep and brushy ravines between the hills. The black flies were a terror on that portage of more than two and one-half miles, with the temperature still hanging in the mid-seventies. Seven hours later we completed the carry and were back on the river for another half mile before one more portage was made after lining *North Star* down along the right riverbank. That's where we decided to call it a day.

We camped on a small sandy island where the Clarke River flows into the Thelon. There were caribou all around us that evening. Frequently they would swim across the Clarke, walk across our island and then swim on to the far shore. They were so intent upon migration that several of them walked between our tent and *North Star*, which was turned up only about twenty feet from the tent. It must have been relatively easy for the Inuit of long ago to kill caribou during their migrations.

THE DOUBLE BEND
IN THE RIVER

The nameless men who nameless rivers travel
And in strange valleys greet strange deaths alone;
The grim, intrepid ones who would unravel
The mysteries that shroud the Polar Zone.

— Robert Service,
To the Man of the High North

Forty-five minutes out of the Clarke River camp we passed the mouth of the Hanbury River. The Thelon flows rapidly through the area below the Clarke and the canoeing was great. During the forenoon we had a change in the weather. Heavy clouds rolled in and a strong wind began to blow out of the north.

"Boy! This Thelon's really a big river now!" said Darrell. "It must have more than doubled in size since we passed the Clarke and Hanbury."

"Yes," I replied. "And if this wind doesn't change soon, we may not get much farther today. I'm getting soaked up here."

We struggled along downriver directly into the wind. By noon we were forced to call it quits. We had been paddling full power down the river with a good current to help us but were making no forward progress. The wind blew us back upstream as fast as we could paddle down. At times like that whenever a strong headwind blows directly in opposition to a strong river current, a strange and savage chop of steep curling waves develops and water easily blows in over the canoe's bow.

Early that afternoon the rains came. The high winds and cold rain continued without letup all night. The downpour stopped before noon of the next day but there was no lessening of the north wind. We huddled around a little fire downwind from some dwarf willows. That was the only place outside the tent where we could find any protection from the cold summer wind. Then more rain fell as the storm continued throughout still another night. Finally in the early evening of the third day the wind lost some of its velocity even though it held, from the same direction.

We soon broke camp. A few minutes later a tan-colored wolf appeared and watched us from the riverbank. Then as we stopped to stretch our legs on Grassy Island we saw a muskox grazing on the opposite shore. This was the first muskox outside of a zoo that either of us had ever seen. We decided not to cross the river to stalk the animal for pictures as we wanted to move as far downstream as possible that evening following our long delay. We managed to move eighteen miles before we pitched the tent at 11 P.M. as darkness began to settle in under cloudy skies.

The rains returned during the night and continued most of the following day, as did the winds which held on our nose out of the north − northeast. We decided to try to move, even though the weather remained bad, as we were falling too far behind our plan of progress.

Only ten minutes out of camp we came upon a huge Barren Ground grizzly. The bear was near the river and as we drifted in to get a better look at him, the shambling giant stood up on his hind legs. It appeared that this huge bear was curious and wanted to get a better look at us, just as we wanted a better look at the grizzly. We did manage to get pictures of him from the canoe, as we

The Barren Ground Grizzly

chose not to go ashore for close up shots. We used no telephoto lens on our cameras so we usually tried to move in for close up shots of most animals we encountered. It's likely that we were the first people that bear had ever seen.

Only a few decades ago, Barren Ground grizzlies were plentiful across the mainland tundra west of Hudson Bay. Now, however, since the introduction of firearms, they have become so rare as to almost be only a memory. We were indeed fortunate to get to see and photograph that huge, light brown colored bear.

In the afternoon as we crossed the 64th parallel, we went ashore and stalked two muskoxen which were grazing over a hilltop. We managed to get pictures. Upon returning to the river Darrell remarked, "We are fortunate to see these strange animals. Just think, Dad, there are probably less than three hundred people in the entire continental United States who have ever seen muskoxen in their natural habitat."

I agreed. Muskoxen, which the Inuit call Umingmak, the Bearded Ones, are strictly arctic animals. Originally they were found all across the arctic barrens, but they were hunted nearly to extinction after firearms were introduced to the native peoples. Today herds are beginning to make a comeback and are found near Bathurst Inlet, between Wagner Inlet and the Boothia Peninsula, on some of the islands north of the Canadian mainland, as well as in and around the Thelon Game Preserve.

The durable muskoxen wear long shaggy coats of thick fur. The side hairs are often two or three feet long on their neck and shoulders. These animals seldom stand more than 5 feet at the shoulder and rarely exceed seven feet in length. The muskox's tail is short and is seldom seen because of the long body hair. They are strictly a herd animal and feed on grasses, willows, mosses and other vegetation. In winter they seek out the ridges and slopes where the wind has blown the snow away. During a blizzard they usually find gullies in which to hide from the frigid winds. The rugged muskoxen are fast on their feet, as we were soon to find out, despite their rather ungainly appearance.

We moved on into the wind and rain. Approaching Hornby Point we made pictures of still another muskox. What a thrill it was, being able to get so close to those unusual animals in their natural wilderness environment. That night we encamped on Hornby Point and while eating supper we enjoyed watching another muskox graze along the shore only a short distance away.

Following supper inside our tent, as the rain continued, we talked about John Hornby, the English trapper who roamed the Northwest Territories during the early years of the 20th century. The place where we were camping is called Hornby Point because that was where John Hornby along with his nephew, Edgar Christian, and Harold Adlard had spent the final days of their lives during the winter and spring of 1926-27.

Hornby had first drifted into the far north in 1908 and spent several years up around the extreme northeast corner of Great Bear Lake. He became well acquainted with the area from there east to the Coppermine River and north to Coronation Gulf. He would often be on his own, away from civilization, for four or five years at a time. In 1924, while in the south, he met J. C. Gritchell-Bullock who had been fascinated by listening to some of Hornby's stories of the Far North.

Bullock had thought, "This may be what I am looking for — unknown country to explore, books to write about it and here is one who knows the North and how to live and travel there." He had asked, "Would there be opportunities for me in this country of yours?"

"Come with me if you like," Hornby had said. "But I promise you only hard travel and a life that will make or break you."

Bullock had met a number of Hornby's friends. They admitted that he was odd but claimed that he had fine qualities and that he was a famous northern traveler. "He has had many narrow escapes," one said, "and one of these times it will be too close. He is the 'lone wolf' type, you know."

"Lone wolf! That should have warned me," wrote Bullock in his diary. "There was no suggestion of any serious purpose to his travels and how could I expect companionship from one who had gone native and preferred to live alone?" But he went along.

Hornby was the leader and set the order of travel. Meals and sleep took no set pattern. "We'll eat when we're hungry," he had said, "and we'll sleep when we're tired but our travel is more important than either."

There were weeks of hard travel by canoe, up rivers and across back-breaking portages to waters that carried them in autumn past the last woods, out to the bleak Barren Grounds at the north end of Artillery Lake, beyond Great Slave Lake. It depressed Bullock. "Where are we going?" he had asked. "What is there ahead?"

Hornby's eyes were glowing like sapphires as his glance swept the country, searching out familiar details. "We are going to do something that has never been done before. We'll den up in a hole in the ground like animals. The snow will make a blanket over us and the gales will sweep past. We'll see caribou and wolves and foxes, maybe muskox, as woodland trappers never dreamed of. We'll be famous because we'll have done one of the few things that have never been done before."

"Mad," thought Bullock. "I should have known then. Sane men do not talk like that nor do they plan such fantastic things. I could not turn back. All my capital of hopes and money was invested in the expedition."

They reached the sand hill where they were to winter. Its bleakness was accentuated by the few dwarf shrubs that were to provide their fuel. The country stretched away over stony hills and tundra flats. Even the sky settled on them in low misty clouds. They dug a hole and roofed it with their tent, covering all with branches and sand. When this was completed, Hornby had said, "Now we'll know how bears and ground squirrels live in winter."

"What a miserable existence that must have been!" said Darrell.

"That's for sure," I replied. "Those two men trapped furs that winter, and took out 358 white foxes, forty wolves and three wolverines. That was during those years when fur prices were high, with white foxes bringing up around $40 each. The next spring they headed east towards Baker Lake, and on July 30th of that year Hornby and Gritchell-Bullock stopped on this same bend in the river, where we are camping tonight."

"Today's July 30th," Darrell said. "What a coincidence. Let's see, that was in 1925, exactly forty-nine years ago this very day!" They had traveled only about 180 miles from Artillery Lake and still had nearly 350 miles to go to reach Baker Lake. In his notes of their trip Gritchell-Bullock wrote —

> *The place where we stopped was at a sharp double bend in the river, where the river turns northeast after flowing west for a few miles. Here on the north side of the river we found an open bank rising up steeply from the water, and a fine stand of good spruce timber 10 to 15 inches in diameter for building and shelter extending northerly more than 200 yards into the barrens. Hornby was much taken with the place and told me that this was a place he would like to come back to, and would build a house there for the winter.*

The next morning they were away early. They traveled about forty miles before their next stop. Gritchell-Bullock, chopping a log to make a smudge, as the mosquitos were bad, let the axe slip and nearly amputated three of his toes on the right foot. His notes say, "It spurted blood and I had difficulty in binding it up. I was very fortunate not to have cut my foot completely off."

With many more difficulties, these two men finally arrived in Baker Lake on August 27, 1925, having been en route since the previous summer. From their winter hole in the esker camp near Artillery Lake, they had traveled about 530 miles in 107 days. That was a feat of endurance considering the way they were loaded down with equipment and furs.

The rain diminished to little more than a mist that evening so we were out of the tent for a better look around. Darrell rekindled the fire and while he heated a pot of water for hot chocolate, I walked up along the edge of the trees and soon found the remains of the old Hornby cabin. Within a few minutes the heavy rains returned as we scurried back inside the tent, each with a cup of hot chocolate in hand. Naturally most of our talk for the rest of that evening was of John Hornby.

In the fall of 1925, Hornby returned to England as he had received word that his father was critically ill. En route, he stopped in Ottawa. He had been hired by the Northwest Territories branch of the government to check on the wildlife during his journey down the Thelon. Part of his official report read:

> *The results of the trip (to the Thelon) show that there is a large uninhabited area where musk ox are plentiful, swans and geese nest and caribou can have their young undisturbed by man. This wooded area possesses no minerals, containing only sandstone and sand, consequently can afford no inducement or excuse for men to go on a prospecting trip. If it is desired to protect the game in this part of the country it is essential to take measures to prevent traders from encouraging natives to hunt in this district. A few years perhaps and it will be too late.*

Darrell remarked, "So that's why this Thelon Game Preserve was established."

"Yes," I replied. "Apparently John Hornby deserves a lot of credit because his suggestion was referred to the Advisory Board on Wildlife Protection on 26 May 1926 and at a meeting of the Board on 28 May 1926 it was resolved that steps be taken to create at the junction of the Hanbury and Thelon Rivers a sanctuary for all game but particularly for the preservation of the few surviving muskoxen. In June, 1927, the Thelon Game Sanctuary was created by Order-in-Council to take effect on 1 September of that year. The Sanctuary, extending from the east shores of Artillery and Ptarmigan Lakes on the west to Beverly Lake on the east, enclosed about fifteen thousand square miles. Almost in the center of this area, and without knowing that the sanctuary was to be created, Hornby had built his cabin."

When John Hornby returned to Canada early in 1926 following his father's funeral, he brought along his eighteen-year-old nephew, Edgar Christian, and another young man, Harold Adlard. The three of them eventually arrived at the double bend in the river about forty miles below Hanbury Junction in early October of that year. Within thirty days they had built a small log cabin in the edge of the trees and in the slope facing the river. This time Hornby had made a big mistake. By the time the cabin was finished, November had arrived and the caribou had moved far to the south to winter below the tree line. Desperately they hunted, day after day without finding either caribou or muskox. They did manage to set some traps and get a net under the river ice.

Early in December they were really beginning to worry about their food supply. Edgar Christian kept a diary. On December 6 he wrote, "On counting our fish we see there are enough for 14 days at two per day and then we only have 100 pounds of flour between us till spring when Caribou ought to come again."

In January, their situation grew critical. On some days they managed to shoot or trap the occasional ptarmigan, fox or wolverine which were used for food to keep them going. January was a bitter cold month. The warmest temperature recorded by Edgar Christian was minus 10 degrees, the coldest was minus 54 degrees.

February began in a more promising style. On February 1, Adlard saw some caribou crossing the river in a northerly direction. He eventually shot one so they had a square meal before they began saving the remainder for later nourishment. Then later in the month they sighted a herd of forty caribou but managed to kill only one young calf. Before March arrived they were digging up garbage they had thrown out early in the winter. On the 17th of March Hornby killed a rabbit and two ptarmigan. On the 19th, they caught a whiskey jack and promptly ate it between them. On March 24th, Christian wrote —

> *Nothing coming in but time is surely passing and although we may go damn hungry we can keep on till caribou come north and then what feasting we can have. Only a matter of patience really but very trying mentally and physically for we are weak and easily tired on 2 meals of hide per day.*

On the 30th of March they shot nine ptarmigan but then for the next seventeen days, they took no more game or fish of any kind.

April 4th was a turning point. That day Hornby made his final expedition into the barrens in a pitiful search for the paunch of the caribou killed in February. Five hours later Hornby returned to the cabin. He had not found what he was looking for. The next day they started burning logs from their leanto because none of them were strong enough to cut wood. On April 10, Hornby must have known he was dying, as he wrote his will while in atrocious pain. He died six days later, leaving the two boys by themselves. They wrapped his body in their old tent and placed it outside, just to the east of the door.

They carried on by themselves until May 4th when Harold Adlard died. The entry in Christian's diary for May 5, 1927 reads —

> *Today I resumed my digging and again had luck in finding more good food which had been discarded, one very fat Wolverine gut and kidneys, heart and liver, and one Fox gut, a quantity of meaty bones, and enough fish for one meal.*

He carried on day by day, always thinking that the caribou would come back in time to save him. On the 20th of May he wrote —

*Have existed by walking and crawling in and
out of the house finding plenty of food, in fact
more than I could eat, but owing to its quality
did not keep me going sufficiently to get rid of it
as I ate it, being insufficient in grease I think . . .
Alas, I got weaker and the weather was blowing a
snowstorm for four days; after that it wasn't
even thawing in the daytime.*

Then his next entry says —

*Now June 1st. I have grub on hand, but am
weaker than I have ever been in my life and no
migration north of birds or animals.*
*Yesterday I was out crawling, having cut last
piece of wood in house to cook me food I had . . .
but while out, I found fish guts and meat in
plenty. At 2 a.m. I went to bed feeling content.*

At 9 a.m. on what may have been June 2nd he wrote

*9 a.m. Weaker than ever. Have eaten all I
can. Have food on hand but heart petering (out)?
Sunshine is bright now. See if that does any good
to me if I get out and bring in wood to make a
fire tonight.*
Make preparations now.

"Make preparations," had been Hornby's phrase for
doing the last things before death.   Part of young
Christian's preparations was to write a letter to both his
father and his mother.

When the fire had died out and he had decided that he
would never light it again, Edgar placed his diary and the
two letters to his parents in the cool ashes of the stove,
together with Hornby's will and the last letters he had
written, and Harold Adlard's few papers.

H. S. Wilson's party of four young men, traveling on
behalf of the Nipissing Mining Company, came upon the

cabin at the double bend in the river on July 21, 1928. They were horrified at their discovery but they decided that apparently they had found the bodies of Hornby and his companions. Then on July 25, 1929, a patrol of Mounted Police finally reached the cabin. On top of the stove they found a note written on a piece of paper. The note said —

WHO EVER COMES
HERE
LOOK IN STOVE

When Edgar Christian's body was found he was wearing a heavy gray sweater over a khaki shirt, gray flannel trousers held up by a silk handkerchief, a muffler around his neck and winter moccasins with puttees. He was in his bunk and had pulled two red Hudson's Bay blankets over him, covering his head.

That night as we were camped near the spot where they had died, we felt close to the Hornby party. We, too, had seen the very country where they had explored. We, too, had been frustrated, cold and hungry. We could only imagine, with feelings of sympathy and fellowship for these men, the desperate hopelessness of their last days during the winter and spring of 1926 and 1927.

Quotations in this chapter from **The Legend of John Hornby** *by George Whalley are reprinted by permission of Macmillan of Canada, a division of Gage Publishing, Ltd.*

CHARGED BY A

BULL MUSKOX

On the ragged edge of the world I'll roam,
And the home of the wolf shall be my home,
And a bunch of bones on the boundless snows,
The end of the trail — who knows, who knows!

— *Robert Service,*
The Nostomaniac

The rain stopped before six the next morning. As we breakfasted on bacon, eggs and toast, we watched a muskox graze along the upper bend in the river. We embarked shortly after eight as low clouds and fog hung near the surface of the river.

Rounding the lower bend, a wolf howled in the low bushes. We put ashore to see if we could get a look at the animal as the howling continued. We finally caught a glimpse of a large, dark-grey wolf as it dashed away over the hill. "Apparently it was sending a message to other wolves on down the river, telling them we are heading their way," said Darrell.

"That wolf could have been keeping an eye on us since we set up camp last night, and for sure it just now told other animals that we are on the move," I replied, as we

A Muskox of the Thelon

again embarked. "You know, we are seeing a lot of animals down through here."

"There are likely about a hundred creatures who see us that we don't see, to each one that we do see. Probably there are many sets of eyes on us most of the time, watching our every move."

"If we stalk another muskox I would like to have my tape recorder along to capture that 'snort' they make as they turn and charge away," I remarked.

"That would be a good idea. I think we have plenty of pictures of them, though," Darrell said. Each muskox we had photographed had taken a look at us, then turned and ran away at full speed, with long hair flowing like ripening grain in the wind. Each one had let out a big snort as it turned to run.

A little later, while approaching an island in the river, we spotted a large muskox. This fellow apparently had the entire rocky island to himself. I decided this would be an opportunity for me to get the "snorting sound" I wanted on my tape.

We nosed *North Star* ashore. I hopped out and pulled the bow of the canoe up on the small rocks. Darrell said,

"I'll wait here for you. I have plenty of pictures of muskoxen."

I hung my tape recorder over my shoulder, picked up my camera, and began to move in on the large bull. I turned on the tape recorder as I approached, then snapped a picture and continued to close the distance between us. When I was about fifty feet away, the animal took a good look at me, but this one didn't charge off as the others had. Instead he slowly walked to one side, took another look at me, and charged, full speed with head down, straight at me! I was astounded!

I didn't know what I should do, and I didn't have much time to think about it. Instinct told me to stand still, then just before the animal hit me, jump sideways, thus dodging the full impact of his charge. That is what I tried to do. As I yelled and jumped to the side, I slipped on loose rocks and fell flat on my back.

For some reason known only to God, the animal abruptly stopped four feet from me. As I lay there with my heart pounding loudly, the muskox stood staring at me.

Darrell was standing in the canoe, frantically hollering "Get up, Dad! Get up, Dad!" Finally, after a full minute or more which seemed much, much longer, the muskox turned his head, and then slowly walked away. My heart was still pounding as I made my way back to the canoe.

Back on the river, the wind soon came up and blew in our faces from the northeast. We didn't talk much for awhile. The sun came out, and by mid-day we were able to dry some of our wet things.

I began to recover from my fright while eating lunch, even though Darrell wanted to know why I was still shaking. He said with a grin, "You're going to be all right, Dad. At least you are beginning to get a little color back in your face."

I admitted, "That was the biggest scare of my life, and as you know, I've had several close calls in the past. I can still see those sharp horns pointing right at me! I'll probably spend the rest of my life wondering just why I was spared, and why the good Lord stopped that muskox from goring me."

"We were both lucky," Darrell said. "If he had hit you, I don't know how I would have managed to get you out of here by myself. The nearest settlement is Baker Lake and that's nearly 340 miles away. There are probably no humans between here and there."

"We can thank the Lord for being with us today," I added. "One thing for sure — I'll stalk no more muskoxen."

That afternoon we dug into it with our paddles and by camping time were thirty-one miles downstream. We feasted on lake trout well above the river opposite some high and colorful cliffs. It was one of those rare warm, windless evenings when the insect life defied description. Consequently we were unable to enjoy our surroundings as much as we would have liked. The black flies were like swarming bees in a black cloud around us. Even with our head nets we could feel them pinging against the mesh like little pellets from air guns. When the flies were joined by swarms of mosquitoes, we had to call it a day. We dove into our tent with a can of Raid to escape the hungry horde.

"Those black flies are worse than the mosquitoes," said Darrell. "They don't just bite, they haul a piece of you away to the nearest rock and then set there and chaw on it." Both of us must have many, many blood relations up there now.

August 1st was another of those rare and beautiful summer days. It was a joy to be alive and canoeing on a river in the barrens that still showed no sign of man's encroachment. "No highways along the river banks, no bridges and no railroads. I really like this," said Darrell.

"Me too! We are fortunate to get to see places like this, and to spend time on rivers that have yet to see the construction of their first power dams. It's also good that we don't have motor boats tearing around, churning up the water and destroying the ecology."

"I like to watch the birds and animals," Darrell said. "But the best of all is just to be able to listen and hear only natural sounds. No matter what time of day or night,

Insect Life Defied Description

there's always something to hear. Some of my favorite sounds are the howling of the wolves, the cry of the loons, and the songs of the various kinds of birds. Then there's that strange, low, throaty sound of the sandhill cranes as they walk along over the tundra."

"I also like to listen to the murmur of the river. Sometimes it makes a peculiar hissing sound as it slides rapidly down over the small rocks on the bottom. Then there's the roar of a rapids! I even enjoy the sound of the wind when it blows from behind us."

"I enjoy the sounds of buzzing insects when we are inside our tent. They lull me to sleep. I've never slept better than when we are bedded down in the tent."

"Yes, I know," Darrell quipped. "Your snoring tells me that! It's one of my least favorite sounds."

"You should wake me up when I snore."

"I don't like to do that. You sound so comfortable! I've always wondered why it is that people who snore always fall asleep first."

That day we moved downstream thirty-eight miles before setting up camp at a place on our map called Lookout Point. The campsite was high above the river and offered a great view of the valley of an unnamed tributary which joins the Thelon across from the point. Scads of ripe blueberries nearly covered the ground. The berries were full size but the little plants they grew on were no more than two inches tall. Most of the luscious berries hung less than an inch off the sandy, lichen-covered soil of the point. We harvested off a spot before setting up the tent. Those berries were excellent quality and flavor, and we munched on them each day from then on wherever we went ashore.

We watched another large muskox graze along the hill behind our tent as we did our usual evening camp chores, and we didn't even attempt a stalk. The "scourge of the north" were out again in full force, and we were driven into our tent before mid-evening.

There were still a few pockets of trees along the river, but here, they were noticeably smaller and further apart than above Hornby Point. The Thelon is the only river in the barrens having trees along its shore. We were by then fully 150 to 200 miles out in the barren lands and we were still finding these islands of spruce trees.

How it is that they can grow along only this river and none other in the barrens is a topic worthy of discussion. The trees along the Thelon were well known to both the Chipewyan and Inuit people for many centuries. In Samuel Hearne's **Journey from Fort Prince of Wales to the Arctic Sea,** he reports on passing well to the south of us, below the tree line, while traveling with his guide Matonabbee and a band of Chipewyans. This was during February of 1772 while on his return to Fort Prince of Wales at the mouth of the Churchill River.

Setting off to the south-east on the 28th, we now proceeded at a much greater rate, since little or no time was lost in hunting. The next day we came on the tracks of strangers, and some of my companions were at pains to search them out. Finding them to be poor, inoffensive people, they plundered them of the few furs they had, together with one young woman.

Every additional act of violence, committed by my companions on the poor and the distressed, served to increase my indignation and dislike. This last act, however, displeased me more than all their former actions because it was committed on a set of harmless creatures whose general manner of life renders them the most secluded from society of any of the human race.

The people of this family, as it may be called, have for a generation past taken up their abode in some woods which are situated so far out on the barren grounds as to be quite out of the track of other Indians. This place is some hundreds of miles distant both from the main woods and from the sea. Few of the trading Northern Indians have ever visited it, but those who have give a most pleasing description of it. It is situated on the banks of a river which has communications with several fine lakes. As the current sets northeastward, it empties itself, in all probability, into some part of Hudson Bay, probably into Baker Lake at the head of Chesterfield Inlet.

The accounts given of this place, and the manner of life of its inhabitants, would fill a volume. Let it suffice to observe that it is remarkably favourable for every kind of game that the barren ground produces. However, the seasonal continuance of game is somewhat uncertain, which being the case, the few people who compose this little commonwealth are, by long custom and the constant example of their forefathers, possessed of a provident turn of mind, together with a degree of frugality unknown to every other tribe in this country except the Eskimos.

Deer are said to visit their country in astonishing numbers both in spring and autumn. The inhabitants kill and dry as much deer flesh as possible, particularly in the fall, so they are seldom in want of a good winter's stock.

*Geese, ducks and swans visit them in great
plenty during their migrations, and are caught in
considerable numbers in snares.*

*The rivers and lakes near the little forest
where the family has fixed its abode abound with
fine fish that are easily caught with hooks and
nets. In fact, I have not seen or heard of any
part of this country which seems to possess half
the advantages requisite for a constant residence
that are ascribed to this little spot.*

Since leaving Hornby Point we had been seeing from
one to five wolves each day. Most of them were whitish
in color, but some were grey or nearly black as was the
one seen on the day of the muskox charge. One evening
while I walked on the tundra, Darrell watched as a wolf
made off with a young arctic tern while its parents put up
a terrific fuss. The tundra wolves do, of course, eat a
wide variety of food as they roam the rolling hills and
muskeg of the barrens. In addition to birds and eggs, they
feed on mice, lemmings, ground squirrels, rabbits, and
other small animals, as well as muskoxen and caribou.
Several times while walking on the tundra we came across
caribou skeletons which had most likely been picked clean
by the wolves.

Tundra wolves are large animals that sometimes
weigh up to one hundred forty pounds, however ninety
pounds is nearer their average weight. They are extremely intelligent animals. The range of a wolf family
may cover several hundred miles excepting in summer
while they are raising pups in their denning areas. There
is no doubt that these animals destroy many caribou each
year. What is too often overlooked, however, is that most
of the caribou taken by wolves are the old, the feeble, or
the crippled. As wolves attack a herd of migrating
caribou, they weed out the poor specimen whose continued
existence would only downgrade the quality of the herd.
In most cases a healthy caribou can easily outrun a wolf,
unless the wolf has hunting partners.

During the middle years of the twentieth century,

wolves were blamed for the diminishing numbers of caribou, but it has now been determined that the real culprit was not the wolf, but man. The deadly combination of man, guns and ammunition, or of man and poison bait, nearly succeeded in the total elimination of these great wolves of the tundra. Today the caribou herds are again increasing and the great white wolves are being respected once more as an essential part of the natural balance.

While the sunny days continued we were seeing many wolves but very few geese. We decided that the shortage of geese was probably due to the high number of wolves in the area. They were likely still denning nearby in late July, and were forced to consume more of the small animals and birds which could be caught in the vicinity of their dens.

During the next couple of days we moved past Ursus Island and the Thelon bluffs, into the District of Keewatin and on out into Beverly Lake. The perfect weather continued and indeed it was an enjoyable bit of canoeing. As we crossed the 102nd meridian, a herd of fourteen muskoxen grazing beside the river moved on up and over the riverbank to the north.

One night we camped near the final pocket of trees along the river about five miles upstream from Ursus Island. Here we found large numbers of stumps from which the trees had been removed many years before. This was the northernmost group of trees in the central barrens. It was also the trees the Inuit people visited to secure wood for their kayak frames, tent poles, sleds, drum hoops and other smaller items. Wood was one of the most valuable items those people could own. They sometimes came from as far away as Victoria Island and other places to the east, traveling hundreds of miles to obtain the precious wood.

Upon investigation, we found that these trees had not all been harvested at the same time. Instead, evidence clearly showed that they had been harvested over a number of years. Due to the slow decomposition of wood at that latitude, it was clear that those trees had been chopped down from fifty to more than one hundred and fifty years before. There were also several stone tent rings a short distance above the tree stumps where the people camped as they hacked down the trees using their crude chopping tools.

Just below the Thelon bluffs a solitary caribou bull came into view and started to swim across the river only about a hundred yards ahead.

"Let's see if we can catch up with that one," said Darrell. We immediately went into action, pulling and swinging those paddles with every ounce of strength we could muster. Sixty seconds later the caribou was in mid-river and we were still thirty feet upstream from him.

We kept digging and *North Star* was fairly leaping along the surface of the river. To our amazement, we were losing the race. That caribou was not about to be overtaken. By the time he lunged ashore, we were still more than fifty feet behind. We had lost the race but in so doing had learned a lesson. The lesson was that caribou are indeed powerful swimmers. We would race with no more caribou.

We arrived in Beverly Lake during the afternoon of August 3rd, another of those perfectly beautiful barren land summer days. It was so calm that the "scourge of the north" followed us all day, even while on the river. Shortly after entering the lake we came upon four canoeists who were camping along the south shore. These were the first people we had seen in nearly three weeks, so we went ashore for a brief visit.

The group, with their two Grumman canoes, had been dropped into Eyeberry Lake on July 1st. They planned to reach Baker Lake by August 17th, so they had been enjoying a leisurely cruise down the Thelon. Those three young men and a young lady were from Maine and New York states. They told us that we were also the first people they had seen on the river. They had been camping in that spot for the past three days.

We soon moved on because we were not too comfortable with those strange New Englanders. Apparently they were also pleased to see us underway again. We could understand their feelings because there is something about the solitude in such a beautiful setting that when a group is alone, they do not like being disturbed by others. We had definitely disturbed their solitude.

"At least we did have nineteen days to ourselves," Darrell quietly remarked as we paddled away.

Now well ahead of schedule, we decided to relax more because we were not expected in Aberdeen Lake for another week. Twenty minutes later we went ashore and found a good campsite with plenty of driftwood along the rocky shore. We soon went for a swim, built a nice campfire, washed out some dirty clothes, baked a cake along with a batch of biscuits, and enjoyed a leisurely evening.

13

BEVERLY TO
ABERDEEN

> *Like winds and sunsets, wild things*
> *were taken for granted until progress began*
> *to do away with them. Now we face*
> *the question of whether a still-higher*
> *standard of living is worth its costs*
> *in things natural, wild and free.*
>
> — *Aldo Leopold*

The insects were no problem that evening as a north wind soon began to pick up. Clouds drifted in and obscured the sun, and the temperature turned much cooler before we crawled into the sleeping bags. I was awakened shortly after midnight by sounds of something or someone banging on an aluminum canoe. Our tent was on higher ground about one hundred yards from where *North Star* was anchored to a rock down near the shore and turned over our packsacks. I charged out of the tent with only my shoes on, thinking someone or something was going through our packs. What I found were two loaded canoes underway just off shore and heading across the wide part of Beverly Lake. They were our New England neighbors starting to cross the lake.

Darrell was out by the time I returned to the tent. When he learned what I had found he exclaimed, "What an hour to start crossing this big lake! Especially after they sat there in camp during that perfect weather!" A few minutes later the rain began and strong gusty winds hit us and continued throughout the night. We never saw that group again so we expect that they made it to shore somewhere.

The rain and strong winds continued throughout the next day, but we went for a hike on the tundra when the rain finally let up. Small groups of caribou moved by several times. The temperature dropped into the 40's as the wind swung more to the northeast during the second night.

Then the sky cleared as wind velocity dropped to a more reasonable speed. We soon embarked and were able to make it across the largest part of the lake before gale force winds again whipped up. That night we camped on an island. Fuel was scarce but eventually we were able to scrounge up enough to cook our supper.

During the next five days we moved forward some each day. Shortly after leaving Beverly Lake the Thelon nearly doubled in size as we passed the junction with the Dubawnt River. At that point we also left the Thelon Game Reserve.

Fuel for cooking was non-existent. Fortunately we were packing a one-burner Coleman stove along with a gallon of white gasoline. It certainly came in handy when there were no sticks to be found. We had plenty of food this time so there was no need to go hungry. Now our only problem was cooking on that little burner in the strong cold winds. The Coleman had no wind break of its own, so we devised a system of arranging our packs around it, close to the tent, to break the wind.

The birds again became more plentiful. There were lots of snow geese and sandhill cranes along the way. Loons, herring and bonapartes gulls, Arctic terns, long-tailed as well as parasitic jaegers, and shore birds were everywhere. Also included were our favorites, the ruddy turnstones and the golden plovers. Each day now we munched blueberries and "eyeberries" nearly every time we went ashore.

The Thelon is excellent caribou country during July and August. From the time we first intercepted the migration of the bulls on the Elk River we were to see caribou every day until we flew away from Aberdeen Lake twenty-seven days later.

Late in the afternoon of August 9th we arrived at the entrance to Aberdeen Lake. We soon found a suitable campsite even though we were exposed to the full sweep of the wind. Our rendezvous with "Pooch" Liesenfeld of Rainy Lake Airways, Ltd. was on August 11th, so we had arrived two days early. If weather permitted us to move again we would follow the north shore of Aberdeen Lake until intercepted by the expected aircraft.

The northeast wind continued without letup night or day. On August 10th we walked along the north shore. There were many places where the Inuit had camped in the past. This had certainly been the "deers way" around the west end of Aberdeen. Most of these old campsites had piles of caribou bones lying around the stone tent rings. Walking east about three miles, we came upon a shack. When we went inside we learned the building belonged to the Canadian Wildlife Service. While reading the shack's log book, we found that the place had been used off and on since 1962. Its most recent use was from April to July 1972 for a caribou tagging project.

"That's more than two years ago," said Darrell, "and look at all the supplies still here." There were several cases of canned foods and cooking supplies including stove and fuel, utensils and many other useful items.

"Son, this has to be the place from where Marlin Perkins and his pilot Max Shapiro filmed that caribou tagging project shown on Mutual of Omaha's **Wild Kingdom** TV program."

"You're right. I'll bet it is! I remember that after Max picked us up above Kazan Falls two years ago he told us that he had just returned from Aberdeen Lake with Marlin Perkins where they had been filming caribou." We were both **Wild Kingdom** fans so we had seen that program during the previous winter.

Cold showers moved in again that evening and continued on an intermittent basis throughout the following day. It was now August 11th, the day we expected to be picked up. We waited all day with everything packed except the tent, but nothing happened. We left the tent up for protection from the cold wind and rain showers. The bad weather continued until early afternoon of the following day. It was a monotonous wait but we had no choice as there was no way to paddle into those high seas on Aberdeen Lake. Several times on both of those days we heard a roar in the distance that sounded like an approaching plane, but each time it turned out to be the wind.

We discussed the fact that no portages were required on the Thelon after the long one made above the Clarke junction back on July 25th. "We've had fifteen days of canoeing without a single portage," said Darrell. "The continuous paddling without a portage would have been monotonous if it hadn't been for the interesting wildlife in the preserve."

"It sure was a leisurely and enjoyable journey. Had we really needed to move we could have probably canoed the final 248 miles in eight or nine days," I replied. "The weather has cooperated with us most of the time. This has been a much warmer summer than two years ago while we were descending the Kazan."

"It has been an interesting trip. I wouldn't mind doing it again. But the next time I'd like to start over in Great Slave Lake, come up over Pikes portage, through Artillery Lake, down the Hanbury past Helen Falls, through here, and then continue on past Baker Lake, all the way out through Chesterfield Inlet."

"That would be quite a trip. Let's do it sometime," I replied.

At 1:30 we were relaxing inside our tent when again we thought we heard an aircraft approaching. We bounded outside, and sure enough, there it was! A twin Beech flying low was heading right over us. While we dropped the tent, the plane circled a couple of times, then splashed down and headed for shore.

An hour later we were landing at Baker Lake. We secured a cabin at Baker Lake Lodge, and learned that the next flight south would not be until two days later. We would again get to spend time in Baker Lake. Next came a hot shower. What a treat! Off came the first layer of camp dirt!

At suppertime in the Lodge we told them that we hadn't heard any news for a month, and asked what had happened in the world that we might be interested in. One man replied, "Well, let's see now. I guess nothing very important. Oh, yes! The Greeks have invaded the island of Cyprus! I can't think of anything else."

Then another man, an Australian, spoke up, "Say, these blokes might be interested in the fact that the President of the United States has abdicated." Indeed we were interested in that news. President Nixon had resigned, turning the Presidency over to Gerald R. Ford.

That evening we had a visit from Ron Hawkins of the Game Management Division of Canadian Wildlife Service. He came to our cabin and his first question was, "Are you the fellows who just came down the Thelon?" When we replied affirmatively, he said, "I've been expecting you. You chaps are in a lot of trouble. I've checked with our office in Yellowknife and they have informed me that you came through the Thelon Game Preserve without a permit."

"We have a travel permit that was issued by the RCMP in Lynn Lake, Manitoba," I replied.

"That has nothing to do with this matter. The Game Management Division allows absolutely no travel by anyone through the Preserve. In fact, they haven't even allowed me to go in there yet and I'm in charge of this side of the Preserve."

"Someone should have told us that ahead of time. We would have obtained a permit if we'd known one was required."

"I don't think you would have been issued a permit. They aren't easy to secure. You see, too many people are traveling through there, and we are worried that animals are being unduly disturbed. We have to put a stop to it. By the way, do you have any guns with you?"

When we assured him that we did not have firearms, he seemed to relax a little. We invited him in and he continued to question us. He asked about the numbers of caribou, muskoxen, bears, wolves, foxes, wolverines, peregrine falcons, and other birds we had seen along our journey. Then he wanted to know just where we had seen them. He took notes of most everything we had to say. He also inquired as to whether we had seen any other people. We told him about the New Englanders and he said, "Yes, I know. Those people don't have a permit either. We have to find a way to get the word out that travel is not allowed in the preserve. Do you fellows have any ideas as to how we could stop these violations?"

"You could start by having the RCMP tell everyone who applies for a travel permit through there," said Darrell.

"Or see to it that all maps printed of the area contain a clearly marked warning," I added, to which Ron Hawkins replied, "Those are good suggestions. I'll pass them along to our headquarters in Yellowknife. I'll also need to see your fishing licenses," he continued.

"Sorry about that," I replied. "We were unable to purchase fishing licenses for the Territories in Lynn Lake. We inquired about them at the RCMP and also at the airbase of Parsons Airways Northern. Both told us that N.W.T. licenses were no longer available in Manitoba. This may be a little late, but can we buy them from you?"

He looked me in the eye, and then glanced at Darrell. Finally, he began to grin and replied, "Well, I guess we could do it that way."

"Wonderful!" I reached for my wallet. Darrell was already reaching for his. So that problem was solved.

Our discussion continued for nearly an hour before he said, "You men have been very cooperative and because you have no guns, I'm not going to write you up this time. However, I will have to report this to Yellowknife and you may be hearing from them later."

We did not later receive any direct message from the

Game Management Division in Yellowknife, but we strongly recommend that a permit be obtained by anyone planning to travel through the preserve.

The north wind continued and the temperature hit a high of 39 degrees the next day while we walked around the settlement trying to keep warm. That was the coldest day we'd seen all summer.

"No doubt about it," said Pooch Liesenfeld. "Winter is on its way. It is time for us to pack up and get out of here as soon as we can."

"By the way," he continued. "If you fellows would like to see the most remote and inaccessible part of the barrens, you should canoe the Hayes River when you come back next time. The Hayes flows into Chantry Inlet from the east."

"We'll consider that, Pooch. Sounds like our kind of river," I replied

Our plans were to again have our canoe shipped either to Churchill or to Montreal as we had done in 1972. At the Hudson's Bay store Bill LaCaptella, the manager, informed us that the company no longer supplied the service. With that information and after a lengthy discussion, we decided to leave our *North Star* turned up and firmly anchored just behind Baker Lake Lodge. "Chances are we will want to use it again up this way in a year or two," said Darrell.

That evening we talked with Allan Simpson from Winnipeg, another guest at the Lodge. He was Chief of Northern Communications in the central region for the Canadian Department of Communications. Al told us some interesting facts about his early days around Baker Lake. He had been stationed there from August of 1950 to September of 1952 while working at the Department of Transports Radio Communication Station.

"I've seen a lot of changes around here," he said. "Back in those days I was one of about thirteen non-Inuit people in the settlement. There were very few Inuits living permanently here then. The only ones that did live here worked for either the Hudson's Bay Company, the Anglican Mission or the Department of Transport. Two of them were special constables for the RCMP. All the other Inuits were living out on the land and came in only at certain times of the year to trade at the Hudson's Bay Company store. Sandy Lunan was in charge at the HBC back in those days."

Darrell spoke up, "Father Joseph Choque must have already been at the St. Paul R.C. Mission while you were here."

"That's right. He was another one of the thirteen of us. Then there was another R.C. missionary, Father Joseph Buliard, who was based here, but he spent nearly all of his time out on the land over in the Back River country around Garry Lake. I met him a couple of times when he traveled to the settlement by dog sled. He disappeared in the fall of 1956 and most likely went through the ice up there somewhere. There is a monument to him up on cemetery hill that you might like to look at. It's only a mile or so across the tundra north of here."

"By the way," he continued. "Would you chaps like to see some pictures I took back in those days? I have some in my room."

We both replied affirmatively. Al headed for his room, saying, "I'll be right back." He returned almost immediately with about a hundred color slides and some black and white photos which he had taken around Baker Lake during the time he was stationed at the Department of Transport.

He showed us photos of Inuit people with dog teams, with their igloos in the background. He had pictures of the few buildings in the settlement at that time, photos of Father Joseph Choque, Sandy Lunan and Canon James, who was the Anglican missionary. There were photos of Bill Carey, the RCMP officer and of Al with a team of sled dogs. All were dressed in their handmade skin and fur winter clothing.

While looking at a picture of some Inuit people Al remarked, "This man building an igloo was known as Scotty. I visited him at his camp at the south end of Kaminuriak Lake while on a dog sled trip in the spring of

1951. Scotty was an excellent hunter and supported a family unit of three adult women, four children and one grandchild."

"You really have seen a lot of changes around here," I remarked.

"That's for sure! In the old days, people frequently died of starvation on the land when the caribou migration routes changed and they missed the traditional hunting areas. My trip to Kaminuriak Lake with Corporal Bill Carey of the RCMP was related to this. Bill was investigating a starvation report from a camp east of Kazan Falls. As it turned out, those people had no caribou. You can see by this picture that their clothing is old and very poor because of a lack of caribou skins. They were surviving, however, on fish, but most of their dogs had died. Survival on the land in those days was very difficult, and almost impossible without dogs."

"This picture of Scotty's camp at Kaminuriak Lake, on the other hand, is quite different. Notice their fine skin clothings, and the big strong dogs. Scotty was getting lots of caribou and even provided us with caribou meat and fish for our return trip to Baker Lake."

"These two sleds from Scotty's camp traveled back here with us to enter the Baker Lake Easter Dog Sled Races. One of the sleds carried Scotty and one woman, and the other was driven by Scotty's son who was about ten or twelve years old at that time."

"Here is a picture of Ooyoomut who traveled with Bill Carey and myself during our trip to the Inuit camps that spring. Several years later Ooyoomut drowned in Baker Lake."

Right after lunch the following day the two of us walked the mile and a half to the airport. Transair's DC-3 arrived on schedule. There was a delay of an hour before take off while a pickup truck returned to the settlement for a sick man whom they were flying to the hospital in Churchill for emergency surgery. He was brought to the airport on a stretcher which was lying crossways on the back of the truck. He was lifted aboard the plane followed by a nurse. The rest of us, including Allan

Simpson, then boarded. Because of the medical emergency the aircraft headed directly for Churchill, canceling the regularly scheduled stops at Rankin Inlet and Eskimo Point.

There were no hotel rooms available in Churchill that night. We were about to set up our tent when we again bumped into Al Simpson. Learning of our problem, he promptly secured a room for us at the Fort Churchill Airbase in the Department of Public Works Reception Center.

Shortly thereafter, following a Transair flight to Lynn Lake and Thompson, Manitoba, we were back in our Cessna 210 and winging our way home.

14

KAZAN FALLS

> *The river swept and seethed and leapt,*
> *And caught us in its stride;*
> *And on we hurled amid a world*
> *That crashed on every side.*
>
> — *Robert Service,*
> ***Barb-Wire Bill***

The spring of 1976 saw us making plans to descend the Hayes River in the District of Keewatin. Our maps of the area were in hand. This time we would fly from Baker Lake into the headwaters of the river starting at Walker Lake, just above the Arctic Circle.

Then in May of 1976 we checked with Rainy Lake Flying Service in Fort Francis, Ontario, to find out if our canoe *North Star* was still in river-running condition behind Baker Lake Lodge where we had left it. We also gave them our planned arrival date and asked for transportation costs to Walker Lake.

When their reply arrived, we learned that Baker Lake Lodge had been destroyed by fire in the fall of 1975 and that Helen Liesenfeld, Pooch's wife, had been seriously burned in that fire. They said that *North Star* was still

there and had been untouched since we left it in August of
'74. Then came more bad news. The cost to fly us to
Walker Lake would be $1,350 and the charge to return us
from Chantrey Inlet to Baker Lake would be an additional
$995.

That news stopped us in our tracks! We expected
transportation charges would be high, but we anticipated
total costs of no more than six or seven hundred dollars.
Their charges were much more than we could afford so we
had to change our plans.

Following further consultation with our maps and
each other, we reluctantly decided to start in Princess
Mary Lake. That would be a much shorter flight. Then
we would canoe the Kunwak River down into Thirty Mile
Lake, where we would intercept the Kazan River. This
would let us canoe the lower part of the river past Kazan
Falls and out into Baker Lake. Once there we would
paddle east through Chesterfield Inlet and terminate our
journey at the settlement of the same name on the
northwest shore of Hudson Bay.

Prior to departure, we invested in a new tent. We
chose a Gerry Fortnight II because it was roomier than our
old pup tent. We also selected the Gerry because the
manager of Bill and Paul's Sporthaus in Grand Rapids,
Michigan, assured us that it was guaranteed to withstand
the strong winds of the Arctic. We also took along a new
stern seat to replace the broken one in *North Star*.

We arrived in Baker Lake on July 19th on the Transair
flight north from Thompson and Churchill, Manitoba.
There were no rooms available in the settlement, so we
slept in our new tent behind the old burned-out Lodge. We
installed the new stern seat in *North Star*, and before we
turned in met Roy Swanson who would fly us to Princess
Mary Lake on the morrow.

The next morning we picked up our travel permits and
fishing licenses from the RCMP. We also bought white
gas for the two-burner Coleman stove Darrell brought
along. We were certain there would be no wood for
cooking anywhere along our route.

By noon we were completing the thirty-minute flight

in the twin Beech. Flying over northern Princess Mary Lake, we found it still completely frozen over. Ahead, however, we could see open water in the southern part of the lake. We were put ashore on a beach on an island just beyond the edge of the solid ice.

When we had completed the unloading, Roy Swanson walked up and down the beach enjoying the scenery.

"Boy," he said. "I envy you fellows. This is great! I wish I could go along with you. You chaps will be living in close harmony with lots of our beautiful unspoiled wilderness. Closer than I have ever been." With that, he returned to his plane and within the next few minutes we watched as he took off and disappeared over the horizon toward Baker Lake.

We selected a spot to set up camp between the beach and a huge snowdrift that had piled up during the previous winter. Ice floes came drifting past all afternoon, blown by a stiff breeze out of the north. The bay below our beach was soon closed in by the ice pack. The temperature rose to 56 degrees, but with the wind out of the north it seemed colder. As I checked my thermometer, Darrell said, "This is not cold for up here. I've read that the average mean temperature for the month of January in Baker Lake is 27 degrees below zero." He shivered.

We walked across the island and on the highest point found a huge inukshuk about seven feet tall. That was the largest stone man we had seen. From its vantage point we could see for miles in all directions. Along the side of a cliff a pair of rare peregrine falcons were nesting. We watched in awe as they circled and scolded while we walked along the base of their cliff.

Darrell remarked, "Those have to be the most awe-inspiring birds in North America."

"It's a thrill to see and to listen to them," I replied. "In years past they were plentiful in Michigan too, but now they are so rare that not a single pair is known to nest in the entire United States east of the continental divide."

That evening as the ice floes continued to drift south, we sat and watched the activities of a family of arctic ground squirrels who lived in the sandy hillside behind our camp. These furry little creatures are plentiful throughout Canada's arctic mainland from Hudson Bay to the Yukon. The Inuit people have a better name for them. They call them "siksiks." These little animals have a loud warning call they give when danger approaches. While upright on their haunches, they let out a series of sharp little calls "shik-shik, shik-shik, shik-shik, shik-shik" to warn colony members to be on the alert. From their call it's easy to understand why they are known as siksiks.

According to Fred Bruemmer, the famous Canadian photographer and author who has spent many years traveling and living in Inuit camps, siksiks were often trapped for food by the people. He says they taste like chicken. He also says, and we agree, that siksiks prefer, and are often found, in well-drained sandy slopes and ridges.

The siksik's most fearsome enemy is the rare Barren Ground grizzly, because he often digs up the burrows to get at the little creatures. Other enemies are the tundra wolf, the Arctic fox, the wolverine, and both the golden and bald eagles.

We watched as they came out to feed. A siksik leaves its burrow very cautiously. First the dark, twitching nose appears, then the head inches up a bit further, the black protruding eyes looking anxiously about, then slowly and cautiously following several retreats to provoke a hidden enemy into betraying itself, the siksik finally emerges, sits upright near the burrow entrance, and inspects the countryside long and carefully. Finally satisfied that all is well, the animal runs off to find some food.

That evening we watched as a pair of siksiks made several trips out for food. Apparently they had youngsters in their burrow, or else they were laying in an extra supply of food, because they returned time after time with mouthfuls of grass, leaves and roots. Occasionally, if we were to move around, they would scoot back into the burrow, but before entering, one of them would stand up on his hind legs to sound the loud "siksik" warning cry,

Arctic Ground Squirrel

then dive into his burrow.

Summer in the barrens is short and the siksiks know it. In four months they must raise a new generation of young, build up a supply of food for winter, and most important of all, store up energy for the foodless winter months in the form of a thick layer of fat to last them through eight long months of hibernation.

"Those siksiks are busy little fellows," Darrell said as he noticed they were still working just before we crawled into our sleeping bags. "It looks like they are going to work all night."

"They are hard workers," I replied. "This time of year they have to keep at it night and day. They're really fun to watch."

The north wind was still blowing the next morning but the ice floes had drifted away from the island. We decided to break camp and have a go at the four miles of open water between us and the outlet of the lake. The wind was directly behind us, so we could get a little help and take advantage of it. Within an hour we had cleared Princess Mary Lake and were shooting the rapids at the outlet. There was so much water flowing down the

Kunwak River that we were able to safely shoot both sets of rapids showing on our map.

The Kunwak is a fast-flowing river all the way down into Thirty Mile Lake. After walking ahead over a mile or so of thick ice and snow, we shot down through some places where the river had recently found a course through the solid ice and hard-packed snow. These solid ice walls sometimes stood eight to ten feet straight up from either side of the channel, and were a little scary. We couldn't help but wonder what we would do if we came to a place where the river competely disappeared under the ice.

By mid-afternoon we had entered Thirty Mile Lake after scooting down the Kunwak, dropping 110 feet nearer to sea level without making a single portage. Along the way that day we saw several caribou, many sandhill cranes, geese and ducks. Then that evening in camp we watched a weasel, some red throated loons, and a pair of golden plovers. Once into Thirty Mile Lake we decided to call it a day as we had moved twenty-six miles in about seven hours.

Thirty Mile Lake is an expansion in the Kazan River. Now things began to look somewhat familiar to us as we had gone through this same lake four years earlier.

The next morning before breakfast we paddled to the island where we found the drum hoop and skull back in '72. Once breakfast was out of the way and the dishes washed up we again explored the island. This time we found a handmade comb with a wooden handle, and an old ice spud. The skull was still there except something had rolled it over and out of the little hole in the moss where we had left it.

A few miles further down the lake and along the south shore we stopped again to explore some other old camps of the Inuit people. At this particular place, three inukshuks stood in a row, and there were many more stone rings. This old campsite was located at a place where the lake was narrow, and undoubtedly was at one time the crossing place for *Tuktu*, the caribou.

In one tent ring near the highest point of the hill we

Inuit Lookout – Workshop Site

found an ancient lookout-workshop area. Judging from the large quantity of stone chips and fragmented rocks littering the surface, the hunters must have put their long hours of waiting to good use. At this workshop site they must have made sharp tips for their arrows and various other kinds of cutting tools. From this spot there was an unlimited view for miles in all directions. On an adjoining nearby knoll we found several graves and we also located a stone meat cache.

There were inukshuks on nearly every hill all along the length of Thirty Mile Lake. By afternoon of the following day we arrived at the rapids above Kazan Falls. We worked our way down towards the falls hugging the right shore until we passed the point where we had sighted the Cessna four years earlier. When the canoeing became impossible, the portage past the falls began.

A misty spiral hung over the falls while we made the nearly two-mile carry to the first good put-in place below. In this distance the river descends a total of about one hundred feet. Just below the falls the Kazan narrows to only one hundred fifty feet. Confined between canyon walls of fifty or sixty feet in height, it thunders, heaves and boils like a river gone mad.

Once back on the Inuit Ku, within a few minutes we located a good camp site on an island in mid-river, and thus ended a perfect day.

Then came an even more perfect day. As it turned out, it was to be a day of unmitigated pleasure. During the first six hours, we moved down the final thirty-four miles of the Kazan and out into Baker Lake. In that thirty-four miles the river drops one hundred sixty feet and best of all, no portages were required. We did, however, make one short portage when we found ourselves on the right hand side of the river at a short bend where the river swings to the left.

From Kazan Falls to Baker Lake, the Inuit Ku averages close to two hundred yards in width and rolls rapidly down around bend after bend. A few miles below our island camp we came upon three Inuit gentlemen who were just breaking camp. We stopped and chatted for awhile.

The man who spoke English was James Kallukt. The other two were father and son by the names of Jacob and James. These fellows were from the Baker Lake Settlement and were out hunting caribou. Jacob, who spoke no English, had James ask us if we had seen any *tuktu*. They offered us tea and smokes and we gave them some peanuts to munch on. These were certainly three friendly people.

We soon departed, but in a little while the three of them overtook us in their twenty foot freighter canoe with a powerful motor. They went right on down river past us but we soon found them again. They were waiting around a bend in the river where the water was really wild. They watched us shoot through. Then they went zooming past us and at the next fast water bend they were waiting again to watch us shoot the fast water. This procedure was repeated time after time until, when they finally passed, waving at us, we realized that we were entering the Kazan delta where it flows into Baker Lake.

While entering the big lake, Darrell said, "Talk about your wild free rivers! This was the best one we've ever canoed."

"Sure is," I replied. "That was the fastest canoe ride of my life."

Once into Baker Lake we headed east and that night we camped on an unnamed island about one-half mile off the south shore of the lake. Thus concluded one of the very best canoeing days of our lives.

The weather remained perfect as we moved to the outlet of Baker Lake. A few miles east of Lofthouse Point we stopped for a visit with four Inuit people from the settlement at the northwest corner of the lake. Samuel Jarah, one of the men, spoke perfect English. He and his wife Martha and a man named Basil, had been down through Chesterfield Narrows hunting seal and caribou.

These people welcomed us ashore and while we chatted they served us a mugup of tea. We opened our food bucket and brought out some of Debbie's homemade chocolate chip cookies which we all enjoyed. (Debbie is Darrell's sister and my daughter.) Samuel was on holiday. He worked as a mechanic for the Department of Public Works in Baker Lake. He told us that he had spent two years in Ottawa where he studied and learned mechanics.

We remarked that we were seeing from one to three aircraft flying overhead every day, and that only four years earlier we hadn't seen a single plane in more than a month. Samuel replied, "There's a lot of prospecting going on around here now. Cominco is test drilling and has found uranium. The country is changing too fast. I hope it's many more years before any mines are opened in this area."

While we chatted and sipped tea, Martha Jarah, who had been in a squatting position, kept swaying from side to side. To our surprise, we learned that inside Martha's pretty *koolitak* (parka type dress) was little three-month-old Valarie Dotie Jarah. That little child had remained perfectly quiet until Samuel had asked if we would like to see his baby. With surprise, we said that we would like to. Martha then slid the little one around until the child's pretty little head popped out an opening in the *koolitak*.

Thanking them for their hospitality, we soon left. That evening we camped on a delightful little island along the south shore, opposite Christopher Island. That island was named for Captain Christopher who was the first European to explore Baker Lake, when he sailed his ship through Chesterfield Inlet in the summer of 1762.

The barrens in the summer sunshine made a gorgeous scene. Arctic flowers of many kinds were in full bloom everywhere. What a beautiful quiet place our island was that evening! The only sounds we heard were the water gently lapping the rocks, the cry of birds, and the steady hum of thousands of insects.

By mid-day of July 27 while paddling down the south channel out of Baker Lake, we were puzzled to find that the water current was flowing west, back into the lake. The map showed the level of the lake to be about eight feet above sea level, so we had expected to move downstream for a few miles into Chesterfield Inlet.

This called for a quick check of the compass and a glance at the position of the sun to verify that we were still heading in a southeasterly direction. True! We were indeed heading in the proper direction. Much to our surprise, the incoming tides of Chesterfield Inlet had turned the huge flow of water coming down the Thelon, the Kazan and numerous other rivers. These waters were being pushed right back up into Baker Lake.

"There sure must be a mighty tide in the Inlet," said Darrell.

"Yes! A lot more than the three or four feet we had expected," I replied. "That rapids which shows on our map at the outlet of Baker Lake must be completely submerged by the high tide."

CHESTERFIELD INLET

> *I rose at dawn; I wandered on,*
> *'Tis somewhat fine and grand*
> *To be alone and hold your own*
> *In God's vast awesome land.*
>
> *— Robert Service,*
> ***The Ballad of Gum-Boot Ben***

The water again was flowing in our direction for the next few miles. We soon passed the site of the original Baker Lake Post. The RCMP base had been established there in 1915. Then a few years later, after the Hudson's Bay Company set up for business near the mouth of the Thelon, the base at the outlet of the lake was moved to the new site at the present Baker Lake Settlement. The reason for this location was that great herds of caribou used to cross the Thelon River near its mouth. Consequently, that is where the inland Eskimos spent a lot of their time.

The late W. O. Douglas, formerly of the Royal North West Mounted Police, says in his last article written for **The Beaver,** "In those days the turbulent water where the Thelon River entered Baker Lake was a favoured caribou crossing. I saw one migration there in later years and the number of animals was staggering. For almost three days an unbroken herd crossed the river."

For the rest of that afternoon we took advantage of the ebbing tide and the water flowing out of Baker Lake. We moved along the south side of the Bowell Islands and encamped for overnight on an island in the lower Bowells. The water flowing past camp was still delicious, cold, excellent for drinking and unaffected by the salt water from the sea. During the following day, however, we found our drinking water to be losing its good flavor. From then on out to Hudson Bay we filled our plastic pail with fresh water whenever we came to an inflowing stream.

The next day we moved past Cross Bay, the mouth of the Quoich River which flows in from the north, and out to Primrose Island. The tide was rolling in when we broke camp. It didn't take us long to learn that if we were to make any progress at all, we had to take advantage of the slower flowing waters in the eddies near the shore. Then for the next six hours, the tide turned and we moved along at good speed, but by late afternoon we were once more hugging the shore and progress was slow as the water again flowed against us.

Primrose Island scenery was gorgeous. From the top of a huge rock nearly two hundred feet above our campsite, we sat and enjoyed the view as the sun moved around past northwest and slowly sank towards the horizon. When we looked to the northwest in the brilliant light, we could see Bowser Island in the Inlet and on up past Terror Point. North and east of us the scene on Primrose Island was even more picturesque.

Four sparkling-clear freshwater lakes between rocky hills added to the magnificent view. Between the hills and down around the campsite, many kinds of flowers were in full bloom with a riot of color. Between the Arctic heather, Lapland rosebay, dwarf buttercups and poppies was the small, dark green of the tundra ferns. Around small pools of water stood thick stands of fluffy, snow-white cottongrass. It is impossible for anyone who hasn't

Cottongrass

seen it to fully comprehend the beauty of the summertime tundra in these remote lands of North America.

The next morning again found us facing the flood tide for a couple of hours as the perfect weather continued. Then we moved along at good speed until mid-afternoon as the tide ebbed. The wind suddenly began to whip up with authority as the flood tide once more began to roll in.

Shortly after leaving Primrose Island we came upon a pair of seals, the first we had seen. They swam towards us and then followed along a short distance behind for the next five or six miles. They appeared to be very curious animals. That pair, along with others we were to see later, were a joy to watch. *North Star*, with its red color and paddles dipping into their water, was likely the first strange sight of that kind those seals had ever seen.

"I think the Inuit used to call the seals *nathek*," Darrell remarked as we hurried along.

That morning we had decided that it would be wiser to wait out incoming tides and paddle with the ebb tides. Now we would put that policy into practice. We sought the nearest shore, which happened to be an island. Inasmuch as the tide was out, we had no choice but to make a portage of about a quarter of a mile over the tidal flats up to the part of the rocky island remaining above the water at flood tide.

To get a little protection from the north wind, we set up the tent on the island's highest point while waiting for the next tidal change. That island was alive with birds. It held the largest colony of nesting terns we had ever found. There were dozens of nests all over the island. Most of them, which were just little hollows in the sand between the rocks, contained two eggs. As we walked about, the terns put up a terrific fuss. There were also several other kinds of birds on the island and along the rocky tidal flats. These included sanderlings, pectoral sandpipers, and several other species of wading birds. As the tide continued to rise, large numbers of pintail and oldsquaw ducks swam along the shore.

That afternoon as we waited, tides and the good weather were the topics of discussion. The weather had been almost perfect for the previous ten days.

"This is turning out to be a most enjoyable trip," said Darrell. "That summer of '72 must have been an unusual year because we had such dreadful weather then. Then two years ago on the Thelon it was almost as delightful as this trip has been."

I agreed. "Four more days of this fine weather would easily see us into Hudson Bay and Chesterfield Inlet settlement as we now have less than eighty miles to go. Maybe this time we'll get home ahead of our due date."

Darrell laughed and quipped, "That would be a first for us!" Then he added, "Let's plan on an early supper and be ready to move at flood tide."

"That's a good idea! Your Grandpa Klein, who in his entire lifetime never saw any part of the sea, used to say to me, 'Time and Tide wait for no man.' That statement applied down in Michigan and it definitely applies here. Let's be ready and we should be able to move several more miles this evening."

"When we decided to canoe Chesterfield Inlet, I looked up 'tides' in our encyclopedia," said Darrell. "I learned several interesting things about them. For instance, as you know, the tides are caused by the moon. The moon's gravitational pull causes a bulge on the surface of the ocean. Then as the moon moves around the earth, that bulge moves toward the land and that causes flood tides. Then as the moon moves across the land and its gravitational force is weakened, the bulge sinks back into the sea and we have ebb tide. That happens on both sides of the globe at once, twice a day. On most shores around the world there occur two high waters and two low waters every lunar day. The average lunar day is twenty-four hours, fifty minutes and twenty-eight seconds."

"That's interesting," I replied. "I never really understood just how the moon's gravity caused the tides, but now it's easy to comprehend. A tremendous amount of water moves back and forth here in the Inlet. It's a wonder our energy-hungry world hasn't developed a way to capture some of that power."

"Let's hope they never do! That would foul up the environment in beautiful places like this, just as they've already destroyed the ecology of many of the once wild free rivers of the earth. I'm sure they've been tempted. The power in some tidal shifts is mind boggling. In the Bay of Fundy, for instance, the tides rise and fall by as much as fifty-three feet twice a day. That makes the fourteen to fifteen feet range of tide we're finding here in Chesterfield look pretty small by comparison. The sea operates by its own set of rules and according to its own physical laws."

"The way I have it figured out," Darrell continued, "Is that this tidal current comes pouring up into the Inlet for about six hours and thirteen minutes at a time. Then it reverses itself and flows out into Hudson Bay for the following six hours and thirteen minutes."

Following supper as the flood tide neared its crest, we again embarked and headed for a point along the north shore about two miles to the east. It didn't take long for us to again be reminded of the power of the tides as we were being swept farther and farther from the north shore. We swung *North Star* more and more to the left and were soon paddling directly toward the north shore

but were still being swept more and more towards the
south shore by the terrific power of the tide. We exerted
all the energy we could muster into our paddling for the
next two hours before we finally succeeded in gaining that
point on the north shore.

We hugged the shore until late afternoon of the
following day until we were well past Barbour Bay. There
we cut across to the south shore and set up camp a couple
of miles beyond Ekatuvik Point. On the top of the high
rock hill behind our tent we found a circle of twelve large
stones, measuring thirty feet in diameter. These twelve
stones were all flat on at least two sides and resembled
seats around the big circle. They ranged from eighteen to
nearly thirty inches in height. The hilltop commanded an
excellent view of the surrounding countryside, up and
down the Inlet, and across into Ranger Seal Bay. Could
this place have been built by the Vikings? Or was it used
as a council circle for leaders of twelve groups of the
Inuit?

There were Eskimo ruins all along those rocky shores.
In the same vicinity we also found some circular stone
walls standing three to four feet high and about ten feet
in diameter. Again we wondered. Could these have been
stone houses centuries ago? If so, what had been used for
their roofs, as no sign of roof material remained. And
who had lived in them? Could those walls have been
shelters constructed by shipwrecked Vikings back in the
eleventh or twelfth centuries? Most likely, we decided,
those structures were built by Eskimos. If so, they
probably had been covered with caribou skins.

Certainly the Inuit peoples used to live and travel all
along Chesterfield Inlet. My journal entry for that
evening, July 30th, reads in part —

> *Tonight the skies are clear. There is no wind*
> *and the temperature stands at 50 degrees. It is*
> *beautiful here. A perfect picture. There's a seal*
> *looking us over a little ways off shore. Flocks of*
> *ducks are flying past. The only thing missing*
> *from the scene are the kayaks of the Eskimos*

*crossing the Inlet or scooting along the rocky
shores, together with the sounds of laughter and
the voices of happy people talking to each other.
Not too many years ago this was surely happening here. But now they are gone — all gone
forever.*

Then came still another day of that unbelievable
perfect canoeing weather in which we moved through the
channels south of Big Island, Moore Island, and dozens of
smaller islands.   More seals were sighted as well as
hundreds of ducks.   Those ducks, mostly oldsquaws and
scoters, would fly past us, make complete circles and fly
by again, looking us over from close range. Both red-
throated and Arctic loons were plentiful. Their call is
much like that of a duck and very unlike that of the
common loon.

South of Moore Island, with a seal swimming along off
our port bow, we heard a motorboat approaching from
starboard. As it came closer, the seal disappeared. Three
Inuit men came alongside and talked with us. They were
from Chesterfield settlement and were hunting seal and
caribou. Fortunately, that *nathek* remained out of sight
and the hunters never knew how close they had been to a
chance to shoot one of those beautiful animals.

Our campsite west of Ellis Island that evening was
memorable. A small stream flowed into a little bay below
the camp. When we first arrived at low tide, water was
flowing out of the stream, dropping in a waterfall of about
five feet.   Then before sunset the incoming flood tide
completely inundated the waterfall as the sea water
poured between the rocks and up into the mouth of the
creek.   We had our own private reversing falls that
evening!

Gorgeous Arctic flowers and dwarf ferns were growing profusely wherever they could gain a foothold between
the rocks. Many were small, some minute, but they grew
in fantastic abundance.   Even the rocks glowed with
colorful lichens in dozens of shades that thrived on their
surfaces.   The colors varied from grays to browns to

brilliant oranges.   We couldn't stay away from those flowers and all of their beauty. We decided that some of those places had to be the rock gardens of God.   We certainly thanked Him each day for allowing us to enjoy all of that serene beauty.

On August first the good weather of the past two weeks disappeared. The morning dawned overcast, with a steady breeze out of the west. We moved along past Ellis Island and Observation Point. Then about fourteen miles short of the settlement we were stopped by a downpour. Once more we put up the tent for protection from the cold summer wind which by noon had swung around to the north at gale force. The skies cleared. White caps were rolling in, meeting the incoming tide out of Hudson Bay.

"If this wind goes down tonight we can still make Chesterfield Inlet in time to catch tomorrow's plane," Darrell declared. "We should be able to paddle the last fourteen miles in about four hours."

"We'll just have to wait and see what happens," I replied. "By the way, if I remember correctly, the Inuit word for 'wind' is *anoke* and their word for 'cold' is *ikee*. That makes this cold wind an *ikee anoke*."

The wind continued throughout the night. By three the next morning, during another downpour, the gale increased in velocity until our tent collapsed on us. We rolled out in the cold rain to re-erect it. Later, another terrific gust snapped the aluminum bracket supporting the tent at the top. Then we really had a problem. Finally, we learned that by turning the tent door directly into the wind, the pressure of the wind blowing into the opening would keep the tent in an upright position. The gale continued all of the next day so we missed our planned flight and the next one was two days later. Surely we could make that flight.

While walking on the tundra with our bucket looking for fresh water, Darrell picked up a wooden kayak paddle which was put together with little square pins made of either bone or caribou antler. That dates it as being constructed before trade began with the Europeans.

We decided that if we were still pinned down by the

weather on the following morning we would attempt to walk into the Chesterfield settlement and try to hire someone with a motorboat to go out and pick up our camping outfit and canoe. That way we would be able to catch the next Transair flight south.

The discouraging cold summer wind was still hitting us with gusts of fifty to sixty miles per hour the next morning, and showed no signs of letting up. We could not canoe on Hudson Bay! We had only one choice and that was to walk the seventeen miles back around the shoreline into the settlement. We packed up our equipment for the flight home and covered it with *North Star*, which was anchored securely to some large rocks, to keep it from blowing into the sea.

The first couple miles of our walk were to the west where we crossed the tip of False Inlet. Then it was nearly a direct line along the south shore of False Inlet, between some lakes and across several areas of tundra where some of the lakes drained into the sea. We arrived at the settlement in early afternoon but were unable to find anyone who would go out and bring in our equipment. However, we finally found a young man who worked for the Chesterfield Inlet branch of the territorial government named Bernie Putulik who promised to move our gear "as soon as the winds slack off."

With that promise, we found a room in the Transient Center and began to relax. The room, with its saggy bed and dirty sheets, was the only one available. We were told that we could only have it for one night because some government dignitaries were expected on the following day.

We replied, "That's O. K. We hope to fly out on the plane to Churchill tomorrow."

There was no restaurant in the settlement so we visited the Bay Company and the co-op store to buy some snacks. Items were expensive. Eggs were $2.20 per dozen. At the co-op store I bought a loaf of bread baked in Saskatoon, Saskatchewan, and dated July 11th. It was now August 3rd. I gave the man a dollar bill, to which he asked, "Will there be anything else?"

I replied, "No, that's all."

Following a lengthy pause he said, "The bread comes to $1.50." We must have looked surprised! I handed him another 50¢ and he added, "I'm sorry about that! Outsiders are often surprised at costs here in Chesterfield Inlet."

The next morning, following a poor night's sleep, we again searched the settlement from end to end for anyone who could be hired to go up the shore and bring down our gear. We didn't want to miss the afternoon's Transair flight! We talked with a lot of people but the best we received were more promises to go "in a little while" or "when the wind lets up."

Late that afternoon after the Transair flight had gone, we were fortunate indeed when Clare Rubidge, who worked for the Ministry of Transport, told us that we could stay at his home. The next flight out was two days later.

"Surely that wind will let up soon. It's been howling steadily now for four days. Maybe tomorrow will be a better day," Darrell said hopefully.

In checking at the Bay Company we learned that we would be unable to ship *North Star* to Windsor, as we had done four years earlier. Our only choice would be to ship it by barge to Churchill. Then there would be stevedore charges to transport it from the dock to the C.N.R. station, plus the rail charges to Michigan. All of that totaled more than the old canoe was worth. After considerable discussion we decided to offer it as a gift to the first person who would go out and bring back our equipment. We spread the word around the little settlement hoping that we could get some action that evening, but we soon learned that when the winds blow in Chesterfield Inlet, nothing moves.

We talked with several Inuit boys around the settlement, and we found them easy to converse with. The girls, however, were very shy. We didn't find a boy who had ever seen a tree, or a cow, or a horse. They only knew about them because of their studies in school, and they had seen them in movies at the Community Hall.

Bernie Putulik of Chesterfield Inlet

Our room at the Rubidge home was much better than the room was the previous night. Clare and his wife welcomed us and made us feel at home. Each meal Diane Rubidge prepared was delicious, especially the dinner of caribou roast with potatoes and gravy, plus apple crisp for dessert.

Following our first supper there, in the evening we all walked to the Community Hall where a movie, **How the West Was Won,** was being shown. It was a pleasure listening to those Inuit people cheer every time the Indians in the movie attacked the wagon trains.

The next morning we again went to visit Bernie Putulik, the man who had been giving us the most promises about bringing in our gear. We told him of our offer of a free canoe if he would pick up our things immediately. That time he really seemed interested and said, "I could use a canoe on my trap line and for early seal hunting. I could tow it behind my Skidoo. If the *anoke* doesn't get any stronger I will go today at noon."

Bernie Putulik did finally leave for our camping gear as he had promised. Darrell went along with him and they returned with everything a couple of hours later. We gave him *North Star* as payment for his services. He was happy! And we were happy that we could finally head for home the next day!

That evening, we watched as young Putulik made several trips across the little harbor at Chesterfield Inlet, happily paddling his many friends out for the first canoe ride of their lives in our good and faithful old *North Star*.

ICE, WHITE ICE

While driving home following the Chesterfield Inlet sojourn, there was plenty of time for discussion and reflection on both the past and the future.

"Well, son! We finally conquered the Kazan, didn't we?"

"Sure did! All of it! From Snowbird Lake we've now seen every one of its 920 miles, down through Baker Lake and out through Chesterfield Inlet into Hudson Bay. Without a doubt we were the first two-man crew in history to canoe that entire route."

"And best of all, we didn't have to drag a guide along to show us the route and to do a lot of the hard work for us. It's too bad we experienced such foul weather in 1972. Other than that, the entire Kazan was a most enjoyable, scenic, and absolutely thrilling canoe trip."

"The area I enjoyed most was that section below Kazan Falls and out through the Inlet. Dad! Did you ever think of writing a book about our travels in the north?"

"Oh, it's gone through my mind a few times. Maybe I could do it some day when I have more time," I replied.

"I think you should attempt it when you can," he said. "In case we're able to make another journey in two years, where do you think we should go?"

"Well, there is one more river I'd really like to run, but the problem is, it's even further than Baker Lake."

"What river is that?"

"It's the Back, also known as the Great Fish River."

"That's the one which flows into Chantrey Inlet, isn't it?"

"Yup! That's the one. We would have to start up north of Yellowknife. The Back is so inaccessible that probably not many people have ever seriously considered it. Best of all, we could luck out and have that river all to ourselves."

"It would be nice, but don't plan on that. I hope we can run the Back. Let's try for it anyway."

With that conversation, the stage was set. The Back River was a challenge we couldn't resist. Its powerful current flows down the longest river in the Barren Lands. It spills swiftly across the Northwest Territories for over five hundred miles into the Arctic Ocean.

Every spare moment during the following twenty-three months found us dreaming, planning, and preparing for our descent of the Back River in the summer of 1978. We read everything we could find on the northern mainland barrens and Back's Great Fish River, including **Beacon Six** by Robert Cundy, **Journey to the Shores of the Arctic** by Captain George S. Back, and **Inuk** by Roger P. Buliard, O.M.I. We even researched the area through early issues of **The Beaver.**

In August of 1976, we took our broken bracket from the Fortnight II tent into Bill and Paul's Sporthaus in Grand Rapids, and told them about our problems at Chesterfield Inlet.

They said, "The bracket must have been faulty to

begin with." They again assured us that our tent was indeed constructed to withstand the winds of the barrens, and they replaced the broken bracket with a new one.

During the summer of 1977, we resurrected our original Grumman seventeen-foot canoe. We bumped out the dents, cleaned it up and checked it over. We then gave the old girl a coat of primer and topped it off with two coats of red enamel. Next came the name *North Star II* which was painted on both sides of her bow. Even though more than thirty years of age she looked like new, and was declared to be ship-shape, and fit to run the five hundred sixty miles of the Icy and Back Rivers.

In January of 1978 we ordered our set of maps from the Department of Mines and Resources in Ottawa. Our plans were to begin the journey in Glowworm Lake and descend the Icy River until it flows into the Back River a few miles above Muskox Lake. Then we would follow the Back all the way to where it flows into the Arctic Ocean at Chantrey Inlet. At the mouth of the river there is a fishing camp known as Camp Chantrey which is operated by Baker Lake Lodge. From there we would have Rainey Lake Flying Service return us to Baker Lake.

In April of 1978 we telephoned the flying service base at Fort Francis, Ontario, and "Pooch" Liesenfeld answered the phone.

He said, "I have retired. I am here alone right now. Albert Bernardi is in charge, but I expect they can fly you back from Chantrey. I'll tell him you called but my suggestion is that you send him a letter requesting a return flight from Camp Chantrey."

So that's what we did. In mid-May our reply came from Albert Bernardi in his letter dated May 9, 1978. This is what it said:

Dear Mr. Klein:

Thank you for your letter requesting trans-portation from the Back River to Baker Lake. Because of our obligations to our guests at Camp Chantrey, we could not make a firm commitment

*to you and suggest that you try to make
arrangements with some other airlines.*

*We are sorry that we could not be of help to
you.*

Yours truly,

Albert Bernardi

That was disappointing news! There was no other air
service operating in that part of the barrens. What did he
mean by "contact some other airline?" We never did find
out. Now all we could do was to descend the Back to the
Deep Rose River or the Amer River, or the Meadowbank
River. Then we would have to ascend one of those
tributaries, cross the height of land and paddle on down
the lower Thelon River into Baker Lake under our own
power.

We each had a complete physical examination just as
we had done before previous expeditions. We both
received satisfactory reports from the doctor and hospital. In discussion with Thomas F. Higby, M. D., as to
whether or not our physical conditions were good enough
to withstand the rigors of canoeing the Back, he gave us
something more to ponder when he stated, "You appear to
be in excellent condition but life at best is a very
uncertain thing."

The big day finally arrived! Early in the morning of
July 1, we headed for Yellowknife. My daughter Debbie
Klein went along. She would drive our Ford pickup back
to Michigan, after leaving us, along with *North Star II* and
our camping gear, at the base of Ptarmigan Airways, Ltd.
By evening of the following day we made our first
overnight stop in Edmonton, Alberta. Then on the third,
we drove on through Peace River and High Level before
crossing the 60th parallel by mid-afternoon.

While making a brief stop to enjoy Alexandra Falls on
the Hay River, Debbie said, "This sure is a long ride. I
think I'll take about a week to drive home. I'd like to

drive a different route too, down through the Canadian Rockies."

We drove on, crossing the Mackenzie River on the free ferry and arriving in Yellowknife during the evening of July 3rd. The total distance traveled in the three days was 2,960 miles. The next morning we checked in with the people at Ptarmigan Airways. They were expecting us and told us that they would have a Cessna 185 ready to leave at about 1:30 that afternoon. They also said that it would be impossible to drop us at Glowworm Lake as the lakes in that area were still solidly frozen over. However, they thought they could probably get us into Muskox Lake.

Back in the city center we bought our fishing licenses, groceries, three gallons of gasoline for the Coleman stove, and checked in with the RCMP. Then we telephoned my wife, Marjorie, who was spending the fourth of July at the home of Ken and Bernice Chappel in Brighton, Michigan, to let them know what was happening in Yellowknife.

Shortly after our return to the airbase, Debbie said goodbye and started the long drive home alone.

Darrell called out to her as she was pulling away from the parking lot, "I hope you don't have any flat tires." We had discovered on the drive north that we had left the spare tire back in Michigan.

Now we were having second thoughts as to whether or not Debbie could make it without a spare tire. She would have nearly three thousand miles of driving by herself, it was hundreds of miles between some of the settlements, and there were very few vehicles on the road. We kept thinking, "What will she do if she has a flat tire?" and "Did we make a mistake in sending her home all that distance without a spare?"

We soon tried to put those thoughts from our minds as Debbie is a level-headed girl who would not panic in an emergency. We were confident she would make it in view of the fact that the pickup had four new tires when we left Michigan.

Two hours later we were flying over lakes still covered with ice from shore to shore. A few minutes

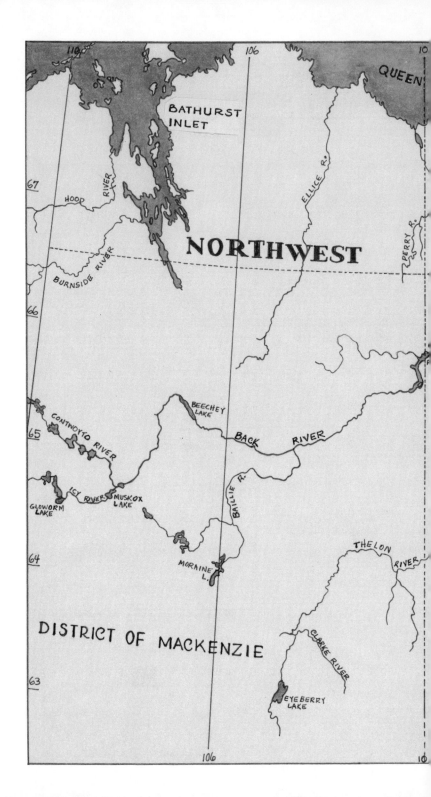

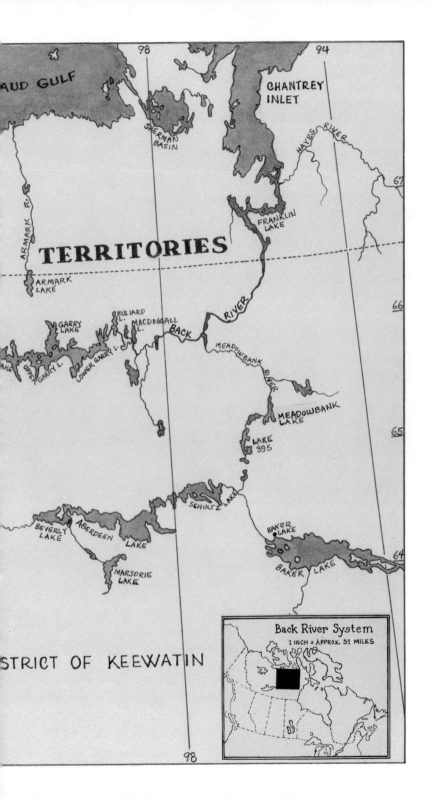

more and we were over Muskox Lake where the same condition existed. There was no open water to be seen. Our pilot continued in a northeasterly direction over Muskox Rapids. Fortunately, just below the rapids and down stream from the junction of the Contwoyto and Back Rivers, we found that Lake 1054 had some open water just below the inlet of the river.

As we circled, our pilot said, "I think there's enough room to set her down in there." We made it, and were soon unloading our gear up over a steep rocky shore to the right of the inflowing Muskox Rapids.

We picked a spot to set up our tent and were hard at it as the Ptarmigan Airways Cessna took off and disappeared into the southwest. It's almost impossible to describe one's feelings as we watched our last link with the outside world disappear, knowing that now our only way home lay more than 650 miles ahead through some of the wildest and most desolate land in North America. And the only way to get there was to dig in and pull those paddles, tens of thousands of times, facing whatever the river and Mother Nature threw at us.

It was a very cold, windy day at Muskox Rapids. No sooner did we have the tent erected than we could see rain coming towards us out across the lake. That evening we did manage to prepare a good supper between the showers, but the strong wind continued and our thermometer stood at 39 degrees. We crawled into our sleeping bags early because that was the only way to keep warm and dry.

The strong winds persisted throughout the night and early the following morning the rain changed to snow. Wet snow continued to fall until it covered everything to a depth of several inches. Wind whipped the tent until it ripped a grommet out of the fly so we had to remove it from over the tent. A few hours later the snow turned back into rain and without the fly, our tent leaked like a sieve. Next, the main shock cord holding up the front of the tent broke from the pressure of the wind.

"It was a mistake to bring this Fortnight II again," sputtered Darrell as we tried to shake water out of the tent door.

I agreed! "I wish we had the little blue pup tent we used on the Thelon," I answered.

"Me too! We didn't know that a tent as large as this one can't be built to withstand the gales of the barrens, but we know it now."

"It's disappointing," I said. "We can stand upright in the center of this tent, but that's a luxury we had no right to expect up here."

We did some repair work in the rain, and then that evening the sun became visible for a few minutes before sunset. We were able to prepare a meal and dry out some of our wet equipment as the north wind continued. While walking on the tundra to get some exercise, we found a rock cairn near the river at the foot of the rapids. Inside the cairn was a rusty tin can which contained a prospector's claim. It was dated 19 August 1959 at 4:55 a.m. and was signed by one J. Rabiscus.

The thermometer stood at 34 degrees when we returned to camp. That evening, in an attempt to get our minds off the weather and our tent problems, we talked about Samuel Hearne and his crossing of Muskox Lake on his journey in search of the copper mines.

"I guess the snow we had this morning is not too unusual for this time of the year," I said. Then I read a clipping I had brought along from Samuel Hearne's **A Journey from Fort Prince of Wales to the Northern Ocean,** in which he said —

> *This night we had no sooner entered our retreats amongst the rocks, to eat our supper of raw venison, than a very sudden and heavy gale of wind came upon us, attended by a great fall of snow. The flakes were so large as to surpass all credibility, and they fell in such vast quantities for nine hours that we were in danger of being smothered in our caves.*
>
> *On the 7th (of July, 1771), a fresh breeze and some showers of rain, with some warm sunshine, dissolved the greatest part of the snow and we*

crawled out of our holes and walked about twenty miles to the north-west by west. On our way we crossed on the ice over part of a large lake, which was still far from being thawed. This lake I distinguished as Buffalo or Musk-ox Lake, from the number of these animals that we found grazing on its margin. The Indians killed many of them but, finding them lean, took only some of the bulls' hides for moccasin soles. At night the bad weather returned, with a gale of wind and very cold rain and sleet.

"Let's see," I said. "That was July 7, 1771. Today is the fifth. Then Hearne went through here just two days short of 207 years ago today."

"That's right! The weather for early July seems to have remained fairly consistent. The lake is still frozen over, the rapids are still here, and the hills look the same as they did when Hearne walked across the ice. Apparently the only thing that has changed is that we don't see any muskoxen around here tonight," Darrell commented.

There was more heavy rain as the north wind continued until the next morning. When it let up, we decided to turn the tent with the door facing into the wind as we had done at Chesterfield Inlet. It seemed to take the strong gusts better that way. By then the little bay in front of our camp was completely filled with heavy drift ice packed tightly against the shore by the wind.

Around noon, we found what looked like an opening in the ice pack at the foot of the rapids. The north shore of Lake 1054 also appeared to be open, so we decided to attempt an escape from our Muskox Rapids camp. The first two miles were directly into the wind to bypass the solid ice that held most of the lake in its grip. What a struggle! Then we moved east down the river past a big drop which didn't show on our map.

That first afternoon we didn't hit it very hard and decided to call it a day at the point where the river swung north, as we were again paddling directly into the wind.

We selected a campsite along the west side of the

river downwind from a steep hill in the Haywood Range of mountains. As we were picking a spot for the tent, Darrell sighted a huge blond Barren Lands grizzly walking out on a point less than a hundred yards upstream from us. We tried to stalk our way back to the canoe to pick up our cameras. The giant bear winded us before we could get to the canoe as we were directly upwind from him. He looked like an immensely powerful brute! He stood on hind legs, took one look at us, turned and charged off up the mountain on all fours at full speed and was soon out of sight. We kept our cameras handy that evening, hoping that he might reappear. However, he must have found business elsewhere because we saw no more of him.

The following twenty-four hours saw us progress only sixteen miles as the cold north wind continued to hit us on our noses. The river flowed mostly north in that area. No portages were required as we shot a rapids where the river dropped three or four feet. We also stopped at an abandoned diamond drilling site on the east side of the river.

"What a horrible mess of junk and litter those people left behind," Darrell remarked, as we walked around and stepped over boards, bottles, cans, stoves, and other junk, as well as racks of test core samples.

"Yes!" I replied. "They really cluttered the beautiful wilderness scenery. The Canadian government shouldn't allow anyone to leave such an untidy mess behind when they move out."

Late that afternoon, we came upon an ice jam that completely blocked an expanse of the river. After looking it over from a nearby hill, we decided that if we crossed to the opposite shore we might be able to get through by making a short carry. Fortunately, when we arrived there we were able to get the canoe through a rocky area where the rocks were holding the ice pack a few feet away from the shore. The temperature warmed up to 41 degrees as the sun came out during the afternoon. That was our first good look at the sun since the day we arrived in the territories. And it was cold! It was so cold that the only insects we had seen since leaving Yellowknife were a couple of fat bumble bees.

That evening after supper, our talk was of Captain George S. Back, the officer of the British Royal Navy who was the first European to descend the river. In the fall of 1833 he arrived at the northeast end of Great Slave Lake where he established Fort Reliance. Then during the following spring he sent his two ships' carpenters, who came along from England, to Artillery Lake to build a wooden boat to be used in their descent of the river. The craft was then hauled over the still-frozen lakes by his men and a contingent of Copper Indians to Muskox Lake. Their boat was not really suitable for river travel. Its empty weight was nearly two tons and she was thirty feet long. Captain Back took along a crew of nine men in addition to himself. When we add the weight of their supplies for the season we find that they carried quite a sizeable load.

In Back's journal for July 1, 1834, he had written —

The boat was conveyed to open water and launched. The river flowing from this lake cuts through a chain of craggy rocks and mountains, thickly strewn with boulders but with sufficient pasturage in the valleys and declivities to attract muskoxen and deer.

Back expected the river might take him to the Arctic coast in the vicinity of Bathurst Inlet, which is almost directly north of Muskox Rapids. He had no idea of the tremendous distance he would have to travel to the east to reach the mouth of the Great Fish River.

"That must have been a real adventure. Think of going down this river with no idea where you would end up," Darrell said. "And the river took them so far east that for several days Captain Back thought it was going to take them out through Chesterfield Inlet. Real adventure was nothing new to him by the time they came down through here. You may recall that he had been a member of the Sir John Franklin expedition down the Coppermine River in 1821 and 1822."

"Yes! That was the ill-fated expedition where several members of the group starved to death during their return walk from Coronation Gulf to Fort Enterprise during the final winter of their travels." We were quiet for a time as each of us saw in imagination that disastrous journey of long ago.

The next couple of days saw us make slow progress down to the north. Lake 1020 was still mostly covered with the winter's ice, but we followed a lead along the west shore which averaged about twenty five yards in width for nine miles. Only once did the lead close completely for a short distance so that a portage was called for. Below that lake we shot some beautiful and exciting drops in the river and for the first time ever, we were paddling north of the 65th parallel. There at last, we had our first sunny day and found an excellent campsite overlooking Malley Rapids. That is where we enjoyed our first big meal of fried lake trout.

Between portages we came upon three muskoxen. Those shaggy animals were just beginning to shed their winter hair, so they were not very handsome even though they were a joy to watch as they came down across a huge snowbank for a drink of water. Then they walked back to the top of a hill where they played a jousting game before resuming their grazing.

The temperature finally warmed up to 56 degrees for a short time, but in the evening the north wind picked up and soon cooled us off again. There is no real darkness north of the 65th in early July. We could see well at any time of the night that we happened to be out and about.

Each evening before crawling into our sleeping bags we had a homemade cookie. Our chocolate chips were packed in a box and made by Darrell's mother, Marjorie, just before we headed for Yellowknife. To our surprise, she and Debbie, plus Darrell's wife, Millie, and our grand-daughters, Kristene and Patricia, had written little notes, folded them and placed one in the center of each cookie before they were baked. Then they were packed in a sturdy box. Once we started finding the notes we decided to eat one cookie apiece each evening with our cup of tea or other hot drink. That way it seemed that we were getting a message from home each day. Darrell's cookie that night was signed by Patty and said, "When you're sleeping it would be funny if your tent fell down."

We didn't think that was funny! My cookie said, "Aren't our messages in these cookies nifty? Cheaper than a call, we're really quite thrifty!" — signed by Deb.

On July 10th we were blown off the river shortly after leaving camp as the Arctic wind continued to increase in velocity. For nine hours we huddled around a little fire of sticks and twigs near the river and down wind from a clump of little bushes which grew near the river, the tallest of which were less than two feet in height. We soaked up and boiled a pot of beans to make some of our delicious three-bean stew. The temperature dropped to the mid-thirties under heavily overcast skies. The wind velocity finally dropped enough that evening after nine to enable us to have another go at the river. From then until 12:30, progress was an additional eight miles. The cold wind, which started hitting us in the faces before ten, continued throughout the night.

Earlier that day we had a real scare. While Darrell was filling the Coleman stove, he discovered that we had already gone through our first gallon of fuel.

"That leaves only two gallons to last all the way to Baker Lake," he said. "We're going to have to take emergency measures immediately or we'll soon be eating uncooked food and raw fish!"

That scare caused us to conserve our remaining fuel, and from then on we heated water for cleaning dishes only every third day, and we cooked in more protected places such as inside our shaky tent. It also caused us to again study our maps. We found that we had progressed a total of only seventy miles in the full week since arriving at Muskox Rapids. And we still had over six hundred miles to travel!

"At this rate it will be mid-September before we reach Baker Lake," I said. "We're going to have to make better time than we've been doing or we may never make it."

"If we don't get out of here before September we will be mighty hungry. We only have enough food with us for about four more weeks." Darrell's voice revealed the concern he felt.

"Son, it may be a good thing that you brought along your slingshot. You may have to do some serious hunting with it."

"I could probably shoot some ptarmigan, but the ducks and snowgeese are so wild that I'd need a lot of luck."

That afternoon while the beans boiled, we also thought of, and again discussed the George Back Expedition. In 1834, weather conditions had apparently been similar to the conditions we were finding. While along the same part of the river we were now in, Back experienced six days in which the sun became visible only "thrice." He had written —

The 11th commenced with heavy rain and a gale from the N.W. which did not lull throughout the day; we were consequently prevented from moving, as the boat could not be taken down the rapids on account of the spray hiding the rocks, as well as the impossibility of keeping her under control. Instead of decreasing with the decline of the sun, the gale freshened, and became far more boisterous. Neither did the morning of the 12th bring any change for the better; the squalls were more violent; and even with the shelter of the high bank, the tent was with difficulty saved from being swept down. In the former expeditions farther west, we had never experienced an extraordinary quantity of rain; indeed the contrary might rather have been remarked; and if it sometimes blew more fresh than usual, the gale seldom lasted more than twelve or twenty-four hours at most, and was generally followed by fine warm weather. But here was a combination of foul and boisterous weather, a very chaos of wind and storm, against which it was vain to struggle.

It seemed that our experiences in this wild barren area practically paralleled those of the Back Expedition.

THE MOST DESOLATE
PLACE ON EARTH

The shores swept faster and faster;
The river narrowed to wrath;
Waters that hissed disaster
Reared upright in our path.

— Robert Service,
The Trail of Ninety-Eight

The cold rain poured down until noon the next day. We embarked as soon as conditions permitted and in spite of the continuing north wind, it was our best day to that point. Not only did we progress twenty-four miles down some good stretches of river, but we also saw and photographed two great white tundra wolves. Then a little later we sighted three more wolves, one of which swam ahead of us to an island. Then a third white wolf stood watching us from a nearby ridge as we paddled across the northwest end of Beechey Lake.

"These wolves must be waiting here for the caribou migration," said Darrell.

"They probably are. More than likely this is the caribou crossing place around the west end of Beechey Lake," I replied.

The Great White Wolf of the Tundra

The only portage made that day was one on the right of about one hundred fifty yards just before entering the lake.   Earlier that afternoon we watched as a bald eagle killed a white fronted goose. A flock of these birds had been swimming on the river ahead of us. As we came around a bend, they hurried ashore, and as they scurried up over the riverbank, the eagle swooped down in a power dive and knocked one goose over while the others scattered. That goose went rolling and flopping as the eagle circled and landed beside its kill.

The wind died down that night for the first time since we were put ashore at the foot of Muskox Rapids. We were out of camp before six the following morning to take advantage of the good weather. We moved down Beechey Lake at a brisk clip as we wanted to complete the twenty-eight mile length of the lake and the portage below it that day.

By mid-afternoon we could see ice ahead and soon came upon a solid cake of ice extending from shore to shore. We worked our way along close to the north shore, sliding *North Star II* over the ice when we had to, from pool to pool of open water near the shore. In some places

Solid Ice in Beechey Lake

we portaged everything up and over the rocks and ice jams along the shore to get to another opening in the ice, where we could paddle again for a short distance. We called it quits early that afternoon. It appeared that the surface of Beechey was solid ice all the way to the outlet.

"I never thought during the last week that I'd ever say this," I quipped, "but what we need now is more north wind to float the ice away from shore."

"Yup! If it would only blow and move this ice just a few feet we could slide right along down through here," Darrell replied.

That afternoon it did warm up to 48 degrees. While we waited we went for a walk on the tundra. We passed a number of sik-sik colonies and amused ourselves by quietly sitting down in the middle of a number of entrances and watching as the fuzzy little creatures popped up from first one hole and then another to look us over.

The wind refused to blow until after midnight. Then a nice breeze came out of the north, and by 6:30 the next morning we found an opening between the ice and the shore. The ice had shifted! We made three portages around points of land where there was no opening in the ice. We also slid the loaded canoe across the ice at numerous other places so that we were able to avoid any other portages. The ice was solid and not honeycombed like the ice we had found at Yathkyed Lake in 1972. Sometimes it was still frozen to a depth of three feet.

"It will have to warm up soon if this ice melts before the end of the summer," said Darrell.

After proceeding along the edge of and over the ice for fifteen miles down the lake, we were surprised again. That was when we came to open water. We found it to be completely free of ice all the way to the rapids at the end of Beechey Lake. At the spot where a peninsula juts out from the south shore, a muskox was grazing in the low bushes. We kept on digging without missing a stroke, as time and miles were of the essence.

But then we did make a stop a couple of miles beyond. Along the north shore we came upon an old Geodetic Survey Camp. There was a dilapidated building with plenty of kitchen utensils and numerous scrap items nearby. There were dozens and dozens of old gasoline and oil drums, and we walked around checking every one as we were concerned about our supply of fuel for our camp stove. The drums were all empty except the last one we checked. On that fifty-five gallon drum, the seal had never been broken. It was marked aviation gas. What a joyful surprise! Darrell soon produced an old screwdriver and hammer lying in the camp rubble. We pried off the seal and under it was a tag saying, "This drum filled in Yellowknife, N.W.T. July 13, 1963."

That was exactly fifteen years ago to the very day. What a coincidence! Naturally we filled our campstove and the empty one-gallon can. Then we closed the drum and put the tag back under the seal just as we had found it. Before replacing the seal we printed our name and address, the date and "Please bill us for 1.2 gallons" which we had removed.

"This is certainly our lucky day," said Darrell, as we repacked the campstove and fuel can back into their proper places.

"Yes!" I replied. "Now if we continue our recently

Captain Back's 'Awful Series of Cascades'

established policy of conservation, we should be able to make it."

Approaching the east end of the lake, Darrell called my attention to the caribou. There were hundreds of them in sight on the hills ahead of us.

Then shortly after six, we began to feel the powerful tug of the current. In the distance we could hear a dull roar. Ahead was the big drop in the river, the drop described by Captain Back as "an awful series of cascades." We moved in close to the right shore and eased our way cautiously forward while watching for the first drop of the rapids. We rounded a bend to the left and suddenly the power of the current increased. Through the clear water we could see huge grey rocks racing beneath us only a few inches below our keel. The roar of the rapids increased and only a couple of hundred yards ahead appeared a line of huge white crests. It was time to get ashore. We pulled up on the bank at the last possible place above the rapids.

A one-and-one-half-mile portage began here. In a river distance of about two miles, the water level dropped more than sixty feet as it curved around a bend to the right. We unloaded the canoe and soon struck out with our packs in an easterly direction across the tundra. The going was good over short, springy moss and grass. Caribou were everywhere. Groups of them ambled off out of our way when they saw us coming. The spot where we returned to the river overlooked more than a half-mile series of chutes, but we could see calmer water at the lower end. We headed for that spot along the edge of a steep hill.

Down by the river we soon located a spot, by moving a few loose rocks, upon which to erect the tent. Then we headed back over the hill for another load of supplies. By midnight everything was moved across the portage except the canoe, and we were eating a rather late supper.

That was a noisy, but enjoyable, camp site. Alongside the roaring rapids we sat watching as thousands of caribou grazed across the nearby hills. A lone seagull flew gently above the turmoil of the bouncing crests of white water, crying an occasional protest against our intrusion into his domain. Arctic terns flitted by, uttering their chattering sounds.

We spoke of Captain Back and of how he had camped at about this same spot almost 144 years before us. In his notes for July 15, 1834, he wrote —

> *The lake which I have named after my friend, Captain Beechey, visibly decreased in breadth; and at length discharged itself by what, from the loud roar that was heard long before we got to it, was conjectured to be a fall, but which was found to be an awful series of cascades, nearly two miles in length, and making, in the whole, a descent of about sixty feet. The right bank was the most favourable for a portage, which we commenced without loss of time, while the two steermen were dispatched to examine the falls.*

He also wrote —

> *The country was still composed of the same variety of rocky hills and swampy prairies,*

*though the latter were far more extensive, and,
near the cascades, might be called plains, all
thickly inhabited by deer.*

"Dad, how many other people do you think have descended this river since the Back expedition?"

"Not very many. My best guess would be less than fifty. In 1855, an officer of the Hudson's Bay Company did it. His name was James Anderson. Then apparently no one else passed through here for more than a hundred years. At least the next recorded descents were not until 1962, when John W. Lentz of Washington, D. C., and three others canoed the river. That same year, Robert Cundy of England, also with three others, passed through here by kayak. Then in 1972, Fred Gaskin headed up the first Canadian team in history to descend this river. Bob and Gayle Greenhill and four others put in at Beechey Lake and ran the river in 1975. Rob Perkens and Bernie Peyton of New England were the first two-man party to make the run. That was in 1976. As far as we know, we are the only ones who will be through here this summer."

Despite the deep roar of the rapids only a few yards from our tent, we slept like logs until six the next morning. Before breakfast we hiked back to Beechey Lake to pick up *North Star II*. Caribou were still grazing or resting all over the hills.

"This would be a great place, here near the rapids, to spend an entire vacation," Darrell remarked as we hurried with breakfast.

"I would sure like to spend some more time here too, but we still have a long ways to go."

It was ten before we slid our canoe into an eddy at the foot of the rapids. Then, at the next marked rapids, we lined the loaded *North Star II* down from the rocks along the right, then shot many other sets of rapids that day.

Caribou were everywhere. Around each bend of the river we saw them grazing, scurrying up the hillsides, looking down at us from a ridge, or swimming across the river. There were thousands!

The Barren Lands Caribou

"This has to be the Bathurst herd," said Darrell. "I read about them last winter. Their range is from the north and east arms of Great Slave Lake to the headwaters of the Yellowknife, Coppermine, Snare and Lockhart rivers along the south, down to Bathurst Inlet and Coronation Gulf on the north."

"That's interesting."

"In 1974 on the upper Thelon, we were in the center of the migration route of the Beverly Herd. That herd winters in northern Saskatchewan and their calving grounds are near Beverly Lake. This Bathurst herd is separated from the Beverly herd by a stretch of geography known as the 'rockpile' or 'rock barrens'."

"The animals around here don't seem to be going anywhere," I remarked. "Some cross the river going south and others swim across going north."

"That's right! This mixed herd of cows, calves and bulls are in a staging area. They will probably rest here for a few days before the bulls lead off in a southwesterly direction toward the tree line. Then about a week later the cows and calves will follow along behind."

We learned later from a game management official in

Baker Lake that we were in a herd of approximately 69,000 animals. It took us more than two days to travel through that herd.

Rounding a bend in the river we came upon a herd of muskoxen grazing in a valley between the hills. We were running so far behind our schedule that again we hurried on past them without missing a stroke of the paddles. The river was fast, and the wind was kind, as we moved forty-three miles before calling it a day. Before turning in, we each found another message from home in our cookies. This is what they said —

Hope you see the migration of the caribou,
They have a long trip, like you two do! — Deb

Don't let a muskox get between me and thee! —
Marge

The next day was another thirty-six mile paddle in which we made two portages over piles of huge water-eroded boulders. Even though these rocks were large, we could not depend on a solid place to step. Frequently during the portages, rocks would roll as we stepped upon them.

"We'll be fortunate if we get out of here without a bad fall or a broken bone," cautioned Darrell.

"This is no place for carelessness. Be sure to watch your every step, and I will too," I replied.

For more than four hours we carefully stepped from rock to rock, trying to keep our balance while portaging over more than a half mile of immense boulders.

During the day as the weather gradually deteriorated, we passed the junction with the Baillie River which forms the northwest boundary of the Thelon Game Preserve. The rain began to fall that evening and continued until mid-afternoon of the next day. We were underway early but found progress slow because the wind began blowing from the east. Another downpour hit us early that evening just after we crossed the 104th meridian.

The cold and rainy weather continued with a strong

wind out of the east, and on July 17 our journal said —

> *The wind whipped our tent all night, and at*
> *about five this morning we heard a loud CRACK.*
> *The main bracket at the top of the tent broke in*
> *two.*

That was the same bracket which had caused the problem at Chesterfield Inlet; the bracket we replaced when we were told that the original had been faulty when the tent was new.

"Now what are we going to do?" I asked.

"Turn the door into the wind right now! Then maybe we can find some way to splice the bracket."

"If we make it out of here we'll send this tent back to the manufacturer* and tell them what they can do with it!"

"That's a good idea."

The wind was so strong that down river progress was impossible. We worked on the tent and did some needed sewing on our clothes, and tried to keep warm in the 37-degree temperature. It had remained so cold that even the dwarf willows were still only in bud stage. No flowers were in blossom, and the insects still hadn't made their appearance except for an occasional bumble bee.

By noon the wind lost some of its velocity, so we broke camp and struggled on into the stiff breeze and rain which continued all afternoon. At the head of Hawk Rapids we were blown off the river as the drizzle increased to a downpour.

While inside the tent that evening we discussed our situation, and Hawk Rapids in particular, as the rapids were less than a half mile down river. We read what Captain Back had written about these rapids —

> *Early in the following morning we pushed out*
> *into the beginning of the rapids, when the boat*

---

* *See Epilogue for conclusion of our tent problem.*

was twirled about in whirlpools against the oars;
and but for the amazing strength of M'Kay, who
steered, it must inevitably have been crushed
against the faces of the protruding rocks. As we
entered the defile, the rocks on the right
presented a high and perpendicular front, so slaty
and regular that it needed no force of imagina-
tion to suppose them severed at one great blow
from the opposite range; which, craggy, broken,
and overhanging, towered in stratified and many-
coloured masses far above the chafing torrent.
There was a deep and settled gloom in the abyss
— the effect of which heightened by the hollow
roar of the rapid, still in deep shade, and by the
screaming of three large hawks, which, fright-
ened from their aerie, were hovering high above
the middle of the pass, and gazing fixedly upon
the first intruders on their solitude; so that I felt
relieved as it were from a load when we once
more burst forth into the bright sunshine of day.
The boat was then allowed to drive with the
current, the velocity of which was not less than
six miles an hour, among whirlpools and eddies,
which strangely buffeted her about.

We decided that we would approach the rapids along
the right.

The next morning, in the cold rain, we embarked and
moved down to the first part of the rapids. We portaged
the upper drop, shot the second drop, and portaged the
third. While we were making the final portage, a pair of
peregrine falcons circled overhead, uttering the unusual
cry of those beautiful birds.

"Do you suppose those birds are descendents of the
hawks that were here when Back and his crew came down
through here?" asked Darrell.

"Could be, but he described them as being large
hawks. Peregrines are medium sized, but they could have
looked large to Captain Back."

"Those birds are telling us that they have a nest of

young nearby. It is probably up there on the side of those cliffs."

The scream of a peregrine falcon over the roar of a rapids is one of those few truly wonderful wilderness sounds. The birds come to meet you upstream of their nest which is almost always overlooking a rapids. They then keep circling with a constant barrage of piercing screams until you are far enough downstream for the nest to again be safe.

The river continued to run through granite hills for several miles below the rapids. The current was swift and there were several unmarked rapids, plus three which were marked. We shot all of those, but late in the evening we shot an unmarked rapids that could have terminated our progress permanently. It was at one of those places where a small island in mid-river divided the water flow. Heavy clouds made the light bad and we did not see that the river dropped several feet in a short distance.

We decided to go to the right of the island but failed to notice that at that same point, most of the water slid sharply off even more to the right. We sped straight ahead until suddenly we were being pulled to the right with shallow water ahead. At that instant we both saw the drop! At the speed we were going our only chance was to cut hard to the right. We shot over a sheer drop of three or four feet, but the bow hardly emerged from the water when we saw that even worse was to come. A standing wave rose ahead of us little more than a canoe length below the ledge.

I started to shout, "Keep her right side up," but the last two words went unheard as water splashed high over the bow and completely filled *North Star II.*

Soaking wet, and with our equipment afloat in the canoe, I kept repeating, "Keep her right side up!" Fortunately, we were able to ease her into an eddy and eventually to the right shore without tipping over. I climbed out on a rocky ledge and the bailing began.

"We're lucky! It was a good thing that everything was lashed in," Darrell remarked from his seat in the stern as he continued to bail water. "I don't think we lost a thing."

I was so cold and disgusted with myself that I could only reply, "Yea, Yea." Then I added, "We can thank the Lord for helping us escape that one."

That evening we named the place "Our Escape Rapids." It was a strong reminder to us that it could be fatal to be over-confident on the turbulent Back. We didn't think we were being over-confident, but from there on we were going to need to be downright super careful.

We found a campsite on the north shore a few miles below "Our Escape Rapids" as a dense Arctic fog closed in. Checking our supplies as we set up camp, we found that the swamping had done very little damage. The plastic liners inside our pack sacks protected the sleeping bags and clothing. The Dry Box containing nearly all our food floated high and dry.

"We're lucky to have this Dry Box," I said. "Even though it is hard to handle on portages, it sure proved its worth today."

"Wow! This fog is thick," Darrell sputtered. Then following a pause, he added, "The Inuit word for Arctic fog is *taktok*."

It turned even colder that night as a strong north wind came up, blowing the fog away at near gale force. We were soon inside the tent in an attempt to keep warm as the Fortnight II whipped and shook all night.

That day also completed our second full week on the river. During the second week we had moved more than two hundred miles. In that distance the Back had become a huge and powerful river. The average width was already more than 150 yards. It flowed with so much power and authority that at each bend the water surface was very noticeably higher at the outside of the bends. There, centrifugal force hurled hundreds of tons of water away from the inside of each bend every minute. The places we had known as eddies on normal-sized rivers had become whirlpools on the Back.

Throughout the night the wind velocity increased even more, along with a driving rain. The cold wind continued with intermittent sleet and ice pellets mixed in with the rain for the next two days. Moving down river in that stiff cutting gale was impossible. We searched for more than a mile up and down the riverbank until we found enough twigs to build a small fire downwind from a pile of huge boulders. We boiled up another pot of three-bean stew, thus conserving more of our precious cooking fuel. We inventoried our food supply and found that we should be able to stretch it another twenty or twenty-one days by continuing to be conservative.

At five in the afternoon of July 20, the gale lost some of its velocity and we were finally underway again. We managed only ten miles that evening while more black clouds were building up in the north.

"We are not the first to camp here," Darrell remarked as we huddled inside the tent and waited for the storm to subside.

"You are probably right. I saw an Inukshuk standing over there on the hill."

"There's a ring of stones just behind our tent too."

The heavy rain let up after about an hour. While we were out of the tent cooking our supper we examined the stone tent ring. It was an ancient one! The stones were sunken deep into the moss and lichens. Some stones were completely covered. It had certainly been abandoned several hundred years before we arrived here. Those were the first Inuit artifacts we had found along the Back. Surely we would find others because we knew that a group of the Inuit people known as Saningayormuit had once lived down around Garry Lake.

Just below camp the river swings to the north and spills out into a wide expanse of shallows and sand flats. For the next twenty-five miles the average width of the flooded sand flats was nearly two miles. The deep water channel that we tried to follow began to twist and turn and we soon lost it. We found ourselves paddling over the yellow shoals.

We were out of camp before seven, but the cold north wind was still blowing dark clouds to the south. We clawed our way north, trying to hug the shores as much as possible. Time after time we found ourselves stranded over huge sandbars, and had to back track and cross that expanse of water in an attempt to find the deep water channel. The windswept waves were running high, and they were especially turbulent when we headed north over the deep water channel.

"This has to be one of the most desolate places on earth," Darrell grumbled.

We battled our way north for the next ten hours, clawing our way into the face of the wind, before we were blown off the river. It was not where we wanted to go ashore, but it was apparently where the north wind wanted us to be. Because of those hours of steady turbulence and malignant chop, we had taken on so much water that we decided we must get ashore anywhere that we could. Our arms ached from the continuous struggle. We headed for a sand dune on the east shore but we hit sandy bottom when still more than two hundred feet from shore. Hopping into the shallow water, we waded the remaining distance and pulled *North Star II* behind us. We were so cold and wet that as soon as the tent was in place, we both crawled inside and into our sleeping bags to try to get warm.

Five hours later the sun came out for the first time in several days, and by eleven P.M. the wind's velocity began to taper off. That was when we should have moved out. Instead, we decided to sleep for a few hours and start again at about three the next morning.

To make certain we would wake up at three, as we were so tired, we again used the Indian alarm clock technique of drinking extra large amounts of water before we turned in. From past experience we had learned the exact amount of water to drink when we wanted to sleep only four hours. Both alarm-clocks went off as planned, except the old one did go off about ten minutes too early.

During that four hours of sack time the wind had again turned against us. To avoid its terrific blasts we cooked breakfast inside the tent. This helped conserve our precious supply of fuel because we were once more well into the second gallon.

On July 22 the sun shone brightly, the first sunny day we had seen in almost two weeks, but we were held prisoners by the north wind. We were pinned down behind a sand dune with drifting sand continually showering down on us. Walking on the tundra was nearly impossible as the chilling wind whipped and stung our faces with blowing sand.

All we could do was wait, and waiting was becoming more and more difficult. An entry in our journal for that day says —

> *We've only had two days, of the eighteen we've been on the Back, that the north wind has rested. Maybe it is trying to tell us something — something like, 'You guys are trespassing in my territory! I want you out of here! In the future, I'll come to you but don't ever, ever try to come into my territory. I don't ever allow anyone to pass through here.'*
>
> *We're now only about a dozen miles above Pelly Lake. Then there are all those other lakes in succession. If the wind doesn't subside soon, we may not make it out of here this summer.*

"Maybe we're beginning to crack up," said Darrell when I told him of my thoughts about what the wind might be howling at us.

"There's little doubt about that! Who wouldn't?"

"There are lots of people down in civilization," he continued with a grin, "who say that we have to be out of our minds to be up here in the first place."

"When they tell me that I'm out of my mind to spend so much time up here, I say to them, 'You don't have to be crazy to canoe up there, but it sure helps if you are'."

That gave us the first good laugh we'd had in several days.

At about nine that evening the wind began to lose some of its velocity. We were soon under way. In a few miles we crossed the 102nd meridian, leaving the District of Mackenzie and entering the District of Keewatin. When we camped at midnight near the geodetic survey marker at the entrance to Pelly Lake the north wind had subsided to a gentle, thirty-four degree breeze.

Another fine day followed a hard freeze during the night. With only an occasional gentle breeze, we made good progress. While crossing Pelly Lake, we came upon numerous flocks of snow geese, the first we had seen on the river. Nearly every group also contained a few blue geese. Along the upper Back there were lots of white fronted geese, but apparently now we had arrived in snow and blue goose territory.

Hour after hour of steady paddling on flatwater caused us to become sleepy. To stay awake, we tried to talk to each other. Now, however, as we crossed Pelly Lake, there were often long periods of silence except for the dip-dip, and swish-swish of the paddles, the chatter of the Arctic terns, or the distant call of the red-throated loon and the quacking of ducks. Hour after hour of those natural wilderness sounds have always had a way of lulling us into a state of lethargy.

In a desperate attempt at staying awake, we started counting the number of paddle strokes we were taking in fifteen minutes. Then we computed that out to the number of strokes per hour and the number per day. A little later, I found myself composing some short lines of verse which I spieled out to Darrell from time to time.

Swing those paddles, pull 'em on through,
Swing those paddles, we've a long way to go.

Swing those paddles under skies of grey,
Swing those paddles through the long, long day.

Swing those paddles through wind and rain,
And as you do, forget your pain.

Swing those paddles, pull 'em on through,
The Back's a big river for a small canoe.

Swing those paddles, move that canoe,
We've still a long haul in North Star II.

Swing those paddles, pull 'em some more,
  The wind's picking up, it's a long way to shore.

Swing those paddles and finally we'll make
  it, with a bit of luck to Baker Lake.

Pelly Lake was full of lake trout. *Islug* were feeding all across the lake and swimming so near the surface that their dorsal and tail fins were showing above the clear, flat water. We were ready for a break. Near an island, we decided to take a trout for our supper. Darrell cast once and pulled in a lively eight pounder.

We arrived at the outlet of Pelly Lake and completed a portage along the north side of the island before six. There we took time to feast on delicious trout with hash browns, pickles and other good things. Then we paddled on into Garry Lake, and before eleven arrived at the beach just below Father Joseph Buliard's mission on an island in the lake.

THE GARRY LAKE
MISSION

> *Teaching them to observe all things*
> *Whatsoever I have commanded you;*
> *And lo, I am with you always,*
> *Even unto the end of time.*
>
> — *St. Matthew,*
> *Chapter 28, Verse 20*

We pulled *North Star II* up on the sandy beach and immediately climbed the steep hill to take a closeup look at Father Buliard's abandoned mission. The building was a small wooden hut covered with black tarpaper. Window and door frames were painted white and a white wooden cross was nailed above the door. Inside the porch door, which was fastened shut by a small piece of rope, we found a heap of rubbish consisting of worn out oil stoves and other old equipment. Inside the second door, we found all the necessities for survival one would expect to find in such a desolate place. The furniture was simple. There was a two-tiered bunk, and a stove in the center of the small room. There were shelves with a few boxes and cans of food, cooking utensils, boot-drying racks, a small table and chairs. The overall measurements of the little hut, including the porch, were only about sixteen by twelve feet.

Behind the mission was a pile of religious books and pamphlets which had been thrown out by someone. They must have been outside for several years for the books could not be opened because the pages were solidly stuck together from exposure to the weather. In rummaging through the debris we found a small plastic medallion of the face of Jesus, the only article of value that could be salvaged.

Lying nearby was an old battered metal boat, several oil drums, heaps of caribou antlers and bones, and directly in front of the mission door was a nearly new Skidoo snowmobile. The Skidoo was hitched to an Inuit's "kramotik" or sledge.

"Apparently someone now uses this old mission as a base for their trapline," said Darrell. "Look! They even left the ignition key in the snowmobile."

Back down on the beach, we soon pitched the tent and were crawling into the sleeping bags. We decided to sleep a few hours even though we both knew the urgency of getting across those big lakes while the weather remained calm.

Most of our discussion the next morning as we paddled on across Garry Lake was of Father Buliard, Oblates of Mary Immaculate, who built the mission to serve the Inuit people living in the area.

"Father Buliard must have lived a pretty rugged life out here," I remarked.

"Yes," said Darrell. "I wonder if he was the same Father Buliard who wrote the book, **Inuk**."

"He must have been," I replied.

"I'm not too sure about that. If my memory serves me correctly, it was a Father Roger Buliard who wrote **Inuk,** published around 1950. Before writing **Inuk**, he had established Kings Bay Mission on Holman Island. It isn't likely that he would have been transferred over here. But then, neither is it likely that there were two Father Buliards working with the Inuit."

"That's a mystery, all right. We'll have to solve it as soon as possible."

Later we learned from Lorraine Brandson, Assistant Curator of the Eskimo Museum in Churchill, Manitoba, that there were actually three Father Buliards serving in Canada. There was Father Joseph Buliard of Baker Lake and the Back River; there was Father Roger Buliard of Kings Bay Mission who wrote the book, **Inuk;** and there is Father Denis Buliard, serving at Iskut, British Columbia. They were first cousins.

Ms. Brandson also supplied us with copies of several back issues of **Eskimo,** a quarterly publication of the Oblate Fathers of the Churchill-Hudson Bay Diocese. The following information was gleaned from those issues of **Eskimo,** which is edited by Fr. Guy Mary-Rousselière, O.M.I., of Pond Inlet, N.W.T. Many of these facts were taken directly from the Garry Lake diary kept by Father Joseph Buliard.

Father Joseph Buliard was born at Le Barboux, France, in 1914; ordained to the priesthood on July 3, 1938; and arrived late in the summer of 1939 at Repulse Bay where he served as companion to Father Lacroix. At his first contact with the Eskimos, he was conquered by them and started eagerly to study their language.

Two months later, a catastrophe took place. On one of his walks on the frozen sea, he broke through the surface, and after a quarter of an hour in icy water, he succeeded painfully in climbing the ice floe and returning alone to the mission in weather of minus 30 degrees. However, his hands were badly frozen. Since gangrene had set in to his fingers it was necessary to send a plane which, on the 9th of December, successfully completed the evacuation. He made a complete recovery during a hospital stay but his hands, with their swollen joints, were always to remain very sensitive to the cold which, in addition to his nearsightedness, obliged him to always travel with a guide.

While he was in the hospital, even if he pulled through fairly well, everyone was convinced that he could never return to an isolated mission of the far north. But he was already fed up with the publicity the newspapers gave his case, and his only thought now was to return to his mission. He said, "Civilization is a burden to me, and I miss my Eskimos so much. It will be an immense sacrifice for me if I'm asked to renounce going back to the Eskimos."

Father Buliard returned to Repulse Bay and during the summer of 1940 he dreamed of evangelizing the various groups of Eskimos scattered over the barrens north of Baker Lake, between Perry River to the west and Chantrey Inlet and Wager Inlet to the east. By the end of the summer of 1942, he settled himself at Wager where there was a Hudson's Bay Company outpost run by an Eskimo, and from there, in November and December, he visited several camps beyond Back River.

Scattered over this immense territory lived a few hundred Eskimos belonging to different groups; the Uk-kusiksaligmiut, of the lower Back River, the Saningayor-miut, living around Garry Lake, the Illuilermiut and a few Netsiligmiut of the Arctic coast. These were extremely nomadic tribes who lived generally in unimportant camps; led by the unforseeable march of the caribou from which they subsisted, these people had to disperse and migrate.

From the missionary standpoint, this region had never been evangelized. A few years previously, Father Lacroix had left for the Back River, but was forced back for want of food for the dogs. For the same reason, from Baker Lake, Father Marcel Rio had not been able to go very far north.

Thus, it was in this territory absolutely un-exploited before, that Father Buliard was to land. To a man as conscious as he was of his limited capacity, there was cause for apprehension. No doubt he must have felt some apprehension, but he was so deeply convinced that he was but an instrument in the hands of God that all his fears vanished.

In February of 1944, he received the order from his Bishop to go to Baker Lake as from there it would be easier for him to visit the region in which he worked. On March 29 he left Wager Bay for the mouth of the Back

The Garry Lake Mission

River and Baker Lake, where he arrived on May 24, visiting Eskimo camps along the way.

From 1944 to 1948 Father Buliard usually lived at the mission in Baker Lake and continued to make the rounds of the Eskimo camps. He travelled by dog team from Wager Bay to the Back River, to Perry River, to the coastal camps along the Arctic shoreline, Chantrey Inlet and down to Baker Lake, time after time. Whenever he returned to Baker Lake he visited camps between the Kazan and Dubawnt Rivers and along Aberdeen Lake on his return to Garry Lake, where he wanted to build his mission.

On the 19th of September in 1948 an attempt was made to build a mission at Garry Lake. Gunnar Ingebrigson and Charlie Weber of Arctic Wings took Father Buliard towards Garry Lake. The object of this first trip was to find a place for the foundation and transport some provisions. The second trip was supposed to bring Brother Maurice with the wood for the foundation of the house. Other trips were to bring the rest of the house and provisions for a year.

Providence decided otherwise. In the first place, the

pilots and Father Buliard never saw a single tent either at Back River or Garry Lake. They had to go as far as Pelly Lake to find two tents; they thought, however, that it was still Garry Lake. They landed on a bay and since the Eskimos said it was a good place to fish, hunt caribou and find driftwood, Father decided to build there. So the provisions were deposited there while awaiting the other trips.

But, as Father would find out six months later, during the night of the 19th, the plane, already loaded and ready to take off on the morning of the 20th, was wrecked by a terrible storm at Baker Lake.

❧

Here is a direct quote from the Garry Lake diary of Father Buliard:

19 September — We unloaded the plane in water well over our knees for we could not go all the way to shore because of large rocks sticking up here and there. When the plane had left, I looked at my new country. The bay where I had been left was immense and fairly cut up. It was surrounded by sandy beaches and hills. About four km from there, two Eskimo tents were visible, but a river, very deep in some places, a little less in others, but always at least a meter deep, separated me from them. Because of this river it was hard for me to go put up my tent near those of the Eskimos, nor could they come and pitch their tents next to mine.

However, two men, not fearing a cold bath, crossed the river to take a close look at the plane and to help me. With them I put up my tent on a hill, took all my things up there, then we looked, without success because the bay was too shallow, for a place the plane could come all the way to the shore. We also looked for a flat gravelly spot on which to build the future house.

In the evening I crossed the river with my two companions to visit their families, one Catholic, the other catechumens. How happy they were to see me come and to know that I would spend the winter with them. Poor people whose entire riches were the game they killed. In their tents no tea or coffee, or tobacco, or flour, or sugar; raw meat and that's all!

That night a torrential rain came and even penetrated my tent but I was so tired that S. had to wake me, for my sleeping bag was wet. He had been awake for some time and had brought up the things left by the shore. All night rain and wind had beaten against our tent which luckily did not give way, but was nonetheless soaked through and through by the rain. The two tents of the Eskimos were torn and flooded. They must have spent a miserable night. In the morning they were laughing about their adventures while drying and sewing up their tents.

I didn't expect the plane that day for the weather was bad. I spent the day levelling the ground preparing a place to build the house. Then days passed. We watched for a black speck in the sky and we cocked our ears in vain. Then I no longer waited. I didn't know what had happened to the plane. The mystery would be cleared up upon my arrival at Baker Lake. In the meantime, instead of worrying I had to assure that I would pass the winter as usefully as possible.

Therefore I planned to visit the surrounding camps as soon as possible, then the Eskimos of Perry River and to return to Baker Lake by dog team for Christmas, visiting the camps not far from the trail along the way. In the meantime I had to live and I had to reconcile the apostolate with the fight for life because I had few provisions, almost nothing for heat and poor clothing.

I spent the end of that September, alone in my tent, on my side of the river but I would go to visit the Eskimo camp on the other bank of the river and the men would also come visit me. I intended to go say my Mass in their camp on Sunday with my portable chapel. "No," they told me, "it is not your place to come to us; we will come to you." And on Sunday my ten parishioners arrived for Mass and stayed with me all day, leaving only after the evening prayers. Therefore I had time to instruct them.

This is how they crossed the river; the head of each family carried his wife piggy-back across the river and then went back to get each of his children, so that he was the only one to get wet. And this whole little band was happy to spend the day with me. They also brought a quarter of caribou and I served tea and biscuits.

Sunday finished, my days were pretty much the same: Mass, breviary, hunting or collecting moss and brushwood, catechism, etc. Thus the last of September was quickly gone.

Snow had already fallen since the 24th or 25th, the edges of the lake and the river froze at night and thawed during the day. Then, when the river was solidly frozen at the beginning of October, the Eskimos came and put their tents next to mine. Other Eskimo families also arrived by sled, and soon where I had been alone, there sprang up a small village consisting of three Catholic families, one catchumen family and three protestant families.

October was cold. So I installed a little stove in my tent, with moss and brushwood, I managed not to freeze too much. The Eskimos made themselves snow houses as early as the 10th of October. I hung on in my tent until the 30th of October, but during the second half of the month it was really cold. I didn't need a blackboard for classes; the sides and roof of my tent served, for *they were covered with a good layer of frost in which one could write with the index. After each night, all our writings had disappeared and were covered over with new frost, so we started over again. It was handy but a bit cold.*

When there was a snow storm, the snow entered my tent like a whirlwind. Many mornings I awoke with my sleeping bag covered with snow and half the tent full of snow. At night there was a terrible noise and the wind set upon my tent in a blind rage. Under the weight of the snow and the efforts of the wind, my tent poles creaked and bent, but luckily they did not break. Often I had to get up in total darkness and shovel the snow that accumulated all along one side of my tent almost crushing it. Weird nights, sometimes awfully long! I could have had a snow house sooner, but I kept thinking I would be setting out. Unfortunately the bad weather, the snow storms, the poor condition of the dogs kept postponing our departure date.

Finally on the 30th of October, I am in a snow house and I find it much warmer but a bit less practical than the tent. It is not very big. It's enough at night for I am alone, but during the day, particularly for the offices, we are packed like sardines. On the other hand, when there are snow storms one is at ease and doesn't worry at all.

On November 3rd, Father Buliard and his guide set out for Perry River on the Arctic coast. They visited Inuit camps along the way and along the coast as far as Sherman Inlet where he bought needed provisions at the trading post located there.

Returning to his camp near the Pelly Lake outlet, on November 22nd they again departed for a camp of Inuit situated on a large lake three and a half days distant. Arriving there, we again pick up an entry from the Garry Lake diary:

I visited the neighboring iglus. In one lives an old fellow who was the victim of an accident and lost one leg from a gunshot wound. Ingenious, he had made himself a wooden leg with a piece of driftwood from a wrecked ship, and for at least twenty years had continued to hunt and earn the food for his family. Now he has lost his wife, and recently his daughter-in-law, and he lives with his son of about twenty years of age. His son goes hunting and traps foxes, while he sews skin clothing, and he is very skillful. While I was talking about one thing or the other, he joins in the conversation joking, saying that a wooden leg is economical because it doesn't need a caribou stocking; it's also practical because it is never cold, while the other leg is often cold. But when I talk about religion, his face becomes hard because he is a sorcerer and a feared sorcerer at that. He seems to listen but doesn't say a word.

Sometimes I am treated as an undesirable. I enter an Eskimo's iglu while he is heating water for tea on a Primus stove. Upon seeing me enter he turns off the stove, saying nobody was thirsty for tea, and he lets the water cool. I had hardly entered someone else's iglu when he says; "It is very cold: I have to bank my iglu," and he goes out, leaving me alone.

30 November — We continue our trip and leave this camp where I was so badly received and where I suffered so much physically and morally. As a first contact with those people, it wasn't great. For a change we are making time today and don't have to walk much. It is blowing snow and the weather is not very clear, but the sled slides well and the rested dogs pull well.

The 1st of December, it is again cold. The sled slides less well than yesterday, and it is black night around 4 o'clock, for the days are

*getting shorter and shorter. We make a mistake
and arrive very late at Sherman Inlet, at the post
of Atanikiktuq and Nuvuslirarjuk. Atanikiktuq
comes to tell me hello; he is very nice but rough
and coarse. In the camp there are about thirty
Eskimos, all came from Perry River when the
trading post was established in the spring. They
are the same type of people as those of Perry. I
will try anyway to do them a little bit of good.
We spent the 2nd of December there. I also
bought some provisions for the trip.*

*4 December — Soft snow and continual
march. It gets very cold and the sky is clear, but
it is the first time my guide comes this way.
They have explained the way to him, but he
hesitates a lot and finally gets lost, for there are
several rivers and we follow the one we should
not have followed. The 5th, 6th and 7th of
December we walk blindly, not knowing really in
which direction, always hoping to find sled
tracks. It is very cold, but we are walking all
day, each taking his turn in front of the dogs, and
each one at his turn beside the sled, we are not
cold except for the face. It is only in the
evening when we stop, perspiration freezing on
our mittens and stockings, that we feel the cold,
and sometimes very much so. We have supplies
for ourselves and make good meals in the
morning and evening, never eating during the day
for it is the polar night, and the days are very
short. Our dogs have nothing left to eat and are
tired. We must excite them and call them often,
for they always want to stop and not start again.
My guide, always so gay when things are well, is
extremely pessimistic when things go badly, and
every evening there are endless lamentations:
"We will never find our way. No caribou, we are
going to lose our dogs and die ourselves of hunger
and cold, etc." I let him talk and try to steer the*

*conversation towards another subject, which does
not always succeed.*

*13 December — We arrive in a new camp, at
the mouth of the Back River, after having
crossed Franklin Lake. There I am in known
territory. There are many people, hospitable and
congenial, but not one is Catholic. There are
still some who have two wives and sorcery has
far from disappeared. One or another believes in
our religion, but finds it too hard to follow.*

*There are eight families there. In this camp,
they have plenty of food, but it is rotten fish. In
the summer, with harpoons and hooks, they catch
a multitude of fish and put them in stone caches.
These fish ferment, rot and get wormy. My
guide likes that and literally stuffs himself. As
for me, I cannot eat that. I have eaten some
these last years in time of famine, and I've been
sick each time.*

*During our stay in this camp, a catechumen
arrives. His family has nothing left to eat. He
has left his five children in the snow house
without food, and all night he has travelled to
come beg some fish here. A good opportunity for
me who must go visit those people. I have little
baggage, I am capable of walking; let's go, while
my guide bucks up the dogs. As for me, I take
the least bit of tea and sugar and some biscuits.*

*When we get to the igloo, we have to knock
on the porch wall, and one by one the children
arrive. Since they had not eaten and it was so
cold, in order not to lose their strength they had
laid under their covers. Upon seeing me they
seem happy. I recognize all these children. I
haven't seen them for a year and a half. Their
faces are not fat, and their clothes are veritable
rags, but they smile at me, they are happy,
there's no doubt about it.*

We enter the igloo. It is so small I can just

barely stand up. No heat, no light; it is cold and dark. They have nothing. Even their caribou skins, their sleeping bags are in very bad shape. It is not just want, it is abject poverty. The man tells me that he did not fish with the others during the summer, and therefore did not have a cache of fish. Since his five children did not have new clothes, he wanted to go caribou hunting to get skins and meat. Alas, there were no caribou, and the winter forebodes suffering. Up until now, he has managed more or less by fishing through the ice, and by going to beg rotten fish from time to time. But it is a hard row to hoe because he is the only one to fish. His children went fishing with him in the fall, and two of them were telling me of their prowess. But now they cannot accompany him, for with their poor clothes they would freeze outright. Now winter is here with its cold, and hunger threatens. No oil or fuel for light or heat, no good clothing or adequate sleeping gear, and yet they are happy.

In the evening after having drunk tea and eaten 'bannock,' we pray and chat for a long time. The children don't want to go to bed, for now it is comfortable in the igloo and they always have something to say. Of course it is after midnight when we go to sleep, packed in like sardines; at the least little movement we make, we touch our neighbor.

When Father Buliard left the mouth of the Back River the 22nd of December, he never suspected that the trip would be one of the most difficult of his adventure-filled life.

Father Guy Mary-Rousselière, O.M.I., of Pond Inlet and the editor of **Eskimo** magazine says, "After forty-three years in the North, the winter of 1948-49 was the coldest winter I can remember." Now back to the Garry Lake diary —

Having left that camp on the 22nd of December, we didn't arrive at my guide's until the 13th of January, whereas I was counting on being there for New Year.

The cold was getting terrible and seemed to get more bitter every day. At Baker Lake, they told me, they were recording temperatures of –50 and –60 degrees F., and as low as –70 in the Yukon. Here the Eskimos say they haven't had such cold in a long time. My nose, my cheeks, my chin and even my neck froze more than once.

Day after day, the travels were all alike; cold, constant walking, lack of caribou, more and more accentuated hunger of our dogs and ourselves. And in the evening the lamentations of my guide who is always so gay in times of abundance and terribly pessimistic in time of trial.

One day it is going up and down hills, another day it is painful walking among the ice hummocks along the Back River rapids (the rapids are so strong that the river remains open for mile after mile during the entire winter). Another day it is walking on thin ice which cracks at each step we take, and finally another day it is rocks that make our way difficult.

25 December — Mass of the day and departure. It is Christmas anyway and despite the cold and the walking, in my thoughts and through my prayer I join all those who are adoring the praying to the Child Jesus.

30 December — These past few days we have walked without stopping. No caribou on the land and our dogs are still without food. As for us, we are living on bannock alone without fat; it is all we have. It is snowing heavily today. We hardly see anything, but we leave anyway for we must. Towards evening, for the first time in a long

*time, we see two caribou. Since it is snowing
and it is dark, my guide misses them though he is
an excellent shot. In unison, we say, "Mami-
anaq!" (What luck) and that's all. We have
arrived at Tasirjuaq, between Back River and
Baker Lake. We make a camp a little later and,
since there seem to be caribou, decide that my
guide will go hunting the next day while the dogs
rest.*

*31 December — Heavy snow storm, even
worse than yesterday. After going out, my guide
says one cannot see 4 m in front of oneself and it
is terrible cold. Then he comes in and suddenly
tells me, "It's useless for me to walk, you can't
even see your tracks, but I want to try anyway.
If I don't come back this evening, don't worry, it
will be because, not knowing where I am, I've
built an iglu."*

*In the evening my guide comes back anyway.
He is chilled to the bone, his face frozen and his
clothes covered with a thick layer of snow. But
he is happy and he tells me about his day. He
couldn't see anything and was just going straight
ahead willy-nilly. But Providence led him, for he
came right up to something black that he had at
first taken to be a big rock. Suddenly he noticed
that it moved. Quickly, he took his gun and shot
it. He had killed a caribou fawn. Despite facing
a terrible wind, he brought it back to the iglu,
dragging it by a rope. Several times he thought
of building an iglu and camping, but thinking of
me and the dogs, he made superhuman efforts,
mistaking his route several times, he finally
arrived at the camp. We end the year with a
grace from heaven. We only saved enough to eat
that evening and the next morning, the rest was
given to the dogs.*

1 January 1949 — My guide wanted to go

caribou hunting on foot again while our dogs
digest yesterday's food and rest. The weather
had cleared but it is very cold. He walks all day
but finds nothing, not even tracks.

2 January — Walked all day in the intense
cold. In the evening I caulk the iglu. My hands
hurt and are very cold, but as that often happens
I pay no attention. The iglu is finished; I bring in
the boxes and am about to make tea and
bannock. I take off my right mitten and am
speechless; three fingers are white as marble,
crushed! A fourth one is not as white, but frozen
even so. All evening, while my fingers thaw, it is
an intolerable sensation of burning. In the
evening, when I go to bed, upon taking off my
stockings I realize that both my feet are also
frozen in many places. When walking a lot,
stockings wear out very fast, freezing due to
sweating and thawing while walking. I have
neither medication nor bandages, so I do nothing.
Once in my sleeping bag my feet thaw but I can't
close my eyes all night. What a night!

3 January — My guide gives me a new pair of
mittens. I put another pair on and we leave
anyway. I don't sit down a single time on the
sled for our dogs are exhausted. In the evening
when I take off my stockings, I notice they are
soaked for my feet have oozed all day long. If I
go to bed like this, my sleeping bag will also be
all wet. So I wrap my feet up in the lining of my
cassock. Later, among the Eskimos, I used
pieces of women's dresses. Scar tissue ends up
forming over more or less all of it after a month
or two, but my fingers will remain hard and
insensible for a long time. That night, my guide
finds two pangniq (adult male caribou) heads and
necks. We share them with the dogs.

4 January — Terrible snow storm! My guide hunts for an Eskimo camp he says is close by but returns having found nothing. Hunger again!

5 January — Taking only our sled and the sleeping bags, we leave in search of the Eskimos. We end up finding a snow house where three families live. We thought we would find people to rescue us from our predicament, but they are as hungry as we are. They have rotten meat but the stomach cannot keep it down. My guide, who eats some, will vomit all night.
Those people were already hungry during the summer. They had been with almost nothing to eat for three weeks, and with nothing at all for eight days. They were skin and bones. Then one of the men, by dragging himself, managed to kill a caribou, and they were saved for other caribou came.

6 January — We were cold last night, for we are in a large, unheated iglu and we are hungry. It is Epiphany! My guide and I pray, while our companions listen. Later, while my guide and another man go looking for caribou, I jig for fish through the ice. I catch a fish which, except for the head, is eaten immediately by everyone there. My guide returns in the evening and wants to go back immediately to our old iglu for they have seen no caribou. "Take the head of your fish," he tells me. "The people have more caches, but don't want to go get them while we are here." And we leave. Late at night we arrive at our camp. We cook the fish head and we eat it, saving the broth for tomorrow morning. We have no more flour.

7 January — We leave without eating anything. As for me, I'm at the end of my rope. I have not eaten my fill for several days. I've been terribly cold, boils and frostbite depress me and fatigue has reached its peak. I walk like an automaton. I can't go on and I feel as if I'm going to drop in my tracks. It is useless to sit on the sled for the dogs can't even drag themselves. My guide is also very tired, but he walks in front of the dogs anyway, for today I cannot do it. All of a sudden, just as I was anxiously asking myself how I would ever go on, my guide stops cold. "Caribou lying on the ice over there," he tells me. While he was cautiously creeping up on the caribou, I sat there resting and watching our remaining dogs, for we had lost two.

We camped and remained there three days, eating, resting and setting up our dogs again. On the 11th we are on the way again, but the dogs have regained strength and from time to time we can ride on the sled. In the evening we arrive at Pituqa. My guide is in a hurry to see his children and leaves right away for his camp, which is now at Tliviak. I stay there and the next morning after Mass I go to my guide's camp. My voyage is over. Deo Gratias!

On the 13th of January Father Buliard finally arrived at Garry Lake. No warm mission post was there to help overcome the fatigue, only life in an igloo and a menu of frozen fish, when available, and cold water, fruit of long hours of waiting on the ice for fish to bite. Then the incessant moving to find a more favorable spot.

On March the 24th, the situation was critical and the priest was out on the ice, as usual, trying to catch a fish, when the plane finally arrived.

At Baker Lake during the months of November, December and January, the thermometer hovered continuously between 40 and 50 degrees below zero, nor did the wind abate. Father Buliard travelled under such conditions for seventy days, with several weeks in the Arctic twilight, lacking most of the time the food he needed to withstand the cold and finding in many camps he visited nothing but ill-concealed hostility. He could have come back directly to Garry Lake from any place on the coast, but he kept on to the bitter end, reaching Perry River, and then the camps along the Arctic shore and inland before returning to his camp near the outlet of Pelly Lake.

19

PRIEST OF
THE BARRENS

Greater love has no man than this,
That a man lay down his life for his friends.

— St. John,
Chapter 14, Verse 13

Father Buliard was brought back to Churchill by the plane which had been sent in to look for him. A short time later, his bishop sent him from there to France to regain his health among his relatives. That was to be the only vacation of his missionary life.

At the beginning of the summer, he was already back at Churchill, which he left on the 6th of August 1949 to build a little house at Garry Lake. The plane flew him in along with Brother Gilles-Marie Paradis and a load of building materials to an island in western Garry Lake which the Eskimos called Siurarjuaq. During the following two days as the plane brought in more materials and provisions, Father Marcel Rio and Father Louis LeMer arrived to help in the construction. By August 9 the house was completed. Father Buliard wrote —

It was hard to find a spot that fulfilled all the desired conditions; central, near the greatest numbers of Eskimos, practical for planes, with good fishing and hunting, and where the moss and peat were to be found for fuel. There will never be a hundred people camped at Siurarjuaq but it is nevertheless a fairly central location situated between the rapids at the exit of Pelly Lake and the open water of Amittuq. The latter two places are habitually frequented by the Eskimos when they are short of caribou caches, but unfortunately impossible sites for an outpost because of the waters that rise in the spring and the lack of a place where a plane can land.

Since the Eskimos around here are essentially nomads, it was impossible to have an outpost in a constantly inhabited place. However, Siurarjuaq is one of the most favourable sites, for there will usually be people nearby. There are fish in the river in the spring and in the fall, but very few during the winter. According to the people from the area, there are also usually caribou, particularly in the summer. Unfortunately the soil is sandy and there is no moss for fuel. The island of Siurarjuaq is little; you can walk across it in ten minutes and around it in an hour. It is fairly close to land on the north, farther on the south. Across from it is another island called Tauja.

9 August — During the morning the door, windows and chimney are done. Charlie Weber arrives late in the morning on his last trip, taking away Father Rio and Brother Paradis who have done a good job in a short time. In the afternoon, it is Father LeMer's turn to leave for Burnside. I'm alone, having sent the Eskimos away after paying them. When the aviators leave they will leave behind the framework of their kitchen and some cases; I will make a small porch out of them. Inside, a partition separates

*a tiny chapel and a small alcove from the rest of
the house.*

*8 September — Feast of the Nativity of the
Blessed Virgin Mary. Altar, tabernacle, pews are
finished and I am glad to conserve the Blessed
Sacrament in my poor little chapel.*

*I leave on foot for a camp some six or seven
miles away to perform a baptism there. After
having crossed over through water up to my
knees and having walked an hour, I meet the
mother of the child who was bringing the baby
herself to have it baptised. I return with her and
her companions. Thus, that evening I do my first
baptism at the out-post; a little John, born in
January. Others came so that ten Eskimos spent
the night here.*

*13 October — It is cold. The door and
windows are frosted and there is a layer of ice on
the water barrel.*

*18 October — I check my nets. The heavy
snowfall of these past two days and the mild
temperature have made the water overflow onto
the lake ice. There are three inches of ice to cut
through in order to reach the wood holding the
ends of the nets, and since the spots are not
visible through the snow, you have to dig over a
large area; real slave labour.*

Early that winter Father Buliard made a trip to the
Inuit camps along the Arctic coast before returning to his
house at Garry Lake, where he labored with the people in
that vicinity until March 22, 1950. Then on the following
day he and his guide left the mission, visiting camp after
camp all the way to the mouth of the Back River,
returning by dog sled to Baker Lake on April 25, 1950.
    Now we return to the Garry Lake diary —

22 August — Charles Weber arrives in Baker Lake around 10 A. M. with the plane, Arctic Wings. It is cloudy and rainy. We leave around four anyway. We reach Garry Lake but the fog is very thick and the pilot cannot see the house. So he returns us to Baker Lake.

23 August — Up since four in the morning, but we don't leave until noon for it is rainy like yesterday. This time, in spite of the bad weather, Charles finds the house. Not being able to land on the water in front of the house, we land beyond the point. Charles gone. I start moving the most urgent things ashore. But soon, in spite of the waves, a canoe arrived with four men to help me move my things. They leave in the evening.
What a jumble in the house for someone has broken in. Everything smells of mildew and almost all my linens are rotten as is the mattress. The cot is broken for the Eskimos have used it as a stool. There is not a drop of fuel left and lots of things have disappeared; cartridges, oatmeal, butter, fat.

24 August — Around seven in the morning I hear the plane. I quickly scramble to beyond the point. There is a strong wind and the unloading is a hassle for Charles is alone. We manage willy-nilly to unload the canoe, two dogs, barrels and cases, while keeping the plane from being swept away by the wind. Finally everything is finished, Charles leaves bidding me adieu for the year. The canoe is not new; it is the old canoe from the Churchill mission. But it seems to be in good enough shape and will be very useful, even absolutely essential. No Eskimos arrive for the waves are too high.

25 August — I put things away, wash and go

*put out the net. Since the dogs have had nothing
to eat, I give them the rotten oatmeal, all I have,
but they don't even want it. I work in the house,
have several visitors and a baptism. Finally
everyone leaves and my guide alone remains with
me.*

*The 30th we finally get four fish. The dogs
are hungry. The next day we lose a net put out
too deep, but we get ten fish in the other nets.*

*September — The month is spent fishing,
hunting and preparing for winter in general. The
wind is often very strong and sometimes lets
loose a real hurricane.*

*23 September — When I woke up the windows
were all red and there was no light in the house.
At 11 o'clock it is still dark and we need a lamp.
The sun is all red and everything outside is
covered with a sort of soot; the air stinks.
People say "Isiriartuq, mamaituq," it smells bad!
It is only in the afternoon that the weather
clears with a strong south wind. Later we will
know there were violent forest fires far to the
south. (The phenomenon was noticed as far as
New York and even in Europe.)*

*26 September — My guide asks us to take him
to the other side of the river, for he wants to go
home over by Kurarjuk. We take him to the spot
he shows us. But when we are leaving he starts
yelling at the top of his lungs for us to come
back; we have left him on an island surrounded
by deep water! We laugh about it and finally
take him to land.*

*28 September — The edge of the bay is
frozen; impossible to get the nets out either
from the land or the water.*

Fr. Joseph Buliard with Four Eskimos

*The next day the wind is not so strong. I try
the canoe but was carried away in the ice and
end up at the point. In the evening I finally
manage to get one net out. I am alone for my
guide has gone caribou hunting with his father.*

*The 30th I take out the second net and thread
my way through the ice pack back to the mission.*
*The netting season is over. We don't have
many fish cached, not even 200, and no caribou.
The boating season is also over. Often when my
guide and I went out in clear weather we had to
come back with terrible waves and we were
afraid more than once. In any case, our biceps
must have grown from the rowing.*

*The 1st of October everything is frozen
almost as far as you can see. We see only rare
patches of open water.*

*3 October — Heavy snow storm. The next
day there is no longer any ice around the island.
The very strong wind carried it out to open
water.*

*5 October — There is new ice almost
everywhere along the shore. The next day I put a
net under the ice.*

*23 October — In the morning, nuptial bene-
diction for T. and L. In the afternoon, marriage
of M. K. and P. The day before I had baptised
four adults; great joy and feasting at the little
post of Our Lady of the Rosary.*

Here we conclude the direct quotes from the Garry
Lake diary. This has given only a sampling of Father
Buliard's diary and of his life at his little house which he
called "Our Lady of the Rosary Mission."

Father Buliard never thought of the Garry Lake house
as anything more than a temporary base of operations, a
warehouse for his food and a springboard from which to
launch off as far as the Arctic coast. Of course, it was
never too comfortable anyhow. In the winter the walls
inside became covered with a coat of frost which his
inadequate heating system could never entirely melt.
"When I can't stand it anymore in my house," he would say,
"I would live in an iglu or go on a trip."

If one were to figure the total number of miles
covered by Father Buliard during his seventeen years in
the north, one would conclude that he had beaten all
records. But the worst part of it was the difficulty of the
conditions which marked his travels.

Travelling in the Arctic by dog team can be, at times,
relatively comfortable. Wrapped in warm caribou skin
clothes, with a good guide and dogs, with lots of food and

sufficient fuel to eliminate anxiety, the traveller can set
out fairly confident.   But how many times did Father
Buliard travel with none or practically none of these
comforts?

One winter the Mounted Police departed by team for
Garry Lake, with plenty of dogs and a heavy load of food
and coal oil, and came back after a dozen days without
having reached their goal.   A few weeks later, Father
Buliard arrived, poorly equipped, his clothing in shreds and
without food, having left Garry Lake and taken in the
mouth of the Back River on his way, a distance of some
900 miles.   If someone had complimented him, he would
have laughed.

That little hut in Garry Lake must have often been
uncomfortable.   To make it conspicuous he had built it on
the very top of the island where there was no shelter from
the gales of winter.   For six years, Father Buliard lived
out his life at the Garry Lake Mission among the Inuit.   On
two occasions his summer re-supply of food failed to
arrive.   Even so, his work continued as he ranged across
the snowbound landscape in search of new converts,
travelling with his dog team as far north as Gjoa Haven on
King William Island and down south to the Thelon River.

When he was at Garry Lake, he held classes among
the Inuit who had gradually come to live in the vicinity.
At night he read theology, and wrote letters to his brother
missionaries scattered across the Canadian north.   He
wrote to one —

> *These primitive people have a wonderful
> philosophy of life, they always look at things
> from the right angle.   Should some misfortune
> strike them, instead of becoming angry, or
> peeved as we white people do, they just laugh it
> off.   This attitude, which I have always found
> rather baffling, greatly helps them in under-
> standing the many blows this rugged northern life
> deals them.*

In another letter he wrote —

Solitude has its great advantages for me. I am more myself, with much more initiative, more of the apostle, and much more ready to sacrifice myself. I am even more practical by myself. I am less the bogged-down one you know me for, because timidity is not there to cut my facilities in half.

His supply plane had not arrived in 1956 and in September of that year Father Buliard wrote his last letter. This letter said in part —

I was going to write a long letter today but I had to paddle the canoe all day, bringing a family from the other side of the river and getting two others, one after the other, both hungry and emaciated. It is 11 o'clock at night but we managed to pray a good while at 8 o'clock.

No caribou at all around here, no more fish and the hungry ones are eating my stock; all we can do is kill the dogs and wait cosily for what will come.

On September 20, he added in a hurry —

No plane yet, but the caribou have come and the Eskimos are making themselves caches.

The **Eskimo** reports in an article written by its editor, Fr. Guy Mary-Rousselière, O.M.I., "The plane never did arrive, and no more word of Father Buliard was known until word-of-mouth news of his disappearance reached Gjoa Haven early in January."

While the Father's family waited with great anxiety, keeping up a spark of hope in spite of everything, three long months went by before the Mounted Police plane finally reached Garry Lake. The plane stayed there twenty minutes and only one Eskimo was questioned, Adjuk, who had built an igloo near the mission in the fall because his wife wanted to be instructed for baptism.

Father Papion gives this report of the questioning of
Adjuk:

> *On October 24, after Mass and tea, Father
> prepared his sled to go and visit his nets about
> twelve or fifteen miles away. Adjuk, who was
> standing by, suggested that he wait a while to
> visit the nets, because the little 'snow flurry'
> looked as if it might become a real blizzard.
> Father did not answer, but set out. During the
> day, there was much blowing of snow. The priest
> was not back at night. The Eskimo looked for
> tracks but the snow was thick and he had no
> dogs.*
>
> *Next day, a howling blizzard. The Eskimo
> looked around a bit but not far, it was impos-
> sible. On the third day of the blizzard, again a
> little hunting around camp without result. The
> fourth day brought good weather. The Eskimo
> went on foot to the spot where the priest's nets
> were set. He noticed that the Father had not got
> that far because the ice was not chopped
> through. He must have got lost sooner. No trace
> of broken ice anywhere in the vicinity. In the
> hunter's opinion, the priest did not drown. After
> a day's search, he went to visit his oldest
> brother's camp beyond the site of the nets. On
> November 14, all of the Father's dogs, except
> one, came back to the mission, thin like tooth-
> picks and without harness. The Eskimos shared
> them.*
>
> *Knowing Father Buliard, I am inclined to
> offer this explanation of his unwillingness to
> listen to Adjuk. All his activity was organized
> around his ministry. He knew the season was too
> far advanced to leave room for reasonable hope
> that the plane would come with provisions. His
> own food was running low and he had to replenish
> it himself. But it would be a big mistake to think
> that this situation would cause him to cancel his*

*parochial rounds. He had to catch as much fish
as possible for himself and his dogs if he intended
to travel. Every fish counted. That is probably
why he set out alone, not asking Adjuk to
accompany him, because he figured he could not
afford to pay him. Most likely, he counted on his
dogs' instinct to find the way back to the
mission.*

*What really happened? Lost in the blizzard,
did he just turn in the wrong direction? Did his
dogs light out after some passing caribou? Did
he fall through the ice as his dogs went on with
the sled?*

A few years earlier, during a visit to Baker Lake he
had said to a friend with a hearty laugh, "Life is hard at
Garry Lake. In five years I will be done for in a fool's land
in which only fools remain. Sooner or later I'll finish by
going through the ice. The rivers up there are tricky in so
many spots."

And so Father Buliard had prophesied his own end.

GOOD DROWNING
WATER

> *Leaping and boiling and seething,*
> *Saw we a cauldron aflume;*
> *There was the rage of the rapids,*
> *There was the menace of doom.*
>
> — *Robert Service,*
> ***The Trail of Ninety-Eight***

During our second nearly perfect day in a row we pulled hard on the paddles all day long. We did, however, take time to catch four lakers, one of which we fried for supper and the others were boiled for future use.

While preparing our fish dinner, several red-throated, Arctic and common loons put up a terrific fuss. That was the first time we had seen all three varieties of loons in the same place. "They must be trying to tell us something," said Darrell.

"There's no question about that," I replied. "They want us to know that tomorrow is going to be another windy day. I hope they are wrong this time, but they usually know what they're talking about."

Entering lower Garry Lake, we thought we saw ice ahead. Then in a little while the ice disappeared from view, so we decided we were getting the "mirage effect" which often comes with calm air over still, cold water. Later, as we approached a small island, we decided that there definitely was ice ahead of us.

As we crossed the 100th meridian, an open water lead took us along the north shore. Our spirits dropped to a new low as we saw that miles and miles of solid ice still covered the lower part of Garry Lake. During the evening the skies again clouded over, and once more we watched a mirage out across the lake as we paddled along the lead of open water.

"Do you see those tall buildings over there at three o'clock?" I asked. "Or am I cracking up?"

"I see them," Darrell said. "There are more buildings back in the southwest at about four-thirty."

Low stratus clouds drifted in over the lake while we watched tall buildings and other strange and impossible-shaped objects come into view during the evening as the mirage continued. It was unreal, almost as if we were in a weird dream as we paddled on and the skies grew darker and darker under the heavy overcast. At one point, for about a half mile, our lead of open water closed with the shore. There, we wiggled our way through, sometimes using *North Star II* as an ice breaker, pushing our way through smaller chunks of floating ice. Shortly before midnight we encamped on a peninsula as a stiff breeze began to whip up out of the east and our mirage disappeared. We were once again forced to face reality as cold rain began to fall.

By early the next morning, the wind had shifted to the northwest and increased to a howling gale, as the rain, now mixed with snow, continued to fall. The temperature dropped again. At noon our thermometer stood at 34 degrees. It was so cold and windy that we cooked breakfast inside the tent. Ice floes drifted into the little bay beside the tent with a grinding roar as they bounced and slid over the rocks along the shore.

Several times recently I'd heard Darrell singing a song from the television show **Hee Haw,** which correctly expressed our feelings. The words are —

Gloom, despair and agony on me
Deep, dark, depression, excessive misery?
If we had no bad luck, we'd have no luck at all.
Gloom, despair and agony on me.

The storm continued throughout the entire day. We were unable to keep warm even inside the flapping tent, and in the sleeping bags with our jackets and pants on. The wind chill factor must have held at down around -5 degrees F. for the next 18 hours. We discussed our situation and checked our maps to find that in three weeks, we had progressed 359 miles from Muskox Rapids. That left us with 97 miles to go down the Back before we would arrive at the junction of the Meadowbank, which we had decided to ascend on our return to Baker Lake.

At 5:30 on the morning of July 26, the gale tapered off to a stiff north wind. We broke camp to follow the north shore from where the wind had cleared the ice. We clawed our way along for only five miles when the north wind stopped us again, so once more we waited, and the waiting was becoming more and more discouraging. We had had enough of the arctic barrens. It was at that location that we wrote and signed our "Pledge to the North" which reads —

We, the undersigned, do pledge and agree, on this the 26th day of July, 1978, to the following:

We do plan to leave the arctic barrens on the earliest possible date and to never, never return for another extended canoe trip at any time in the future.

With God as our witness.

Signed: Darrell Klein   Signed: Clayton Klein

Recorded: North Shore
Lower Garry Lake, Back River
4:15 p.m. C.D.S.T.
July 26, 1978

Rocks were more plentiful than usual at this camp, so within a few hours we had built a stone cairn. We placed our "Pledge to the North" in an empty almond can and installed it inside the cairn.

Following a nine-hour wait we had another go at it into the face of the north wind. During the next four hours of steady clawing we gained four more miles before we again had to give up.

On July 27 the wind rested. This made it one of the best days of the summer, even though it rained nearly all of the time. We were underway before six and shot the rapids at the outlet of lower Garry Lake. We crossed Buliard Lake before noon. The first set of rapids were around a hard right turn just below the lake. Then we descended a succession of strong rapids. In places we were carried along with extraordinary rapidity, shooting over large boulders upon which certain disaster would have occurred had we struck one of them. Four portages had to be made in that stretch of river.

Late that afternoon in a steady drizzle, we arrived at the northernmost point of our journey. We paused for a shore break, and to celebrate the milestone, we prepared a cup of hot Kool-Aid.

"This is probably the farthest north that I will ever get," I remarked. "We're now within forty-six miles of the Arctic Circle."

Early the next morning we crossed MacDougall Lake, portaged an unmarked rapids, and by noon had arrived at Rock Rapids. Our reconnaissance of those rapids required nearly two hours. Canoeing progress has to be slow on any river in the barrens. To have headed into that rapids without looking it over in detail would have been certain suicide. From noon until midnight we made three long portages along the right side of the river, and finally camped about a mile above Sinclair Falls.

"The Back is a mighty big and powerful river," Darrell said thoughtfully. "I hope we can get off from it soon. It's so powerful and wild that it scares me!"

"I know exactly what you mean. This is by far the largest and most difficult river we've ever canoed."

We found Rock Rapids to be much the same as Captain George S. Back described it when he passed them on July 22, 1834. Here is a quote from his journal —

Bending short round to the left, and in comparatively contracted channel, the whole force of the water glided smoothly but irresistibly towards two stupendous gneiss rocks, from five to eight hundred feet high, rising like islands on either side. Our first care was to secure the boat in a small curve to the left, near which the river disappeared in its descent, sending up showers of spray. We found it was not one fall, as the hollow roar had led us to believe, but a succession of falls and cascades, and whatever else is horrible in such "confusion worse confounded." It expanded to about the breadth of four hundred yards, having near the centre an insulated rock about three hundred feet high, having the same barren and naked appearance as those on each side.

From the projection of the main western shore, which concealed the opening, issued another serpentine rapid and fall; while to the right there was a strife of surge and rock, the roar of which was heard far and wide. The space occupying the centre from the descent to the island was full of sunken rocks of unequal heights, over which the rapid foamed and boiled, and rushed with impetuous and deadly fury.

At the part it was raised into an arch; while the sides were yawning and cavernous, swallowing huge masses of ice, and then again tossing the splintered fragments high into the air. A more terrific sight could not well be conceived, and the impression which it produced was apparent on the countenances of the men.

Early the next morning while we were eating breakfast, once more a cold rain began to fall which continued without letup until late in the afternoon. During the rain we shot another rapids and completed a lengthy portage past Sinclair Falls. That was a desolate but beautiful place! We would have liked to have taken some pictures there, but it was raining far too much to even consider removing our cameras from the Dry Box.

Then in mid-day our old nemesis, the cold north wind, decided we were having it too easy. Wanting to have one more whack at us, the villain returned with its usual barren lands vengeance. We hung in there in spite of the blowing sheets of rain, scratching our way along directly into the face of the wind, until late in the afternoon when we were once more buffeted off the river, this time on an island just south of the 66th parallel.

To get some protection from the wet, frigid blasts, we set up the tent after securing our canoe to a large rock. We crawled inside to get out of the wind, and the thermometer stood at 37 degrees. We cooked up a big pot of beans inside the tent, had supper, and for four very windy hours after the rain stopped, we dried out wet clothing and equipment.

There had not been much conversation that day between us, but at suppertime Darrell said, "When we reach the Meadowbank and head south up that river, I expect this north wind will finally quit blowing. In fact, most likely then we will have the first south winds of the summer."

"That would be just our luck to be going upstream and bucking a headwind. If a south wind doesn't arrive soon, this could be known as the year without a summer. Here it is, nearly August and the little bushes are still in the bud stage. There are no insects except an occasional bumble bee, and even the usual Arctic plants and tundra flowers haven't blossomed. I've heard that we had a year without a summer down in the United States once. I think the year was 1816. It was caused by erupting volcanoes in Indonesia which formed a high altitude cloud that circled the northern hemisphere all that summer. Perhaps something like that happened again just about the time we left Yellowknife."

"If we could only make it to Escape Rapids, which is four miles ahead, we could probably complete the portage tonight before we make camp," said Darrell.

"That would be great, but how can we make it into the face of this northeaster?"

"It won't be easy, but let's try it one more time."

I was ready for another attempt, so at 7:30 that evening we shoved off and rounded the corner of the island into the full force of the wind. We gave it everything we had, digging continually without missing a stroke. Three hours later we were still digging but making no further progress. That gale was sweeping us to the southwest faster than we could paddle northeast toward the rapids. To make it more difficult, high waves frequently broke over the bow and we were in danger of being swamped. In that condition we finally made it to shore but were still nearly a mile short of our goal for the day, Escape Rapids.

Having had all we could take for one day, we set up camp and soon turned in to warm up and get some rest. Next morning there was no improvement in the weather. We waited hopefully for a drop in the wind's velocity. When it didn't come by noon, in desperation we decided to continue on anyway. That called for another rigorous effort, and for an hour we battled the wind and waves before we finally arrived at the head of Escape Rapids.

Next came a difficult carry of a mile and a half along the left shore where the Back plunges thirty-six feet nearer sea level. By then our load was light enough so we completed the portage in two trips. Earlier, three trips were required to make a portage. The wind gusts were so strong that on two occasions, terrific gusts blew *North Star II* right off from Darrell's shoulders as he struggled along with it. It was impossible to hold on to it when those powerful and sudden gusts hit us.

Halfway across the portage we found a heavy green wooden box. On the cover was printed "PLEASE OPEN ME." We opened it and found the box to be packed full of clothing, books, a twenty-two calibre rifle, ammunition, a saw, hair lotion, pills and numerous other articles. Nearby we found several jars of food, a prospector's hammer, and a length of nylon rope. Everything was soaking wet and probably had lain there for several years. A sheet of paper attached to the inside of the cover of the box was apparently a message with a person's name and address at the bottom, but the weather had rendered it impossible to read.

We forced open some of the books. One had been borrowed from a library in Medford, New Jersey, in 1974. We wondered and speculated, "Why had someone left that box there? And what conditions would cause someone to abandon everything?"

The only thing we removed from the box was the cover of the book with the library card, which we would turn over to the RCMP when we reported to them at Baker Lake. We replaced the contents of the box, closed it and tightly tied it with the nylon rope, just as we found it.

By the time we completed the Escape Rapids portage, the velocity of the wind had started to drop. We immediately embarked and moved twelve miles before we set up camp just above another rapids. The temperature was 39 degrees, but that seemed warm because the wind had finally calmed down. With our cup of hot chocolate before turning in, we enjoyed the last of our cookies from home. The message in my final cookie* was from Debbie. It read, "In that rapids up yonder there's a hidden rock. Now the big crash won't be such a shock!"

While sipping on the hot chocolate, once more we hashed over our need to be extremely careful in our every move. Darrell cautioned, "In a place like this a fall on the rocks during a portage, or an upset in the river, could finish us off once and for all."

"That's probably another reason why our progress seems to be slow down through here," I replied. "An accident of any kind could easily turn into a real catastrophe."

---

* *See Appendix for more on cookie notes.*

For those reasons we often carried around rapids that at other times and in other places we would have run with little hesitation. On the Back, the cold water could have numbed too quickly to risk a capsize. An upset on the Au Sable or on the Suwannee could be an inconvenience, but on the Back, it would have been sheer disaster. With that in mind we continued to move carefully and to discuss the situation time after time.

Early the next morning after carefully looking it over from shore, we decided to shoot the rapids below camp. Underway by only about one hundred yards, and while maneuvering into position in the fast water to line up with the slick of the rapids, there came a sudden and surprising WHAM! We had hit a hidden rock, which bounced *North Star II* almost out of the water. Neither of us had detected the rock which must have been hiding only about an inch below the surface. The warning on Debbie's cookie message suddenly came true!

The force of the rushing water spun us around and there we hung, on top of that boulder nearly 200 feet from shore. The canoe was facing upstream with the drop of the rapids only thirty feet behind us, or downstream. There we hung! We talked it over, trying to decide on the best procedure. Then we tried to pry ourselves loose with paddles. The canoe wouldn't budge. The only alternative was for me, being directly above the submerged boulder, to step out into the river and stand on the rock without slipping off, and lift on the loaded canoe until it floated free. Then I would jump back in and we would have to shoot the rapids going down backwards, as there would not be time to turn around in that swift water before we would be swept over the drop.

We took our time and talked over the situation as it had to be done perfectly. There was no room for error. The slightest mistake by either of us would be fatal. We said a prayer and carefully made our move. All went as planned! Thank the Good Lord! We made it through without further mishap. Once below the drop, we soon brought *North Star II* about and again headed downstream.

The remainder of the day was one of almost

Portage Past Sandhill Rapids

continuous river thrills. We were in very fast and turbulent water most of the time, with frequent whirlpools and underwater boulders to avoid. There was a portage of a half mile at Sandhill Rapids, and another past an unnamed swoosher a few miles below. Once back on the river following the carry of over a mile past a nameless rapids, and while taking a drink, I said, "This sure is good drinking water."

The reply I heard from Darrell was, "It could also be good drowning water!"

"Let's not try for that!"

"This river really scares me. I'll sure be happy to leave it!"

"Me too!"

That afternoon there was a short portage at Wolf Rapids, which were also named by Captain Back in 1834. In his journal, he had written —

> *Within a few hundred yards of us, nine white wolves were prowling round a herd of musk oxen, one of which was shot; but, being a bull, was too strongly scented to be eaten. As there was no possibility of making a portage, should it be necessary, on the side where we encamped, at*

Mealtime at the Mouth of the Meadowbank

daylight of the following morning we pulled up stream to cross over, and see if it was more favourable on the other side. The descent broke over a fall five feet deep, opposite to a gloomy chasm in a rock; but as it did not reach quite to the eastern side, the boat was enabled to pass it, and then ran the Wolf Rapid. Some of the animals whose name it bore seemed to be keeping a brisk look-out for what might happen.

The highlight of the last day in July, however, came at 6:30 that evening when we pulled into Lake 137. That was where we finally left the Back River. Putting the Back behind us called for a real celebration. We went ashore on a rocky ledge, prepared a big supper, and topped it off with a second cup of coffee, chocolate chip candies and an extra spoonful of honey. Then with the help of a gentle breeze at our backs for the first time since leaving Muskox Rapids, we paddled to the south end of Lake 137 and camped near the point where the Meadowbank River flows into the lake. We had completed 456 miles down the Back in twenty-eight days, and now it was good to be leaving it!

THE KING OF
THE BARRENS

> *The wind bloweth where it listeth,*
> *And thou hearest the sound thereof,*
> *But canst not tell whence it cometh,*
> *And whither it goeth.*
>
> — *St. John,*
> *Chapter 3, Verse 8*

August 1 began a new phase of our journey as we began the climb up the Meadowbank River. To escape the north completely, we still had to ascend the 137 miles of the Meadowbank River, carry over the height of land, descend an unnamed stream until it joined the Thelon River, and then follow the Thelon down into Baker Lake. We still had a total of 212 miles to travel.

"If we can have a period of several days of this weather when the winds are kind, we could conceivably make it out of here by August 10," said Darrell.

"That isn't likely to happen," I replied. "Upstream travel at best is going to be slow. I don't think there's a chance that we can average twenty-one miles a day up through there, even if the weather is good."

As we paddled southeast into the lower Meadowbank, Darrell asked, "Dad, have you noticed anything different about the scenery around here?"

"Yes, I have. The area looks greener!" Then looking around further, I added, "I don't see any ice or snow either."

"That's right! Maybe summer has finally arrived. This is the first time since leaving Muskox Rapids that we don't have ice or snow in sight. Maybe we have finally left the long Arctic winter behind us."

The lower Meadowbank was a good-sized river. We made good progress until we arrived at an island near the west end of an esker. There the real work began as we made a portage over the island. Upstream travel on Arctic rivers was new to us. We would paddle as long as we were making forward progress, usually near shore or in an eddy. When the oncoming current started pushing us backward at a greater speed than we could move forward, we would go ashore. Then with forty-foot tracking ropes tied to either end of the canoe, we would walk along the shore, stepping or jumping from rock to rock, maneuvering the loaded canoe upstream.

Most of the rocks, regardless of size, were lying loose along the river bed, and they rolled when stepped on. Even those weighing several hundred pounds could not be depended on. We had learned from previous experience along the larger rivers that one must always expect every rock one steps on to roll, and if that rock doesn't move at all, then that was a lucky step. The Meadowbank contained more than its share of loose rocks, so wet feet and legs now became commonplace.

We soon learned that to guide the canoe away from shore with tracking lines, we should tighten up on the stern rope leaving some slack in the bow rope. When we needed the canoe to come closer to our side of the river, we would reverse the procedure by doing some forward pulling on the bow rope, with slack in the stern line. This was just the opposite of tracking a canoe downstream.

That first day we moved up through six miles of very fast water. Frequently, we came to places where the forty-foot lines were not long enough to keep the canoe in deep water, as there were rocks of all sizes everywhere. In those places, our only option was to make a portage, or, where possible, manually lift and slide the loaded canoe up and over the rocks.

"This upstream business is extremely hard work," Darrell sighed that afternoon. "It's hard on our paddles too."

We were both so exhausted that we camped early that evening. Our boots and socks were soaked from stepping on rocks just below the surface of the water. During that day we moved a total of fourteen miles and climbed sixty feet above Lake 137. Before turning in for the night, Darrell set his alarm clock for 4 A.M. because we needed to get an early start in the morning.

We were back on the river by 5:15 the next day, but there was more tracking than paddling for the next ten hours. At lunch time we could look back down the river valley and see the place where we had camped overnight, a distance of about five miles. Progress was difficult. We did make it into Lake 261 by supper time after completing a difficult portage over some high hills. That carry cut off three miles of extremely fast and turbulent water around a bend in the river. The portage was well marked with a line of large inukshuks.

That evening we paddled to the south end of Lake 261. The next day more of the same from sunrise until after sunset. We were making progress and the progress was gratifying. Early that evening, we noticed a heavy bank of clouds moving in from the northwest. We ended the day by making another lengthy portage over high ground, across a lake and back down to the river, by-passing three more sets of cascades around another bend in the river. By the time we had completed the last portage and found a place to set up camp, darkness had settled in and the rain began to fall.

The "hungry horde" met us in full force as we made the carry over those hills. Strange as it may seem, we almost welcomed them as they were the first swarm of mosquitos to bother us that summer and it was further proof that summer in the far north had finally arrived.

The next morning as the rain continued, the wind began whipping up. Before we could break camp, gale force winds from the north again hit us. Camped as we were on the south side of that sizeable lake, we had no choice but to wait inside the tent. It had again turned cold, and the north wind continued to fire some of its heaviest shots at us all day long. It blew the tent down on us, so once more we rolled out and turned the entrance towards the wind as we re-erected it.

That day we both came down with another bad case of "tent fever." In discussing our predicament I voiced my feelings. "We've seen a lot of bad canoeing weather, but today has to be the worst day of all."

"Yup! This is sure miserable. But it could be worse. How would you like to be hung up here in December or January?"

"That would be something else! The average mean temperature for the month of January in Baker Lake is 27 degrees below zero and that's too cold for me!"

"It probably gets even colder than that here along the Meadowbank. Maybe this is the beginning of winter. If so, we had a mighty short summer. I hope we make it out of here before the lake freezes over."

We were silent for a time as we contemplated being stranded in this barren land in winter. Finally I said, "We are most likely the only non-Inuit people to have ever canoed this river."

"That's probably right, especially going upstream."

"Certainly last night as we portaged over the hills behind camp, we walked where no other non-Inuit had ever been."

"That all sounds great," Darrell replied. "But the reason we are the first to pass through here is that no other white men were ever as stupid as the two of us."

During the afternoon we set up the camp stove inside the tent and made up three dozen slices of cornbread to use for future lunches. We couldn't resist eating a half dozen of them while they were hot. Then a little later we had a big supper as the gale howled on. The only good

thing about that day of misery was that it gave us a
chance to take on some extra food and rest our weary
muscles. We both had lost a lot of weight and were now
as skinny as rails.

That afternoon Darrell occupied himself by writing in
his journal —

> *When the north wind howls on the barren land*
> *The canoeists must stop — you understand.*
> *When the sun doesn't shine and it begins to rain,*
> *The cold and the wetness, Oh! What pain!*
>
> *With the waves three feet high and roaring in*
> *We set up the tent and climb right in.*
> *That's the only way to keep warm and dry,*
> *But it's still pure misery and that ain't no lie.*
>
> *It's been five weeks since we've seen a man*
> *We're locked right in, to this barren land.*
> *But sooner or later we will escape,*
> *And let me tell you, that'll be just great.*

The north wind died during the night so we rolled out
at four o'clock in 36-degree temperature and were
underway within a few minutes. Up and up the river we
went. By noon we had arrived at a series of several more
cascades just below Meadowbank Lake. Another carry of
a mile and a half over a very high and picturesque hill, and
we had by-passed those rapids. Once more we followed a
line of inukshuks across the hills and in doing so, cut off
more than three miles of river.

Completing the portage in late afternoon, we paddled
on down the length of Meadowbank Lake before encamp-
ing on an island. There we found another place where the
Inuit had lived. In addition to the usual stone tent rings,
we also found thousands of little twigs piled in a crevice
between some huge boulders. The largest twigs were less
than one quarter inch in diameter. Apparently they had
been gathered many years before and stored for firewood,
then never used. Undoubtedly the twigs had been

collected by someone who searched over a huge area of
tundra, hills and valleys and spent many, many days in
their search.

That had been our best day since heading upstream.
We had advanced thirty-two miles and climbed to 389 feet
above sea level. In the evening a breeze started to blow
from the southwest. By noon of the next day the
southwester had picked up so much velocity that we were
blown off the water for the succeeding six hours. That
was the first time in nearly five weeks that the wind had
blown from the south. During the afternoon we inventoried our remaining food and found that we had to get to
Baker Lake within the next few days or we would once
more really be going hungry. We were about ninety-six
miles from the settlement. In checking our maps, Darrell
found that we were still twenty-six miles from the height
of land and from there on the canoeing would all be
downhill.

Once more we faced a headwind as now our route led
southwest toward the Thelon River. That evening the
insects came out in full force sounding much like a swarm
of bees. They hit the tent in such numbers that, to us
inside, it sounded like a downpour of rain.

Then came another day of perfectly sunny weather
with the wind still strong out of the south. Progress was
slow. We struggled along into it until we completed a
second portage and entered the big lake at the top of the
Meadowbank River system which we called Lake 395
because its elevation was 395 feet above the Arctic
Ocean. From the south end of that lake we would make
the portage over and then down into the Thelon. There
was no possible way to continue into the gale, so once
more we set up the tent.

Here is a quote from our journal for the afternoon of
August 7 —

We baked a batch of bread inside the tent as
we anxiously await a drop in the wind. We do not
have time to wait here. Our families at home
now have to be worried as they were expecting

to hear from us by August 1st. This is so distressing! We have certainly learned our lesson, this time. We will never enter the barrens again!

We broke our afternoon camp, following an early supper, as the wind's velocity dropped a little. After about a mile of progress in heavy breakers on the nose, the velocity once more increased. Waves broke over the bow time after time as we struggled toward the lee of an island about a quarter mile ahead. By the time we finally succeeded in reaching the island, everything in the canoe was awash in nearly two inches of water. How disheartening! We bailed out the water and waited again.

A couple of hours later we tried again and managed to keep fighting on until darkness settled in. In all, we moved a total of eleven miles, and would easily have made thirty or more miles without this wind.

The wind did a 180-degree turn with a downpour of rain early the next morning. Before the rain let up the north wind's velocity had increased into a howling gale. Once more it smashed the tent down on us. We rolled out in the cold and blowing rain to again turn the front of the tent into the face of the gale while re-erecting it. Quickly I checked the temperature. The mercury stood at 38 degrees.

Back inside the tent again to get warmed up a little, we came down with another bad case of Tent Fever.

Darrell shivered and moaned, "What a disappointment! If that wind could only be reasonable, within four hours we would be at the south end of this lake and begin the portage over into the Thelon."

"It wants to take one more crack at us to remind us that we are definitely not welcome here and that we must never again return to its realm."

"I don't need another reminder like this. Believe me, I have learned my lesson. I want to get away from here and when I escape, I will never return. What I long to see are some trees! Some nice green trees!"

"Me too! Trees would slow this surface wind down, but up here the wind is the undisputed ruler of the barrens domain. It has no competition from anything and it wants us to realize that it, and it alone, is the King of the Barrens."

In checking our journal we found that it was now August 8th. It had been thirty-five days since we flew out of Yellowknife.

"It was five weeks ago yesterday," said Darrell, "that we started this miserable trip and in that five weeks we haven't seen another human being. This has to be one of the most desolate places on the face of the earth."

"That's for sure! And in that five weeks the days have shortened up too. The sun sets before ten and it rises at about four in the morning, so instead of two hours between sunset and sunrise, which we had up near Muskox Rapids, we now have six hours, and now it really gets dark at night too."

"I hope we can soon get going again. We only have enough food to carry us three or four more days," Darrell remarked as we were preparing lunch of Red River cereal, toasted corn bread, honey and coffee. "Baker Lake is still nearly ninety miles away."

I didn't reply, but the situation didn't look good.

Early that evening the north wind lost a little of its velocity, so in desperation we had another go at it, even though our safety was in question. The one thing in our favor was the fact that the wind was at our backs and would help push us to the south end of the lake.

After rounding a point about a mile and a half from where we had been camped, we thought we could see another big snowbank because they had been so plentiful along our route that summer. The snowbank was south of us and we headed for it as it was on our route across a large expanse of the lake. After another fifteen minutes of paddling and bouncing over huge waves, Darrell said, "I don't think that is a snowbank. It looks like several white tents to me." I looked again. They were white tents!

"Thank the Lord!"

Thirty minutes of paddling brought us to the hillside of tents. We went ashore and soon introduced ourselves to Brian McClory, the cook, and Antoine Yassa, his assistant. These men were part of a five-man crew with the Geological Survey branch of the Canadian government. We told them our problem, and within a couple of minutes Antoine was on the radio calling Baker Lake, asking the operator there to place a collect call to our families in Michigan. We wanted them to know that we were on our way home and A.O.K.

They served us coffee and cakes and told us that the next morning they would try to find someone with an aircraft to come in and pick us up.

We set up our tent on a level spot and soon crawled into the sleeping bags to get warm. We took our remaining food into the tent and immediately ate our planned lunches for the next two days. We were ravenous. The food was gone within a few minutes.

The next morning dawned bright and clear with no wind at all. It would have been a perfect day for canoeing. At breakfast we filled up on delicious french toast, sausage and whole wheat muffins, along with fresh orange juice and coffee. Young McClory kept bringing on the food as long as we could eat it. His food was excellent. While eating we also met the other members of the survey team, John Adshead, project leader, David Halliwell, assistant, and Danny Sateana of Rankin Inlet. The others were all from Ottawa and vicinity.

Antoine was on the radio early, talking to Boris, owner of the Iglu Hotel in Baker Lake, to arrange a pick up for us. Nothing was confirmed.

After lunch John Adshead said, "There's a good chance that Boris will have a plane drop in here at anytime." We were certainly ready. We had given *North Star II* to Brian McClory who said that he would try to take it back to Ottawa with him.

We waited! Just before six a message came in that a Twin Otter on a return flight from Amer Lake would pick us up in ten minutes. By the time we could get to the lake shore and say our goodbyes to those friendly men of the Geological Survey crew, the Twin Otter turboprop had splashed down a short distance from shore.

We arrived in Baker Lake just thirty minutes too late to catch the three-times-weekly Transair flight to Churchill.

We spent two nights in the Iglu Hotel, resting and eating. I had lost eighteen pounds on the trip and Darrell had dropped twenty pounds.

On the following morning at breakfast, Bruce McKnight, exploration manager for Western Mines Limited of Toronto, asked us if we would like to ride with him to Lac La Ronge, Saskatchewan. He had chartered a Cessna 310 to come and pick him up that morning. Of course we jumped at the chance!

We were soon underway. Following a fuel stop at Stoney Rapids on the Fond du Lac River, we arrived in La Ronge by mid-afternoon and connected for a flight to Saskatoon that same day.

After our weeks in the desolate Barrens, things looked strange at Stoney Rapids for there were a few trees. Then when we arrived at La Ronge, what a beautiful and gorgeous sight. It was sunny! It was warm! There was no wind blowing! Everywhere we looked there were trees, trees, trees! Beautiful green trees! We will never leave them again.

EPILOGUE

In late September of 1982, Ragnar Jonsson finally came south to Winnipeg. That was his first trip to southern Canada since 1923, when he passed through lower Manitoba as a twenty-five-year-old immigrant from Sweden. He returned to the south for long-needed cataract surgery on his right eye. "My shooting eye," he said.

While at the Health Sciences Center in Winnipeg, Mr. Jonsson caught up on some of the latest news. "There's nothing left but disaster everywhere," he said. "Sometimes I think it would be better if we didn't have to hear all those things." About the speeding downtown Winnipeg traffic, he said, "They all seem to be in such a horrible hurry to get somewhere, and they burn up a lot of precious gas."

In his fifty-nine years along the tree line, he has gone as long as two years without human contact, but he says, "I'm no hermit. I just enjoy the simple life up there.

"I no longer have to come down to Brochet to pick up my mail." He also says, "Now there are bush pilots who happen by every few months, and they drop off my mail and the other supplies that I need. Sometimes they even fly out whatever furs I have ready for market."

In early October of 1982, we tried to telephone Mr. Jonsson at the hospital in Winnipeg, hoping to arrange for an interview. He had already left for the north. The nurse that we talked with said, "He seemed like a fine old gentleman, a super patient. He just didn't like this city life." When asked if she knew where he was staying, the nurse replied, "I think he has headed back up north to his camp in the Northwest Territories."

We talked with Robert "Bob" Ferguson of Parson's Airways Northern in Flin Flon, Manitoba, in March of 1983. He said, "While Ragnar was in the hospital, his dogs were kept on an island in Cranberry Lake, near Cranberry Portage, Manitoba. When he returned from surgery in Winnipeg, Ragnar wanted us to fly him and his dogs right back up to his camp. We couldn't keep him down here. He kept saying, "There are just too many people around here and I don't like all of this noise."

Bob Ferguson also told us that Ingevar Stolberg of Chiupka Airways and the old chum of Ragnar Jonsson, had died suddenly several years ago, and "I attended his funeral. I think that it was about twelve years ago."

We asked Bob if his Company was still using the old Fairchild Husky which they had used to fly us into Snowbird Lake back in 1968, to which he replied, "No! That old relic is now in the museum down in Winnipeg."

.

On April 29, 1980, Verlen Kruger began an even greater canoeing effort than his record-breaking 7,000-mile cross continent canoe safari with Clint Waddell in 1971. This expedition, still unfinished, is a 28,043-mile odyssey by paddle and portage, known as "The Ultimate Canoe Challenge."

This time, Verlen and his son-in-law, Steven Landick, travel in their one-man canoes, the *Loon* and the *Monarch*. These canoes were designed by Verlen and built by Sawyer Canoe Company of Oscoda, Michigan, and by Mad River Canoe Company in Waitsfield, Vermont.

Even more spectacular than the mileage are some of the unique challenges these men have undertaken and completed since their present adventure began at Red Rock Lake in Montana at the source of the Missouri River in the spring of 1980. First it was the entire length of the Missouri and up the Illinois River through Chicago and into

Lake Michigan. Then through the Great Lakes to the Erie Canal and across New York State and down the St. Lawrence River to Quebec City, where they headed up the Chaudiere River, over the height of land and down the Allagash and St. Johns Rivers into the Bay of Fundy by October of 1980.

To keep ahead of the gales of winter, they immediately headed down the Atlantic coast and saw plenty of rough water before picking up the Intercoastal Waterway south of New York City. Then it was south to Florida into the Gulf of Mexico and up the coast to the mouth of the Mississippi River.

On February 17, 1981, Verlen and Steve headed up the Mississippi and arrived in Lake Atasca, Minnesota, eighty-three days later on the eleventh of May. That had been 2,300 miles of upstream paddling. They were the first canoeists ever to complete the entire Mississippi River going upstream.

For the next 3,900 miles, they headed into the fantastic wilderness country of Canada. They picked up the old fur trade route on Lake Winnipeg and from Great Slave Lake followed Alexander Mackenzie's historic route down the river bearing his name, all the way to Tuktoyaktuk on the Arctic Ocean.

Then it was back up the Mackenzie to the Rat River, through McDougall Pass and down the Porcupine into Alaska and the Yukon River. By October, they had ascended the Yukon to Chilkoot Pass where winter caught up with them.

In 1982, Kruger and Landick entered the Pacific Ocean at Skagway and canoed down the inside passage to Vancouver, then into the open Pacific and along the coastline to Cabo San Lucas at the tip of the Baja California in Mexico. This was where they established another record. They were the first to canoe the west coast from Alaska to Mexico. January, 1983 found them paddling up the Gulf of California to the mouth of the Colorado River and on upstream to Yuma, Arizona.

In March of 1983, after a short break, Verlen and Steve again tackled the Colorado River, heading for one of the most difficult parts of their journey, going upstream through the Grand Canyon, something that has never been attempted by anyone in history.

When asked just how they expected to negotiate those boiling rapids of the Grand Canyon, Verlen replied, "We'll paddle what we can, and climb, drag or haul the rest. We may have to climb all the way out of the canyon, walk on the rim and get back in, if that's what it takes."

That's what Kruger and Landick are doing as **Cold Summer Wind** goes to the publisher. Can they make it? With their stamina and determination, we think they will succeed.

Once above the Grand Canyon, they will ascend the Colorado River up through Lake Powell and the Green River to its headwaters. Then there will be a 66-mile portage over the continental divide through 7,400-foot South Pass and into the Bighorn watershed in Wyoming.

The Bighorn flows into the Missouri River. After about one hundred miles down the Missouri, they will portage over into the Souris River and from there they will follow the historic route of the French Canadian voyageurs through Manitoba, Ontario, Minnesota, and on into Lake Superior.

They will follow the Superior shoreline around to the Au Train River in northern Michigan and up that stream and down the Whitefish River back into Lake Michigan. Then it's the shoreline of that lake, scheduled for late October of 1983, to Grand Haven and the Grand River upstream, to Verlen's home, which overlooks the Grand River near Lansing, Michigan.

Verlen and Steve are covering the entire 28,043 miles under their own power, without guides, motors, or support team on land or water. In places where it is impossible to paddle or line their canoes, they actually carry their own equipment the total distances by themselves. These two men are establishing canoeing records, some of which will certainly stand well into the twenty-first century. We are proud of Verlen and Steve, and we are also proud to be one of the sponsors of "The Ultimate Canoe Challenge."

While in Baker Lake following our Thelon River journey in 1974, we again met Father Joseph Choque of St. Paul's Mission. He wanted to know what we had been doing during the past couple of years. We had another good chat, which as it turned out was to be our last visit with him.

Father Choque was transferred to Frobisher Bay on Baffin Island shortly after our visit. He continued his work there until the summer of 1978, when he was attacked by the disease which ended his life on March 4, 1978.

On our 1976 journey, we had our problems with the Gerry Fortnight II tent. We had even more serious problems with it as we descended the Back River in 1978. Following that ordeal, we shipped the tent remains back to the manufacturer. We also enclosed the following letter.

August 31, 1978

Dear Mr. Cunningham:

We are returning this Gerry Fortnight II to you so that you may know what happens when your tent is used in Canada's Arctic Barrens. This tent was only used on two camping trips.

We purchased it from The Sporthaus in Grand Rapids, Michigan. The men there assured us that this tent would withstand the strong winds of the Arctic. That was during the first week of July in 1976. That summer we camped for two weeks in the Baker Lake-Chesterfield Inlet area of Northwest Territories. Fortunately, we had good weather until the final couple of days. Then a storm hit us which blew the tent down, breaking the top bracket between the two poles.

When we returned the tent to The Sporthaus, they replaced the bracket and said that we must have purchased a tent with a faulty bracket.

We next used the tent from July 4 to August 9 of this year on the Back River of N.W.T. That was when we decided that we should send the tent to you.

This summer a storm whipped up at our first campsite at Muskox Rapids, and the top bracket was broken again. During the next five weeks we worked our way down the river, traveling more than six hundred miles, not seeing another human. The tent gave us endless problems, for we had strong winds at least five or six days out of every week. The only way we could keep it standing was to pitch it on level ground, which was often impossible to find, and the front had to face directly into the wind. Many times we were forced to get out in the cold rain or snow and turn the tent until it again faced into the wind, and then make repairs. We managed to survive, but it wasn't easy.

When you inspect your tent, you will notice the way we repaired the bracket, the damaged fly, the broken expansion cord in one of the aluminum poles, and other things which hopefully will enable you to design and build a better tent in the future. In those strong winds we were unable to keep the fly on the tent, and every time it rained the tent leaked like a sieve.

Our suggestion is that it might be wise to check your tents out in a wind tunnel to learn how they can take it. Another suggestion is that

your dealers should not tell prospective custom-
ers that these tents will withstand strong winds.
This letter is meant to be constructive criticism.
We do hope that your company may learn from
our unhappy experiences.

Sincerely,

Clayton Klein

A reply to our letter arrived a few weeks later in the form of a new and better-constructed Gerry Fortnight II tent. Our thanks to Jerry Cunningham!

.

Darrell Klein is now the president and general manager of the family fertilizer business. He still does some canoeing with his wife, Millie, and daughters, Kristene and Patricia. At times, David Schneider of Marne, Michigan, also canoes with him.

At the present time our canoeing ventures in northern Canadian waters, as a two-man team, are on hold, because Darrell is presently unable to get away from the business long enough for any extended trip. Possibly sometime in the future we will have another go at it.

I still have a strong urge to see more of the waterways of Canada. My wife, Marjorie, says I'm hooked on the north. Our daughter, Debbie Klein, who works in the Department of Food Science and Human Nutrition at Michigan State University, is my present camping partner.

In recent years, she and I have canoed across Everglades National Park in Florida, down the Otoskwin River in Ontario, and the upper Dubawnt River in

Debbie Klein at Fort Hall

Northwest Territories. Then in 1981, Debbie and I ran the upper Thlewiaza River in northern Manitoba, going down as far as the old, abandoned Fort Hall Trading Post on the west shore of Thanout Lake.

From there we headed back upstream to the south and into Blue Lake. Then it was over the ancient trail used for hundreds of years by Indians, trappers, traders, and the occasional brave Inuit, to the Cochrane River.

The old trail is seldom used anymore, and will probably disappear completely before the end of the twentieth century. We are indeed fortunate, and thankful, to have been able to travel that Old North Trail, both back in the sixties while it was still in use, and again recently when Debbie and I were probably the only people to use it that summer.

OUR COOKIE BOX

Inside the box of Marjorie's homemade chocolate chip cookies, we found this note from her —

Dear Darrell and Clate,

Eat each cookie with tender care,
You may find a message hidden there.
Millie, Deb, Kris, Patty and Marge
Have written messages for you as you sail
your barge.
Enjoy your canoeing, be happy, have fun,
And come back to us all at the end of your
run!

Here are a few of the messages we found as we enjoyed our daily cookie. It seemed as though we were receiving a message from our homes.

Debbie Klein wrote —

1. *Hope 'Expedition North Star II'*
   is lots of fun for both of you.

2. *While waiting for that big wind to hit,*
   pray all those tent stakes will stick.

3. *Dig right in — take that stroke*
   Wow, what power, the paddle broke.

4. Aren't our messages in these cookies nifty?
   Cheaper than a call, we're really quite
   thrifty.

5. When you're pooped and the canoe won't go,
   Just hitch a ride on the next ice floe.

6. While you're in the land of Farley Mowat,
   At home they wonder how many brains
   you've got.

7. Bet you're wondering about the news.
   Too bad they don't put TV's in canoes.

8. Don't get between that bear and her cub,
   You'd make yummy grizzly grub.

9. We're down here in the summer heat!
   Doesn't that Arctic wind feel neat?

Kristene Klein wrote —

1. Hope you're enjoying your soft beds,
   running water, and all the comforts
   of home.

2. Don't let your tent fall down, don't let your
   canoe float away, and don't be late.

Marjorie Klein wrote —

1. It's lonesome here at home without you!
   The nights are long!

2. How are the itchy whiskers?
   Are they a haven for the flies?

3. Don't let a muskox
   Get between me and thee!

4. *Wouldn't you like a night in your own bed about now?*

5. *We've asked the Lord to ride with you
All the way in that canoe!*

Millie Klein wrote —

1. *We're missing you! Sob! Sob!*

2. *I'd write you a love note,
But I'm afraid Dad would eat it!*

Patricia Klein wrote —

1. *Have fun without me — the great Patty!*

2. *When you are sleeping, it would be funny
if your tent fell down.*

3. *Ha! Ha! You can't tease me for a month.*

BIBLIOGRAPHY

BOOKS

Back, Sir George. **Narrative of the Arctic Land Expedition to the Mouth of the Great Fish River.** London: John Murray, Ltd., 1836.

Bruemmer, Fred. **The Long Hunt.** Toronto: Ryerson Press, 1969.

Buliard, Roger P., O.M.I. **Inuk.** Farrar, Strauss & Young, 1951.

Caras, Roger A. **North American Mammals.** Galahad Books, 1967.

Cundy, Robert. **Beacon Six.** London: Eyre & Spattiswoode, 1970.

Douglas, George M. **Lands Forlorn.** G. P. Putnam's Sons, 1914.

Douglas, William O. **My Wilderness.** Doubleday & Company, Inc., 1960.

Freuchen, Dagmar. **Peter Freuchen's Adventures in the Arctic.** Julian Messner, Inc., 1960.

Gordon, Bryan H. C. **Of Men and Herds in Barrenland Prehistory.** National Museum of Canada, 1975.

Harper, Francis. **Caribou Eskimos of the Upper Kazan River, Keewatin.** Lawrence, The Allen Press, 1964.

Hearne, Samuel. **A Journey from Prince Wales Fort in Hudson's Bay to the Northern Ocean.** London: A. Strahan & T. Cadell, 1795.

Jenkinson, Michael. **Wild Rivers of North America.** E. P. Dutton & Company, Inc., 1973.

Langer, Richard W. **The Joy of Canoeing.** Saturday Review Press, 1973.

Morenus, Richard. **Crazy White Man.** Rand McNally & Company, 1952.

Mowat, Farley. **The Snow Walker.** McClelland & Stewart, Ltd., 1975.

———. **Tundra.** McClelland & Stewart, Ltd., 1973.

Olsen, Siguard F. **The Lonely Land.** Alfred A. Knopf, 1961.

Pryde, Duncan. **Nunaga.** Walker & Company, 1971.

Rasmussen, Knud. **Across Arctic America.** Greenwood Press, 1927.

Rutstrum, Calvin. **North American Canoe Country.** Macmillan Publishing Company, Inc., 1964.

Service, Robert. **The Complete Poems of Robert Service.**
Dodd, Mead and Company, 1947.

Sevareid, Eric. **Canoeing with the Cree.** Minnesota
Historical Society, 1968.

Tyrrell, James W. **Across the Sub-Arctics of Canada.**
Dodd, Mead and Company, 1898.

Whalley, George. **The Legend of John Hornby.** Toronto:
Macmillan of Canada, 1962.

A R T I C L E S

Anderson, Ian Stuart. "Bathurst Inlet Patrol." **The
Beaver,** Spring 1972.

Blanchet, Guy. "The Letter." **The Beaver,** 1963.

————. "Exploring with Sousi and Black Basile." **The
Beaver,** Autumn 1964.

Branson, Branley Allen. "Messages of the Clouds."
Canoe, April-May 1980.

Breckenridge, W. J. "Naturalists on the Back River." **The
Beaver,** Spring and Summer 1955.

Bruemmer, Fred. "Autumn on the Edge." **International
Wildlife,** September-October 1981.

————. "Siksik." **The Beaver,** Spring 1972.

————. "The Tree Line." **The Beaver,** Autumn 1978.

Buetow, David. "The Dismal Lakes." **The Beaver,** Summer
1978.

Deeks, John F. "Ecstasy Is a Monster Storm." **Audubon,** July 1981.

Douglas, W. O. "All in a Winter's Patrol." **The Beaver,** Winter 1978.

——. "The Quangwak Affair." **The Beaver,** Summer and Autumn 1976.

——. "Last Resort." **The Beaver,** Summer 1972.

Hall, Alex M. "Encounters with the Tundra Wolf." **The Beaver,** Winter 1976.

——. "Seven Rivers North." **The Beaver,** Summer 1976.

Hall, Alexander MacLennan. "Alone in the Barrens." **The Beaver,** Spring 1980.

Herfindahl, Orris C. "Across the Barrens by Canoe." Travelarctic Division of Tourism, Northwest Territories, April 1978.

Hoobyar, Paul. "Paddling with the Possessed." **Canoe,** April 1983.

Lentz, John W. "Inuit Ku." **The Beaver,** Spring 1968.

——. "Be Prepared." **Canoe,** August 1976.

Luste, George J. "Eskimos of the Kazan." **The Beaver,** Spring 1975.

Mason, Bill. "Off the Rocks." **Canoe,** September 1981.

McManus, Patrick F. "Two-Man-Tent Fever." **Audubon,** May 1981.

Mead, Margaret. "Eskimo Life a Century Ago." **The Beaver,** Autumn 1980.

Oswalt, Wendell H. "Caribou Eskimo without Caribou." **The Beaver,** Spring 1961.

Pelly, David. "A New Historical Site in the Northwest Territories." **Arctic in Colour,** Vol. VI No. 4, 1978.

Repp, David. "Down the Coppermine." **The Beaver,** Summer 1972.

Rogers, E. S. "The Chipewyan." **The Beaver,** Winter 1970.

Ross, Gillies W. "On the Barrens 1934." **The Beaver,** Autumn 1968.

Rossbach, George B. "By Canoe Down the Thelon River." **The Beaver,** Autumn 1966.

Rousselìere, Guy Mary, O.M.I. "Traveller for Christ in the Barren Lands." **Eskimo,** all issues from Spring-Summer 1978 to Fall-Winter 1980-81, and from Fall-Winter 1981-82 to Fall-Winter 1982-83.

————. "Fr. Joseph Choque, O.M.I. (1912-1979)." **Eskimo,** Spring-Summer 1980.

Steenhoven, Geert Van Den. "Ennadai Lake People 1955." **The Beaver,** Spring 1968.

Viehman, John. "Real Bernard's Rivers Out of Time." **Canoe,** December 1977.

Voigt, Dennis R. "Seven Rivers North." **The Beaver,** Summer 1976.

Wilkie, R. J. "Naturalists on the Back River." **The Beaver,** Summer 1955.

INDEX

271